Y0-AAB-101

Palgrave Studies in Literary Anthropology

Series Editors
Deborah Reed-Danahay
Department of Anthropology
The State University of New York at Buffalo
Buffalo, NY, USA

Helena Wulff
Department of Social Anthropology
Stockholm University
Stockholm, Sweden

This series explores new ethnographic objects and emerging genres of writing at the intersection of literary and anthropological studies. Books in this series are grounded in ethnographic perspectives and the broader cross-cultural lens that anthropology brings to the study of reading and writing. The series explores the ethnography of fiction, ethnographic fiction, narrative ethnography, creative nonfiction, memoir, autoethnography, and the connections between travel literature and ethnographic writing.

More information about this series at
http://www.palgrave.com/gp/series/15120

llo • Gibrán Güido
Editors

Fathers, Fathering, and Fatherhood

Queer Chicano/Mexicano Desire and Belonging

palgrave
macmillan

Editors
Adelaida R. Del Castillo
Department of Chicana and
Chicano Studies
San Diego State University
San Diego, CA, USA

Gibrán Güido
Department of Literature
University of California at San Diego
La Jolla, CA, USA

Palgrave Studies in Literary Anthropology
ISBN 978-3-030-60879-8   ISBN 978-3-030-60877-4   (eBook)
https://doi.org/10.1007/978-3-030-60877-4

This Palgrave Macmillan imprint is published by the registered company Springer Nature Switzerland AG.
The registered company address is: Gewerbestrasse 11, 6330 Cham, Switzerland

To our writers who mined unexpected depths to give voice to the unwritten and unsaid and to the youth, in all their irreducible difference, in search of community and love.

SERIES EDITOR PREFACE

Palgrave Studies in Literary Anthropology publishes explorations of new ethnographic objects and emerging genres of writing at the intersection of literary and anthropological studies. Books in this series are grounded in ethnographic perspectives and the broader cross-cultural lens that anthropology brings to the study of reading and writing. By introducing work that applies an anthropological approach to literature, whether drawing on ethnography or other materials in relation to anthropological and literary theory, this series moves the conversation forward not only in literary anthropology, but in general anthropology, literary studies, cultural studies, sociology, ethnographic writing, and creative writing. The "literary turn" in anthropology and critical research on world literatures share a comparable sensibility regarding global perspectives.

Fiction and autobiography have connections to ethnography that underscore the idea of the author as ethnographer and the ethnographer as author. Literary works are frequently included in anthropological research and writing, as well as in studies that do not focus specifically on literature. Anthropologists take an interest in fiction and memoir set in their field locations, and produced by "native" writers, in order to further their insights into the cultures and contexts they research. Experimental genres in anthropology have benefitted from the style and structure of fiction and autoethnography, as well as by other expressive forms ranging from film and performance art to technology, especially the internet and social media. There are renowned fiction writers who trained as anthropologists, but moved on to a literary career. Their anthropologically inspired work is a common sounding board in literary anthropology. In the endeavor to foster writing skills in different genres, there are now courses on ethnographic writing, anthropological writing genres, experimental writing, and even creative writing taught by anthropologists. And increasingly, literary and reading communities are attracting anthropological attention, including an engagement with issues of how to reach a wider audience.

Palgrave Studies in Literary Anthropology publishes scholarship on the ethnography of fiction and other writing genres, the connections between travel literature and ethnographic writing, and internet writing. It also publishes creative work such as ethnographic fiction, narrative ethnography, creative non-fiction, memoir, and autoethnography. Books in the series include monographs and edited collections, as well as shorter works that appear as Palgrave Pivots. This series aims to reach a broad audience among scholars, students, and a general readership.

Deborah Reed-Danahay and Helena Wulff

Co-Editors, Palgrave Studies in Literary Anthropology

ADVISORY BOARD

Ruth Behar, University of Michigan

Don Brenneis, University of California, Santa Cruz Regina Bendix, University of Göttingen

Mary Gallagher, University College Dublin

Kirin Narayan, Australian National University Nigel Rapport, University of St Andrews

Ato Quayson, University of Toronto

Julia Watson, Ohio State University

Buffalo, NY	Deborah Reed-Danahay
Stockholm, Sweden	Helena Wulff

ACKNOWLEDGMENTS

This book would not have been possible without the vision and encouragement of Mireille Yanow from Palgrave Macmillan who believed in this project from the very start and mentored our initial steps through the publication process as did Madison Allums whose guidance helped us marshal the project to its completion. Daniel Enrique Pérez, José H. Cadena, and Omar O. González receive our gratitude for their generosity and constructive participation in this project. José H. Cadena allowed us special access to his collection of artwork and helped us prepare the illustrations for the book. We also want to thank and especially mention the great heart, bold honesty, and daring of the contributing authors to this collection. Many of who wrote and wrote draft after draft giving voice and literary form to the present as well as recollections of the past, some of them long left unspoken or forgotten yet crystalized herein as insight and awareness of fathers and fatherhood. Gibrán also thanks Ana Castillo for inviting him to her *ranchito* (small ranch) as a writer-in-residence where she shared her wisdom, knowledge, and courageous spirit. He thanks his mother, Maria Lozano, and brother, Omar Güido, for their unconditional support, love, and insight on all his endeavors. He particularly thanks his father, Abel E. Güido, for finding the inner strength and courage to let go of all that was keeping him from his sons. Adelaida thanks Joanna Brooks at San Diego State University for her inspiration and advice, the Emeriti professors Dr. Juan Gómez Quiñones of the

University of California at Los Angeles, Dr. Rudy Acuña of the California State University at Northridge, Dr. Gustavo V. Segade of San Diego State University, and Walter O. Koenig for his kindheartedness, encyclopedic awe, and laughter.

CONTENTS

     Jesus D. Mendez Carbajal

Part VI   Fatherhood Patterns and Passionate Fathering   231

27   **Like Father, Like Queer Son?: Gay Chicanx and Latinx
     Males and Their Fathers**   233
     Daniel Enrique Pérez

28   **My Padrino**   255
     Xuan Carlos Espinoza-Cuellar

29   **God Is Never Ashamed of Us**   257
     Xuan Carlos Espinoza-Cuellar

30   **You Will Love**   259
     Xuan Carlos Espinoza-Cuellar

Select Bibliography   263

Index   277

NOTES ON CONTRIBUTORS

Eddy Francisco Álvarez Jr. is an assistant professor in the Department of Chicana and Chicano Studies at California State University, Fullerton. His scholarly and creative works have been published in *Journal of Lesbian Studies, Aztlan, TSQ: Transgender Studies Quarterly, Label Me Latina/o, Bilingual Review/Revista Bilingüe*, and other journals and edited books.

R. Allen Baros holds a PhD in English and teaches English at Skagit Valley College in northern Washington State. He is interested in Chicana/o literature, culture, politics, and inclusive pedagogy. Utilizing a queer of color *joto* perspective, he is especially interested in how queers of color reimagine the boundaries of family, identity, and personhood. He grew up in Albuquerque, New Mexico, and now lives in Seattle Washington with his partner and their two dogs.

Larry T. Baza was involved since the 1970s in civil rights causes, social justice issues, art/artists advocacy, and fundraising specifically related to race, class, and sexuality concerns across local, regional, and national networks of activism. Some of the organizations he worked with include Chicana/o, Latina/o, Art, and LGBTQ organizations such as the United Farm Workers (through work with El Teatro Campesino), El Centro Cultural de la Raza, Chicano Federation, Association of Latino Arts and Culture, and San Diego Pride. He was born and raised in San Diego. Larry passed on February 20, 2021.

Fredy Caballero holds a Bachelor of Arts in Philosophy from the University of California at Los Angeles. Through his work with the UCLA organization Improving Dreams, Equality, Access, & Success (IDEAS) he has advocated on behalf of the immigrant youth movement through education. He also did volunteer work for the political and civic campaigns of women congressional leaders promoting socioeconomic justice.

José Héctor Cadena is a writer, poet, and collage artist. He grew up along the San Ysidro/Tijuana border. He has a bachelor's degree from San Diego State University and Master of Fine Arts degree from San Francisco State University. He is a PhD candidate in American Studies at the University of Kansas. José is a *Voices of Our Nation Art Foundation (VONA)* Fellow.

Adán Campos is a graduate student in Arizona State University's Gender Studies PhD program. His thesis draws on key aspects of Chicana feminist theory, Jotería studies, and biopolitics. Raised in Las Vegas, Nevada, it is there that this jota first engaged in community-based activism concerning im/migration issues.

Adelaida R. Del Castillo is an associate professor and former Chair of the Department of Chicana and Chicano Studies at San Diego State University. Her interests bring together rights discourse, culture, and gender/sexuality studies. She has written on sex/gender meaning and economic survival strategies in Mexico City and postnational notions of Mexican immigrant citizenship. She is the editor of *Between Borders: Essays on Mexicana/Chicana History*, and co-editor of *Queer in Aztlán: Chicano Male Recollections of Consciousness and Coming Out* (Lambda Literary Awards Finalist).

Cuauhtémoc Peranda M.F.A. (Mescalero-Apache and Mexica-Chichimeca/Cano) of Santa Cruz, California, is a Critical Dance Studies doctoral student at the University of California, Riverside. Cuauhtémoc holds a bachelor's degree from Stanford University, Master of Fine Arts (MFA) from Mills College, and is Overall Prince of the Legendary House of Lauren, International.

Christian Emmañuel works in the human services sector providing homeless and low-income San Francisco Bay Area residents with opportunities for self-determination, shelter, financial stability, creative expression, and community building. Being the first in his family to navigate higher education, he is an emerging writer. His work has been featured online with *The Huffington Post* and *Black Girl Dangerous*. He is working on his first novel, *Now We Burn*.

Xuan Carlos Espinoza-Cuellar is a third-world xueer/ista, *indigenista, mexican@, xingon/a!, activista,* educator, radical, proud *GORDA!, intelectuala, estudiante, poeta y bruja*. A xueer who believes in social justice, a pansexual jot@ *que cree* (that believes) poetry has the potential to revolutionize the world, *cada palabra* (each word) is a spark of consciousness, *cada poema una transformación profunda* (each poem a profound transformation). His performance ranges from cabaret to slam poetry. His vision is one of reclaiming art from and to the margins, dignifying our forms of expression and use of laughter to heal and interrupt/resist oppression and exploitation.

Marcus H. Fisher is a native of San Diego where he works as an advocate with People Assisting The Homeless (PATH). In his private life he serves as an intuitive reader and modern brujo.

Robert Jude Frausto "Corky" Frausto holds a bachelor's degree in Psychology from the University of Texas at San Antonio and a master's in Special Education from the University of New Mexico. He teaches Psychology, Chicano Literature, and Chicano Studies at an Albuquerque inner-city high school. His artistic endeavors include painting, mosaics, and photography. For the past fifteen years he has hosted "Corkfest," an annual art and music festival at his home in the South Valley in Albuquerque, New Mexico, in the company of his three dogs and two cats.

Miguel Garcia Jr. a Detroit native, is a master's student at the Harvard Graduate School of Education. As a first-generation college student, he helped to establish one of many LGBT centers at Harvard at Harvard and has worked for over six years providing support services to black and brown LGBTQ youth of color in his community. His undergraduate studies focused on the Harlem Renaissance and the Chicano Arts Movement and he is writing a creative, non-fiction work on Latinidad and mental illness. He has contributed to TheBody.com, *Bipolar Magazine*, Harvard's *H-Bomb Sex Magazine*, and the Gran Varones Project.

Omar O. González is a native of the indigenous community of Ysleta, Texas. He completed his doctoral dissertation focusing on the work of John Rechy at the César E. Chávez Department of Chicana/o Studies at the University of California, Los Angeles, under the direction of Professor Alicia Gaspar de Alba. He teaches in the Department of Chicana and Chicano Studies at California State University, Northridge.

Gibrán Güido is a PhD candidate in the Department of Literature at the University of California at San Diego and a founding member of the Association for Jotería Arts, Activities, and Scholarship (AJAAS). He is a recipient of the National Association for Chicana and Chicano Studies Frederick A. Cervantes Student Premio for best graduate paper and twice the recipient of the San Diego Human Dignity Foundation's PFLAG Richard P. Geyser Ethics Memorial Scholarship for his commitment to LGBTQA equality and ethics. He co-edited *Queer in Aztlán: Chicano Male Recollections of Consciousness and Coming Out* (Lambda Literary Awards Finalist).

Carlos Manuel is Associate Professor of Theatre and the Chair of the Drama Department at Contra Costa College in San Pablo, California. He is a produced and published playwright, theatre director, and actor. Comedic or dramatic, his work addresses issues on immigration, gay/queer sexuality, and Latina/o identity.

Joe Earvin Martinez was born in the suburbs of Sylmar, California, and grew up in San Fernando Valley and Antelope Valley. He earned his Master of Arts in Communication Studies with an emphasis in Performance, Language, and Cultural Studies from California State University, Northridge. He lives with his family, partner, and dogs in Palmdale, California. His father resides in Rosarito, Mexico, where he and his family visit.

Jesus D. Mendez Carbajal is a graduate in the Community-Based Block (CBB), Multicultural Counseling & Social Justice Education Master of Science Degree Program in the Department of Counseling & School Psychology at San Diego State University. Born in Guerrero, Mexico, Jesus was raised on the Kumeyaay lands of San Diego, California.

Daniel Enrique Pérez holds a PhD from Arizona State University. He is an Associate Dean in the College of Liberal Arts at the University of Nevada, Reno, and author of *Rethinking Chicana/o and Latina/o Popular Culture and the edited collection Latina/o Heritage on Stage: Dramatizing Heroes and Legends*. Born in Texas, he was raised in Phoenix and now resides in Reno.

Yosimar Reyes is a nationally acclaimed poet and public speaker. Born in Guerrero, Mexico, and raised in Eastside San Jose, Reyes earned a BA in Creative Writing from San Francisco State University. His work explores themes of migration and sexuality and has been published in various anthologies and online journals. His first collection of poetry, *For Colored Boys Who Speak Softly*, was published through collaboration with the legendary Carlos Santana. He is working on the one-man show, *Prieto*. He is a Lambda Literary Fellow and the recipient of the Undocupoets Fellowship.

Luis A. Chavez Rodriguez is a native of San Diego, California. He is completing a master's degree at the School of Leadership and Education Sciences in the Counseling and Marital and Family Therapy program at the University of San Diego.

Gustavo V. Segade is Emeritus Professor of Spanish at San Diego State University (SDSU), a literary critic, poet, translator, and activist. He was born in New York City of a Puerto Rican mother and Cuban father. He completed his doctoral studies from the University of Arizona and in 1969 became the first chairman of the Department of Chicana and Chicano Studies at SDSU. He has translated the works of Latin American, Mexican, and Chicano writers including Mónica Lavín. *Points of Departure*, Gabriel Trujillo Muñoz, *Permanent Work: Poems 1981–1992*, and Sergio Elizondo, *Perros y Antiperros*.

Daniel Vidal Soto is a poet, lecturer, and multimedia essayist. As a teenager his interest in science led to research work on high particle physics at the University of Texas, Arlington, and FermiLab through the University of Chicago. His writing appears in *The Border Crossed Us: An Anthology to End Apartheid*, the multimedia "Latino Rebels, Nerds of Color" (under the penname Professor Mex), La Bloga Floricanto, and Cloud City Press. He has performed his work at the Smithsonian Institution in Washington, DC, and for the Danspace Project at St. Mark's Church-in-the-Bowery. He received a bachelor's degree in English Language and Literature from Macalester College, St Paul, Minnesota, and taught at the Department of English at Long Island University, Brooklyn. He is from Barrio North Side in Fort Worth, Texas, and works out of Brooklyn, New York.

CHAPTER 1

Introduction: Queer Chicano/Mexicano Accounts of Fathers, Fathering, and Fatherhood

Adelaida R. Del Castillo

In many ways this book is about telling. A telling that may not be fulfilled or accomplished as originally intended perhaps because the use of the written text may not always be easy or necessarily the most capacious means of

---

I use the terms Mexican and Mexicano to refer to Mexican nationals. However, I may use the term Mexicano in this essay when referring to individuals born or residing in the United States who may also identify as Mexican in addition to other cultural or political monikers of self-identity. For example, for cultural and political reasons when in this country I identify as Mexican, Mexicana, Chicana, and Latina. The terms Mexican American, Chicano, and Chicanx refer to individuals of Mexican descent born or raised in the United States. I also may use the terms Latino and Latinx to refer to different generations of Mexicans collectively or individuals of Latin American descent born, raised, or residing in the United States.

A. R. Del Castillo (✉)
Department of Chicana and Chicano Studies, San Diego State University,
San Diego, CA, USA
e-mail: delcast1@sdsu.edu

© The Author(s), under exclusive license to Springer Nature
Switzerland AG 2021
A. R. Del Castillo, G. Güido (eds.), *Fathers, Fathering, and Fatherhood*, Palgrave Studies in Literary Anthropology,
https://doi.org/10.1007/978-3-030-60877-4_1

conveying human access to knowing and being in the world. We might perhaps conceive of or compare the writing process, as does Anzaldúa (1987), to a shamanic act with a life force of its own capable of tapping into different ways of knowing and altered states of awareness. Or take Barthes at his word when he tells us the power of text *is not representation* but rather the ability of the text to exceed its purpose as the object of fixed, predetermined, or closed practices of meaning (Moriarty 1991). And it is fixity and restricted ways of arriving at meaning that we want to veer from in this collection so that much of it—visual art, prose, or verse—gives expression to the quality and incongruity of being in human relationships linked to aspects of kinship, sexuality, culture, and class that may not easily fit quotidian patterns of the typical or the ritual ideals of society. The decolonizing of ethnography[1] is taken to heart and further tweaked by theoretical concepts of decolonizing reality[2] to better comprehend the lived experience of radical others and their states of being marked by inter-actional registers of outsider positionalities.[3] Encounters with difference are conveyed as authentically as possible allowing authors to voice and construct their lived and inner experience as they must. Master categories of kinship, sexuality, culture, class, or even notions of time may be ren-dered provisional for a fuller description of being in the world according to its own aesthetics of making sense of particular realities even when out of sync with the ordinary or the practices and procedures of authority.

Different aspects of time, and memory, and the very act of writing appeared to be significant to several contributors some of who took these notions apart and reassembled them as if hieroglyphs of stress, the meaning of which should not or could not easily be spoken. Such is the metamor-phosis of temporal reckoning in the work "A Performance Recovery: Cruising Fathered Memories Through Dependency Circuits" by Joe E. Martinez (Chap. 20) where time and homelife quickly come undone to a textual beat that grows more and more disconcerting as things come into and out of the household leaving it bare of large items. The incessant pace of fleeting things, deeds, and kin—father, uncle, mother, perceptive son, his dear siblings, that aunt, cousins—is … is what, for what? Time loses that numerical force that once linked it to the hours of a normal day and morphs into very specific repetitive acts of acquisition, ingestion,

---

[1] See Tuhiwai Smith (2012) and Mohanty (2003).
[2] See Anzaldúa (1987) and Keating (2015).
[3] Some of which include race, class, ethnicity, skin color, gender identity, and sexuality.

release, and fatigue. And because of it the household too must now regroup as it relocates from neighborhood to neighborhood, each move a temporal beat of infinitesimally sharp slivers of embodied pain, remembering, and change in the precocious queer boy who is watching and is growing up.

Temporal reckoning takes a different form in the work *"Querido Padre: Things I Want to Tell You and Other Thoughts"* by Adán Campos (Chap. 23). As if code for spoken and unspoken knowledge, time shifts between here and there as the author finds his way through moments of loss and longing for the father. One might even say, time plays an agentive force in this process of recollection by making impossible any further renewed or persisting relations between father and son. Campos writes, "Years after your death I realized part of me felt robbed. You were taken suddenly, without notice". Death as fixed and finite time cheats and removes the potential for what might possibly have turned out to be a more gratifying relationship between the two. The author then complicates time and memory by questioning their reliability in the face of contrasting versions of the father by those who knew him better than did the son or at least knew him longer. But enough. The son will speak of and to his father any which way he pleases. Memory takes the son back to a body of water, a vast ocean, then startingly Adán reveals his father *once saved his life*. But the father is angry and the child is cold and distressed. That was father who pulled me out of the water, wasn't it? The emotional strength of the work outmaneuvers the fixity of time through sheer, unrelenting longing. Father is back! And we too are made to feel a son's complex feelings for the complicated person father *is*.

The very act of writing is generative for other reasons. In "Unwriting the Father" (Chap. 5), R. Allen Baros suggests the process of crafting written work may take the author in unexpected directions that may be instructive. Such a turn may let the author see his father in a different light by adding to those perceptions he may have held about his father before he began the project. In no way does this suggest such insights are necessarily ameliorative or take the place of stronger, more ambivalent feelings regarding the father and his choices. In *"Todo sobre mi madre/*All About My Mother" (Chap. 8), the writing process brings clarity to Carlos Manuel. After years of preoccupation with matters having to do with the father and questions imploring the revelation of his authenticity comes the realization through the very act of writing that it is his mother who has been the vital force in his life and in the survival of their family. Is it any wonder writing has such vitality? Long ago, our native ancient ancestors examined truth through the wisdom of writing[4] and in her own work Anzaldúa integrates such concepts to reconceptualize contemporary imperatives on self-awareness.[5]

Why This Book?

Not long after Gibrán and I completed work on *Queer in Aztlan: Chicano Male Recollections of Consciousness and Coming Out* (Del Castillo and Güido 2014), Gibrán suggested we turn our attention to queer Chicano men and their fathers. Unresolved issues between queer Chicano men and their Chicano/Mexicano fathers suggested generative encounters between them. In a previous work,[6] Gibrán's coming out to his father did not turn out well and consequently communication between them ended for many years. In the essay for this collection, "Our Shimmering and Ephemeral DNA" (Chap. 22), Gibrán suggests fatherhood may be an integral part of oneself expressed through the personhood of the father who, although estranged from the son for many years, somehow remains connected to him not only biologically, but emotionally, cognitively, and through spiritual links that transcend time and connect the pair psychically as if one. Here the son makes use of other sensibilities to make sense of vulnerabilities in himself that may be a reflection of the father's own but for which there is no point of origin for these and other liabilities or for where the father's being ends and the son's begins or for who's to blame for what. If the son, in moments of despair and anxiety, returns to the self and its alien terrain, he may be surprised to find that it is there that he inadvertently links to the father, supporting and sustaining him as he does the self. To do otherwise is to remain fragmented and alienated from a much vaster and more varied personhood. Here the son acknowledges and accepts a profound link to the father. Still, how does a queer son come out to a homophobic parent? In "No Last Name" (Chap. 24) Yosimar Reyes doesn't get the opportunity to speak to his father about such matters because he was still a child when his father came by to see his boys intending to establish a promising relationship with them that did not pan out. Perhaps the boys called too often, the phone line eventually was disconnected. And when

---

[4] See León-Portilla (1963), especially Chaps. 1, 3, and 5 on these themes among the Nahua.
[5] See Anzaldúa (1987), Chap. 6.
[6] See Güido (2014).

the father returned years later to pick up where he left off, the boys were no longer invested, Reyes writes, "we are men now, Pelón and I have demons of our own. We made men of ourselves without a blueprint". In the poetry of Jesus Daniel Mendez Carbajal, the son, too, is no longer in a waiting mood, in "Chrysalis" (Chap. 26) the son confronts the father by telling him "I'm now 21 years old and I'm through with staying silent / I'm here to cash in my overdue father-son time, father-son love, cash in my endless coupons and redeem lost time" but in "Communion" (Chap. 25), the son is attentive and compassionate when he writes, "If we forgive our fathers, we humanize them, put them back together / Piece by piece, limb by limb, help them become whole again". And the poetry of Xuan Carlos Espinoza-Cuellar lets us know others have stepped in as father figures for him, in "God is Never Ashamed of Us" (Chap. 29) Espinoza-Cuellar writes, "My grandpa said, 'ask me anything' / So I asked / 'Why don't you wear shoes instead?' / 'Because I'm going to the house of god, and he sees us as we are—poor, brown, Indian, fat'". In the poem "My Padrino" (Chap. 28) it is his godfather Espinoza-Cuellar speaks of, "My godfather is an organic intellectual/ He knows hundreds and hundreds of sacred plants / He sings to them, summons their energies / He says to me '*la primera alabanza es el canto*' (the first form of worship is song)." Someone, too, is mentoring him in "You Will Love" (Chap. 30) with all the tenderness and regard we expect from those who gave us life.

Gibrán was right, turning our attention to notions of fathering and fatherhood made sense for several reasons some of which were the near absence, quality, and timeliness of literature on straight Chicano men and their fathers let alone literature with any attention to gender identity and same-sex desire. We have much to learn about queer Chicano/Mexicano male kin relations in the United States especially with regard to relations with fathers and notions of fatherhood. My own ethnographic fieldwork (Del Castillo 1993, 1996) on sex/gender meaning in female-headed households in Mexico City revealed the performance of gendered scripts by heterosexual men in these households that were more expansive of traditional ideals of Mexican male-dominant gender ideology. This led me to better understand and appreciate the greater tolerance and flexibility gendered behavior among lower income groups is allowed at the local level especially resulting from economic survival strategies. However, my work was not meant to be representative of Chicano culture or Chicano men and their families.[7] Although Mexican and Chicana/o cultures are related in many ways, their situatedness and development in different nation states result in distinct historical, socio-political, economic, cultural, linguistic, and other variations. Gibrán and I sought first-person accounts on the topic of fathers, fathering, and fatherhood open to greater levels of complexity through, if possible, the interplay of queer sexuality, kinship, culture, and/or class. Such would enrich and contribute to the social science literature and family studies on queer sexuality and especially the emergent field of Jotería studies.[8] Even if not exclusively on Chicanos or Latinos, Andrew Gottlieb's studies on queer sexuality's impact on the family published in the books *Out of the Twilight: Fathers of Gay Men Speak* (2000), *Sons Talk About Their Gay Fathers* (2003), and *Side by Side: On Having a Gay or Lesbian Sibling* (2005) helped to establish a particular direction in LGBT family studies. All three are framed by psychoanalytic theory and based on structured surveys and participant interviews. The first two offer participants' stories crafted by the psychoanalyst granting him final authority and assessment over the representation of the other's lived experience, which is not uncommon in social science literature with its deference to professional certainty. The third book is an edited collection by Gottlieb that allows participants to tell their own stories. Alfredo Mirandé, a sociologist, also takes a survey approach in *Hombres y Machos: Masculinity and Latino Culture* (1997), which includes a discussion on Mexican men and fatherhood based on survey data collected by the author and ultimately seen through his analytical perspective. The question of power, agency, and the construction of the text matters significantly if we take to heart what theorists such as Foucault, Deleuze, Barthes, and others have found wanting in modern "objective" constructs when having to give expression to the language of sexuality, desire, love, loss, the evocative, and the emotive. The anthology *Muy Macho: Latino Men Confront Their Manhood* (1996) edited by Ray Gonzalez allows its contributors, prominent Latino authors, greater creative freedom in the format and content of essays that address the patriarch and masculinity but none has a father writing about a gay son. In our own collection, the prose poem "My Two Sons" (Chap. 11) by Gustavo V. Segade represents the only contribution among our 30 chapters written by a father about his gay

---

[7] For a different approach in this direction, see the work of Richard T. Rodriguez (2009) and its literary critique of constructions of male sexuality in Mexican American and Chicano families in the imaginary of the Chicana/o Movement, art, film, music, and other media.

[8] See Álvarez and Estrada (2019), and Güido (in progress).

sons. We're not sure exactly what to make of this or what it suggests about Latino fathers and the public recognition and praise of gay sons but it may be due to the younger demography among which we made our call for papers.

Perhaps one of the most suggestive and complex statements on Mexican fatherhood is represented in Richard Rodriguez's *Days of Obligations: An Argument with My Mexican Father* (1992). His work is particularly pertinent to our project because, although never directly acknowledged in the text, one is aware, as perhaps is the father, of the author's closeted homosexuality and the implicitly coded approach to same-sex desire in the book. Already in his previous book, *Hunger of Memory* (1982), Rodriguez provides the reader with subtle, sophisticated registers to his sexuality and tends to depict his father as a rather cold and removed father figure. In contrast, explicit same-sex desire and longing are the subject of Rigoberto Gonzalez's *Butterfly Boy: Memories of a Chicano Mariposa* (2006). The book tells of the author's troubled relationship with his frequently absent Mexican father exposing tension of various kinds between a Chicano queer son and his Mexican father. There occurs, for example, an erotically charged episode between the father and son that remains inexplicable. This raises the topic of fathers and father figures as objects of sexual desire. Desire of the father or father figure is raised in "Border Crossings" (Chap. 18) by Omar O. González where the author's married uncle is desired. In the essay a 12-year-old Omar begins a sexual liaison with his uncle who refers to Omar as "mi'jo" (my son) as young men often are by older others in Mexican culture. Omar is a willing participant and seems to take partial responsibility for the act by referring to his "hypersexuality." Might this disposition explain sex with a stepfather when Omar was a child? The author seems to suggest such could have been more compelling had the stepfather not been so unresponsive to the sexual needs of the boy. In a previous work[9] González recalls the occurrence of man-boy sex possibly with this same stepfather. For many of us such acts and encounters are unthinkable, indefensible, and criminal. González, however, uses normative incongruities that appear to be ironic or silly that disarm us and serve to distract our attention to what is taking place. For example, the sexual encounter between the minor and his uncle is rendered with attention to mannered behavior or appropriate social deference as culturally expected of and prescribed for minors when addressing their elders or

[9] See González (2014).

social betters. In a second contribution to the collection, "Make Me Your Toxic Son, Daddy": The Bio-Familial Bonds Created by Gay Men Vis-à-vis 'Bug Chasing' and 'Gift Giving' (Chap. 21) González fetishizes Daddy as the object of desire among gay men of seropositive status and their imaginary of father-son constructions.

One of the most enigmatic treatments of the father in Chicano homo-erotic literature remains John Rechy's in the first chapter of *City of Night* (1963). One understands the boy in this chapter is based on Rechy himself and the family on his own family. The father's emotional and physical treatment of the boy is complicated in many ways not the least of which is the result of Rechy's own varied rendering (through changes in the galleys for the book) of in incident involving the game "give me a thousand," which the father plays with the boy (Del Castillo, 2014, p. 196). Rechy prefers to recall the particulars of the game, when his biographer asks about it,[10] as an example of a Mexican male's expression of fatherly love even though others may see the game as more disturbing.

Finally, in this collection, a discussion on scholarship on Latino queer sons and fathers is offerred in "Like Father, Like Queer Son?: Gay Chicanx and Latinx Males and Their Fathers" (Chap. 27) by Daniel Enrique Pérez. He reviews literature and film media on Chicano and Latino father-son relationships with particular attention on queer sons that also includes and examines the author's relationship with his own father.

Approach, Voice, and Style

In our call for papers we asked potential contributors to write as raw, bold, straightforwardly honest, and/or unapologetically daring as they pleased about how acts of fathering and/or notions of fatherhood—whether physical, emotional, psychological, sexual, spiritual, or other—marked their lived experience as gay, queer, or transgender persons. We asked contributors to think about how their lives and notions of manhood, masculinity, and/or gender identity were shaped by their relationships with their fathers, father figures, and/or the absence of fathering. We asked about personal recollections of the dynamics between heterosexual fathers and/or father-figures and gay/queer or transgender children. And we asked about how gay, queer, transgender positionality functions in the contestation of traditional notions of manhood and/or masculinity. Having

[10] See Casillo (2002), pp. 40–41.

worked on the previous collection on queer Chicano sexuality, Gibrán and I were prepared for the possibility that first-person accounts of sexuality might prove difficult for contributors having to recall and relive matters now being written about. Soon after submissions began arriving, it became clear to us the selections were remarkable in many ways, some for their stunning clarity and compassion, others for their literary approach, or for their irony and humor, or earnest urgency, and still more for their regard of fathers, father-figures, and queer sons in addition to raising issues of ethnicity, culture, class, spirituality, indigeneity, HIV/AIDS, desire, erotics, belonging, and coming to terms with loss.

THE PRESENCE OF BEING

The verse and prose in this collection remind us of the negotiated quality of meaning-making that may or may not resolve what is true or real when uncertainty is a possibility. For this reason we begin Part 1, *"Can I write about my father?"*: Representations of the Presence of Being with the poetry of Daniel Vidal Soto and his signification of the father and the station of fatherhood in "Sky Maps," "Journal 2," and "January Spirals" as troubled, unstable notions. Soto approaches the presentation of the father cautiously as if unsure of his authenticity giving us the sense that both the father and fatherhood are not true enough but rather a simulation of a positionality and project located somewhere in that garage-hyperreality where the father bangs away most nights on expensive cars he repairs for a commission. From this vantage point the reader of "Journal 2" (Chap. 3) can tell that although the pater is without form, he is at least associated with a kind of presence linked to the sound of clanking tools and the sharp light of a blow torch. This is not to say the son is emotionally removed or physically distant from his father. In "January Spirals" (Chap. 4) both occupy the same house where the son, ever unable to sleep, has gotten used to the trail of sounds his father leaves in his early-morning departures to work and late-night arrivals from work, only to exit once again to the garage where more work awaits him. The son comes to understand that broader structures of social injustice and racial discrimination undermine his father's best efforts to protect and provide for the family in having to reside in a small racist Texas town. We detect, nonetheless, a feeling of affective ambiguity and perhaps ambivalence on the part of the son toward the father and we are not quite sure what the cause of this might be until we recall the young man in Soto's fourth poem "How to Compromise

Yourself" (Chap. 19) in Part 4 mentions his parents would disown him if they knew he was having sex with a man. In "Sky Maps" (Chap. 2) the father is incapable of physically reaching the boy whose movements he is attempting to control and by the end of the poem the boy, now a young man, is leaving home under the duress of a homelessness that awaits him. In "January Spirals" we learn his father's father was an exegete and practitioner of the Christian faith. But what is to be made of all this when the son in the poem "January Spirals" questions his ability to write about the father if it leads to the creation of false memories and to what purpose? Tellingly, the poet is reluctant to write about the father if what results is self-serving and subjective. But if he must, and he must for the father is a vital part of the many things the poet holds fast to in his arsenal of memories; if he must then let it be the ephemeral that gently evokes that slippery ground between fatherhood and fatherlessness.

In "Unwriting the Father" R. Allen Baros was clear on who he thought his father was only to have this confidence disrupted by changing circumstances and the writing process itself. The author once knew his father as buoyant with winning attributes and American Dream achievements; this father is charming, loves his wife and children as they do him, and is a loving son to parents who hold him in high regard. The father's fine character and qualities endure years and years to the continued admiration of his family and adult son. Then comes a change of focus that grows sharper now on this page and then on another, clarity zooms in and out as if looking through an optical lens and the son comes to feel he might not know this father at all. This can't be. The author suggests there is an underlying morality to the performance of family relations that hinge on the father's promise to fulfill normative and cultural ideals. It is the father's enactment of the roles of father, son, and husband that sets into motion a moral economy that sustains a social network of family relationships making it possible for each member of the family to play their respective gendered and cultural roles. So it is unlikely a proper father would renege on such a vital and moral commitment. But it appears this father has, even if a bit late in life. But if this is true and the father is no longer conforming to family expectations, the strongminded son will have it out with him and force the father to do the right thing. The intended enactment of such resolve culminates for the son in a searing epiphany of laser beam lucidity, the kind that shatters ideals and patio furniture. The writing process itself brings further clarity and irony as the author wonders if the father has exercised the kind of freedom to make choices that the son wants for himself especially because as a queer man he is unwilling to fulfill the gender and cultural ideals he expects of his father. The difficulty of this situation, the author reminds us, is what comes of hero worship and the construction of the father, husband, and son through the uncritical narrative accounts of loving and devoted members of the family. Even so things don't bode well. Now when father and son meet, the son conveys to the reader they no longer assume or interact with each other through traditional kinship roles of father and son. Instead two men sit across from each other estranged by developing circumstances as they tentatively devise ways of being with each other.

Not unlike Soto, Peranda, too, is wary of master narratives of the Mexican father and traditional notions of fatherhood. In "Overall Prince, Now Father Lauren: On Becoming a Two-Spirit Butch Queen Father" (Chap. 6), he queers decolonial ways of conceptualizing and practicing expansive notions of fatherhood informed by different registers of indigeneity and sexuality first through sacred rituals of transformation that change young men into warriors through the Mexika/Aztec Ocelotl ceremony then through Peranda's own reading of the divine duality of ancient Mesoamerican deities as an affirmation of two-spirit sexual identity. To queer the notion of fatherhood in this way is to make it "exceedingly excellent" and "ovah" the top while simultaneously allowing the notion to serve as a disruptive force against the very institution of fatherhood and its oppressive tendencies. But before these experiences, there was another—Peranda's first contact with fatherhood as the son of an exceptional man who was open to and excited about his sons' curiosity, capacities, and learning. Together these experiences help introduce the reader to the Ballroom Scene culture where Black and Latino gay, queer, and trans participate and compete in vogueing and other categories as part of groups known as "houses" modeled on the family with a father and mother. In this essay Peranda suggests alternative ways of fatherhood that deploy inclusive and compassionate strategies of being and consciousness in the making of what he refers to as a "House butch queer Father." Of the latter, Peranda writes, "what is most amazing and warm is that the ballroom children and parents see and acknowledge traditional forms of creating oneself, and honor is served. Because of my Ocelotl status, some Ballroom Icons and Pioneers seem to be a little more open in sharing their knowledge because they know, understand, and trust that I follow a sacred, ancient code of ethics that always protects the communities in which I find myself."

FAMILY SETTINGS

A sense of the culturally familiar is evoked in Part 2, Fathers, Father Figures, and the Family by unfolding father/father-figure-son relationships within the context of the family and traditional Tex-Mex, Mexicano, Chicano, or hybrid culture. In "Tommy Paved the Way" (Chap. 7) Robert Jude "Corky" Frausto uses humor to tell about the ups and downs of growing up a frail, effeminate boy in Eagle Pass, a Texas border town where his father is a community leader. The father is tough and intolerant but cares about his son and teaches Corky to deflect the perception of weakness and powerlessness through norms of masculinity. But it is not until the boy, now an orphan adolescent, goes to live in his uncle Tommy's household that Corky comes to value and accept himself as he is. Tommy is a large, ex-military, flamboyant elder uncle and friend of Colonel Frank Dixon, a survivor in the Philippine theatre of the unspeakable Bataan Death March during WWII. Both veterans are now openly gay and Dixon frequently drops by the house to drink, enjoy music, and play card games with uncle Tommy and friends. Corky learns that queer men even if effeminate are capable of becoming brave war heroes by overcoming truly insurmountable challenges. Uncle Tommy's large presence and outrageous humor, his love of being alive and acceptance of his sexuality serves the growing boy well.

But such is not the case for the Mexican boy who is Carlos Manuel in "*Todo sobre mi madre*/All about My Mother." This boy is a watcher of people who also listens when people least expect it to what they share and fear about boys without fathers, like himself, growing up to be gay. The boy's inquisitiveness drives him to search through his mother's things. This results in questions about his real father, his past fathering experience at the hands of a hater, and a provisional father figure—his maternal grandfather—a gun-wielding macho who serves as the head of a family clan of uncles, aunts, cousins, and step-siblings. The boy does grow up to be gay and he often wonders if fatherlessness had something to do with it. No thanks to the clan, the young man's life is one of denial and "doubt, fear, uncertainty, shame, guilt, self-mutilation, [and] internalized homophobia". Resilience comes through creative expression and writing. And it is through the process of writing this particular account that the author realizes it is senseless to think about the father when it is the mother who has been the most significant parental figure in his life. It is she, Carlos insists, who is worthy and deserving of honor and respect as a guiding figure.

Love and respect for an open-minded and honorable father is the subject of "Tito—A Remembrance of My Father" (Chap. 9), Larry T. Baza's tribute to his father. Tito Cepeda Baza, a Guamanian "Chamorro" youth, arrived in the United States during WWII to train in San Diego. He along with Filipino trainees were assigned as "Stewards" and functioned as servants and cooks in the barracks of non-commissioned officers, naval kitchens, and the private homes of high-ranking naval officers. Although Tito achieved the rank of Chief Petty Officer he would not speak to his sons of his naval experience but he was aware of and supported civil rights activism and was proud of his sons for being participants in such causes. When Tito came to San Diego he met and married Larry's mother, Hortensia Jenny Celaya, a Mexican American girl, before departing to serve his new country. Thereafter, the bride, the bride's sisters, and mother, Eloisa, turned Tito's household into a matriarchal domain where the women, and Eloisa's African American husband, Ernest, loved and nurtured Larry. Ernest was Larry's only father-figure until Tito returned home. The family allowed Larry to grow as he pleased until his Uncle Dooney teased the teenage Larry for being effeminate. By the time he was in high school Larry had learned to fit in by acting straight and having girlfriends while still having sex with men. In time Larry married a woman he, his father, and family admired and with whom Larry remained friends after their divorce. Finally, Larry came out to his brother and he persuaded Larry to speak to their father as well and he was right to do so. Later the father would bond with Larry's husband through their mutual love of gardening.

José H. Cadena's art is featured in this collection because of its attention to themes on fatherhood and queer Chicano/Mexicano sexuality. His narrative "Deddy" (Chap. 10) is situated on the US-Mexico border region between San Diego and Tijuana, an exopolis of hybrid Mexican, American, Mexican American, and Latino cultural attributes[11] and transborder dynamics.[12] Although assimilated to American ways, José is considerate and deferent to his father as traditionally expected of a Mexican son. The day comes when José opens up to his father allowing him to learn of a part of the self that José has kept secret. But the father is stunned by the revelation as if something in him stopped. Of what use is a father's influence? Of what use is all that cultural capital that goes into the formation of a son? But the son cannot possibly abide by his father's commandment, it is not

---

[11] See Adelaida R. Del Castillo and Jose Manuel Valenzuela Arce, (2004), "The Transborder Exopolis and Transculturation of Chican@ Studies" *Aztlan*, (29)1, 121–123.

[12] See Norma Iglesias Prieto, 2017, Transborderisms: Practices that tear down walls. In R. Real (Ed.), *Border wall as architecture* (pp. 22–25), University of California Press.

something you fix. Time comes and goes as it must, but what is time without quality? That day his father called, could he have done so because of our capacity as sentient beings to know that life diminishes when once it dazzled in the life force energy of a child no longer there? The father called and because of it both father and son trek through mundane swap meets and thrift stores where they've been before giving expression once more to immediate moments of knowing; the father alert and mindful of the surprising qualities and depth of the other.

In "Punched in the Stomach" (Chap. 12) Marcus H. Fisher recalls unique aspects of his relationship with his father in a matter-of-fact manner as if told from a young boy's perspective that invites more open cognitive possibilities. We are told, for example, that his father met Marcus in a vivid dream before he was born and that his father told Marcus he had a purpose in life. An artist and reader, Marcus did well in school but the kids were intolerant of effeminate boys who could not throw a ball or ride a bike. The father enrolls his son in a self-defense class but the rigor of the training turns out to be too painful and demanding, the boy just could not take a punch to the stomach. Later on, it seems as if the young man wonders if he had stayed in the class and endured the demands of painful training would he have been better prepared for the demands of life?

NEURODIVERSITY

A topic we had not anticipated emerged explicitly in many of the essays. Issues of mental health, in particular, bipolar disorder and schizophrenia, were identified as impacting fathers, sons, both fathers and sons in the same family, as well as other members of the family, and were vividly discussed as influential in shaping parent-son relationships. In response to the need to openly address matters of mental health as part of self-identity Part 3, Fatherhood, Queer Consciousness, and Neurodiversity was created although not originally envisioned as part of the book.

In the opening chapter to the section, "'¿Cómo estás, mi niño? (How Are You, My Boy?)': Memories of Father and Fatherhood—Mental Illness, Enforced Masculinity, and Loss" (Chap. 13), Eddy F. Álvarez Jr. tells of the death of his father during which the elder women of his extended family expect him to step into the cultural role of head of the family. The situation, the author reminds us, is not unlike the matriarchal power expressed in *The House of Bernarda Alba* by García Lorca. Since his childhood the women in the family anticipate that Álvarez, the family's only boy, will fulfill the traditional familial duty expected of the oldest son so they groom him as the *hobrecito* (little man) of the household. But the boy's interests and sexuality lay elsewhere and it is not until the impending death of his father that Álvarez, now a young man, becomes head of the family. Although his father loved him and accepted his queer sexuality, as a youth Eddy could be short or become frustrated with him because his father suffered from schizophrenia and could be obsessively overprotective of Eddy. In part, guilt and moral obligation compel the author to assume leadership over the family during this difficult period. However, given the sexism and homophobia of family members, Álvarez makes it a point to police the expression of his own queer sexuality so as not to appear unmanly to grieving relations who already suspect his sexuality. In addition, the author suppresses any affective expression of grieving for his father, which he feels would be inconsistent with the expected hypermasculinity of his new cultural role. These restrictions on his personal sensibilities and behavior subject the author to exceptional moments of pain and anguish, isolation, and subsequent need for emotional relief and support. None of which he receives except perhaps when he gets on the freeway, turns up the volume on the radio, and breaks out into uncontrollable sobbing. This situation may lead us to suspect the author has rendered an affectively negative experience suggested by the policing of queer sexuality, the family's homophobia, the cultural imposition of heteronormative masculinity on males by females, and the sorrow with which the essay ends. But could something else be taking place? In "Race, Sex, and the Incommensurate: Gary Fisher with Eve Kosofsky Sedgwick" José Estevan Muñoz (2009) tells us "queerness" is about the incalculable of being alive suggestive of the "incommensurate" or infinitude made evident or accessible to us as *a sense* and not as *a politic*.[13] As such, although "queerness" does not yet exist in our world, queer people of color can engage in what Muñoz calls

---

[13] This mode of "queerness" is not to be confused with the queerness that has yet to exist in a "queer futurity" where it performs as a particular way of being in a world not yet manifested. It is also not to be confused with what Muñoz designates as "queer politics," which takes place in life or as part of lived experience and gives expression to concern over matters of social rights and social equality by individuals and groups who acknowledge and understand they are signified by their sexual difference. An example of a group engaged in queer politics, Muñoz tells us, is the LGBT movement in North America. It's important to note that queer politics is linked to the notion of "value as equivalence" which explains the social significance of notions of equality in contrast to "queerness," which can't be measured or achieved by notions of equality because being incalculable it is beyond politics.

"a queer politics of the incommensurable" (p. 193) that involves an agentic dynamic partly mobilized by queer people of color to manifest, share, or make accessible aspects of the "incalculable sense of queerness" (p. 193). That is, we can trace possibilities of the infinite through finite notions of the expansive and capacious as *a sense* available to all of us because sense is a kind of knowing that has no limits so it is not surprising that emotion is a means by which the incalculable is shared.[14] If we were to read Álvarez's text reparatively and not as a hermeneutics of suspicion,[15] we could say that in sharing his grief and lamentation—in part the outcome of his own collaborative but troubling undertaking of patriarchy and Latino performance of hypermasculinity—Álvarez gives expression to a queer of color grieving as a particularity of queerness that is not entirely limited to young queer Latino men sobbing in their cars but which Álvarez has made his own by sharing it as such with all of us. In effect, this finite sense of the infinite incalculable of human sorrow is healing and works as an expression of love and compassion capable of involving us all.

In contrast, the certainty in Miguel Garcia Jr.'s "My Dead Father" (Chap. 14) makes the reader feel as if the word "dead" in the title lays to rest not only its object but quite possibly any ontological exercise or religious creed that might reason or advocate for notions of fatherhood if fathers turn out to be like the author's own. So even though Miguel Sr. is not actually dead and gone, he is to Miguel Jr. Then, as if "dead" were a substance or contagion capable of spreading from father to son, it lodges in the son in the form of bipolar illness that subjects him to episodes "governed by an insatiable desire to feel deeply and to dare significantly". Feeling low about losing his physical attractiveness through the intake of lithium and feeling elderly about losing his sense of self through changes in the brain, the author likens bipolar illness to a rehearsal for death. But it is his grandmother, with whom he would garden as a boy, that he remembers telling him, "just like the wild weeds, [your mad] cousin served a purpose in our family; and though he was ill, he could recover and blossom into something beautiful and purposeful".

In "*Alchemistas* (Alchemists)" (Chap. 15) by Christian Emmañuel there also exists a certain vulnerability that prevents his mother's

---

[14] The other five, according to the work of Jean-Luc Nancy from which Muñoz borrows to explain the incalculable, are art, love, friendship, thought, and knowledge, see Muñoz (2009), p. 194.

[15] See Sedgwick (2002).

household from keeping the family together when faced with state orders allowing the father possession of the children. Though the mother's mental fragility is not the focus of this essay there is an underlying sense that it as well as poverty had something to do with the economic instability of the household, impending homelessness, and the father's success in destabilizing the family. What is made clear is the absolute power and sheer terror enforced on others by the machinations of a father who does not love nor is truly invested in his children. A reprieve from these troubles takes place when the author goes to live with his grandmother. There he learns of the power of self-determination (a possible foil to patriarchal ploys and painful subjectivity) and is given unconditional love. He writes of his grandmother, "She told me that my queerness is evidence of god's love, and that the pain I was born into was simply a matter of turning lead into gold. '*Es mi alchemista, con agencia puede transformar cualquieres*' (You are my alchemist, with agency you can transform anything you want)". Through the power of self-actualization the young man learned that hate and resentment were not useful, that fatherhood is an open concept consisting of different genders, and that queer masculinity and queer sexuality are particularities invested with difference and human dignity.

As mentioned above, the act of writing is generative in ways Mesoamerican ancestors linked to wisdom and divine truth, Anzaldúa finds the act of writing sacred because of its healing and transformative capacity.[16] In "Coming Home to Myself" (Chap. 16) by Luis A. Chavez Rodriguez this kind of healing lets the author examine inner and outer aspects of his life and relationships in his family and with his father that invite change. Through the writing process the author reveals experiences with depression since childhood that others in the family may not have wanted to acknowledge by addressing it given the fear of stigmatization. Yet he strives to find answers through therapy and medication, a sense of hope, open-mindedness, and readings that allow him to embrace a father with whom he has had a fraught relationship due to his own issues with mental illness. Lastly, having been schooled in San Diego, Chavez Rodriguez's transnationality and transborder sensibilities and capacities make possible his grasp of critical differences between sexual, class, and cultural beliefs and practices on both sides of the US International border that contribute to his transborder sexual identity.

---

[16] See Anzaldúa (1987), Chap. 6.

Finally, in the piece "The Best" (Chap. 17), Fredy Caballero resolves to negotiate challenges posed by mental health issues troubling his father who he has not spoken to in years. The author doesn't tell us why he and his father became estranged but we accept this silence as his decision. It's as if Fredy has chosen not to add to the list of wrongs that already mark his father's relationships with family members or perhaps he doesn't want to further burden his father. While attending undergraduate studies in this country, the author becomes engaged in social justice activism but experiences bouts of depression himself, which leads him to question whether he can help others if he can't help himself. It occurs to Fredy that perhaps his father drinks to alleviate his depression as does he. This allows Fredy to see his father in a new light and to become his father's champion among family relations who feel he has much to answer for.

Conclusion

It is evident the topic of fathers, fathering, and fatherhood has led our contributors in diverse directions and to new realizations that could have resulted in different ways of organizing the book. We chose six ways of dividing the collection with particular attention to presence and being in the world, the influence of the family, the impact of neurodiversity on queer sexuality and consciousness, Daddy issues and taboos, the quest for and reclaiming of the father, and fatherhood patterns and passion. The individual works by our contributors are reflected in the six parts of the book but are not meant to be captured exclusively by them due to the complexity of subjects they raise, some of which I have addressed herein. But one thing is clear, the essays in this collection are expressive of heartfelt knowing, urgency, resolve, compassion, and humor about authors's experiences with fathers and notions of fatherhood. And although no longer moored to normative realms, when Artaud considered what could be discussed publicly or privately he expressed this was no longer of concern to him because he insisted, "I know what is, that is all."[17]

[17] See Sontag (2009, p. 399).

REFERENCES

Álvarez, E. F., Jr., & Estrada, J. (2019). Jotería Studies. In H. Chiang & A. Arondekar (Eds.), *Global Encyclopedia of Lesbian, Gay, Bisexual, Transgender and Queer (LGBTQ) History* (pp. 863–867). Charles Scribner's Sons.

Anzaldúa, G. (1987). *Borderlands/la Frontera: The New Mestiza.* Aunt Lute.

Casillo, C. (2002). *Outlaw: John Rechy.* Alyson.

Del Castillo, A. R. (1993, Fall and Winter). Covert Cultural Norms and Sex/Gender Meaning: A Mexico City Case. *Urban Anthropology, 22*(3–4), 237–258.

Del Castillo, A. R. (1996). Female Breadwinners, Male Rage, and Gender Accommodation in Mexico City. In C. Pallán Figueroa, J. W. Wilkie, & J. A. Alejandre (Eds.), *Mexico and the Americas: VIII PROFMEX-ANUIES Conference Proceedings* (pp. 362–372). Mexico, DF: PROFMEX-ANUIES.

Del Castillo, A. R. (2014). [Review of the Book *City of Night: 50th Anniversary Edition,* by John Rechy]. *Aztlan: A Journal of Chicano Studies, 39*(2), 195–199.

Del Castillo, A. R., & Güido, G. (Eds.). (2014). *Queer in Aztlán: Chicano Male Recollections of Consciousness and Coming Out.* Cognella.

González, O. (2014). Constructing an Ofrenda of My Memory: A Poz Queer Chicano Indio Finds His Way Home. In A. R. Del Castillo & G. Güido (Eds.), *Queer in Aztlán: Chicano Male Recollections of Consciousness and Coming Out* (pp. 173–227). Cognella.

Gonzalez, R. (Ed.). (1996). *Muy Macho: Latino Men Confront Their Manhood.* Anchor Books.

González, R. (2006). *Butterfly Boy: Memories of a Chicano Mariposa.* University of Wisconsin Press.

Gottlieb, A. (Ed.). (2005). *Side by Side: On Having a Gay or Lesbian Sibling.* Routledge University Press.

Gottlieb, A. R. (2000). *Out of the Twilight: Fathers of Gay Men Speak.* Routledge University Press.

Gottlieb, A. R. (2003). *Sons Talk about Their Gay Fathers.* Routledge University Press.

Güido, G. (2014). My Shadow Beast. In A. R. Del Castillo & G. Güido (Eds.), *Queer in Aztlán: Chicano Male Recollections of Consciousness and Coming Out* (pp. 105–122). Cognella.

Güido, G. (In progress). Association of Jotería Arts, Activism, and Scholarship. In A. R. Del Castillo & N. Iglesias Prieto (Eds.), *Chicana and Chicano Encyclopedia: From Aztlán to Zapatistas.* Movements of the American Mosaics Series. Greenwood/Praeger.

Keating, A. L. (Ed.). (2015). *Light in the Dark/Luz en lo oscuro: Rewriting Identity, Spirituality, Reality / Gloria E. Anzaldúa.* Duke University Press.

Lamb, M. E. (2010). *The Role of the Father in Child Development.* Wiley.

León-Portilla, M. (1963). *Aztec Thought and Culture.* University of Oklahoma Press.

Mirandé, A. (1997). *Hombres y machos: Masculinity and Latino Culture.* Westview Press.

Mohanty, C. T. (2003). *Feminism Without Borders: Decolonizing Theory, Practicing Solidary.* Duke University Press.

Moriarty, M. (1991). *Roland Barthes.* Stanford University Press; New York University Press.

Muñoz, J. E. (2009). Race, Sex, and the Incommensurate: Gary Fisher with Eve Kosofsky Sedgwick. In *Cruising Utopia: The Then and There of Queer Futurity.* 10th Anniversary Edition. New York University Press.

Rechy, J. (1963). *City of Night.* Grove.

Rodriguez, R. (1982). *Hunger of Memory: The Education of Richard Rodriguez, an Autobiography.* Bantam.

Rodriguez, R. (1992). *Days of Obligation: An Argument with My Mexican Father.* Viking.

Rodríguez, R. T. (2009). *Next of Kin: The Family in Chicano/a Cultural Politics.* Duke University Press.

Sedgwick, E. (2002). Chapter 4: Paranoid Reading and Reparative Reading, or, You're So Paranoid, You Probably Think This Essay Is about You. In M. A. Barale, J. Goldberg, & M. Moon (Eds.), *Touching Feeling: Affect, Pedagogy, Performativity* (pp. 123–151). Duke University Press.

Sontag, S. (Ed.). (2009). *Antonin Artaud: Selected Writings.* Berkeley and Los Angeles: University of California Press.

Tuhiwai Smith, L. (2012). *Decolonizing Methodologies: Research and Indigenous Peoples.* Zed Books.

PART I

"*Can I Write About My Father?*": Representations of the Presence of Being

INTRODUCTION TO SECTION

Views of father/queer son relationships as ephemeral, unfolding, remade, and beloved. Fatherhood assumes a time and spatiality unsettled by illusive registers of affectivity and new cultural performativities of identity and desire.

Hardness was Diluted

CHAPTER 2

Sky Maps

Daniel Vidal Soto

Abstract Recollections of a father's vigilance over his mischievous child but as time passes the father can't or won't prevent a son's life elsewhere. We're not sure why the young man is leaving home; could it be due to his sexuality, intellect, or independent spirit? Possibly all three. This homelessness appears to remove the son from material loss, the familial domain, and rejection.

```
--------when I was young
------and haciendo males--------------------
----------------too distant-----------
For my father--------
------------------------to reach------------
------he'd grab a stone---------
--------------------------not so large that it'd damage
------not so heavy---------
-------------it wouldn't lift off the ground -----------
And throw it---------------------
```

D. V. Soto (✉)
Brooklyn, NY, USA

© The Author(s), under exclusive license to Springer Nature
Switzerland AG 2021
A. R. Del Castillo, G. Güido (eds.), *Fathers, Fathering, and
Fatherhood*, Palgrave Studies in Literary Anthropology,
https://doi.org/10.1007/978-3-030-60877-4_2

--------------------at my ankles---------------
Upon my impending homelessness
-------------he tells me----------------
----a hope for resolve-------------and a
-------------------goodbye---------------
-----& this was all Saturn--------
----------------could ever say--------------
Recounting I'd push his hugs-------------------
--------even after a lifetime, thinking -----------
----------------he never hugged me--------------
The night my phone cut off
-------------was the first--------I wished--------
------for my mother's voice----------
Stupid luck, this is how it works
------------I want her to lie-------------
-------------------tell me everything
Will be better------------
-----------& I am--------------
---not the only one on the train
Without a pressing fear---------
--------sometimes my own
Eye recounts a memory
That is not my own
-----------and soon, in this self vanishing-------
Does the foreign memory appear
-------once more stepping-------
--through the gate----------
----------------------a piece
------of self unseen
In a face's mirror-------------
------------a quickening depth------
I've found, on the street---------
----------a friend of mine-----------
-------a home that can't be taken------
---all the earth, the alien buildings & what----
--------------can't be forsaken----------

CHAPTER 3

Journal 2

Daniel Vidal Soto

Abstract Thoughts of past events framed by a tenuous present that grows darker perhaps due to some malady or experience portending pain and dying. But the past itself was deeply disappointing. A young boy is rejected by his grandparents and must return to a home without fixed meals or speech or presence of parents because one is seriously invalided and the other is overworking himself to dangerous levels of ill health.

I
I always say
The North Side
Was my first home
But it's not
It's River Oaks
A small shit town
Just outside the city
The city I'd thought
Was bigger than life

D. V. Soto (✉)
Brooklyn, NY, USA

A. R. Del Castillo, G. Güido (eds.), *Fathers, Fathering, and Fatherhood*, Palgrave Studies in Literary Anthropology,
https://doi.org/10.1007/978-3-030-60877-4_3

II
It wasn't until 3rd
That we moved
Really, just another extension
Of my father's story
Going north
From Coahuila, to El Paso
To Fort Worth, NYC, and even in my thoughts
Begin to wonder what the separation is
Between our paths

III
Seeing all the Mexicans
In the city made me happy
Me thinking all along
It was only white people
In the town
& got slapped back to reality
Seeing a white hand
Hit a brown face
At the sound of his mother's
Tongue

IV
Special education,
ESL,
I would have stayed
Were it not for my mom
Were it not for a teacher
With a heart
Who heard my answers
And responded with a prayer

V
But are such grants
Given to every apple?
When was the last time
One of them saw the new waves?
Made more brilliant and moving
By the ship's plowing

VI
I nearly forgot my deaths
But never thought
Poor me

VII
Or that time
Grandma rejected me
For her carnivorous son
My grandfather soon following
And my beginning century
As a child, as a human
Without them

VIII
& after this rejection
Came home
To a house with mother
Bedridden, neck & spine broken
Unable to cook or speak
Silent nights indeed

IX
& coming home again
To the blackness
That was my father's absence
Marked only by the sound
Of metal and flashes of fire
A howl of power tools
Channeling the powerful
Flow

X
All this I learned
Learning death and dying
And the ways to summon
The North Side
This brown curse or gift
Of skin, too deep for my knowing
Releasing heat from metal

Keeps the sword at aim
& I keep this river
Somewhere between
The sun's plasma
& my own semblance
Of what is common
For growing pains

CHAPTER 4

January Spirals

Daniel Vidal Soto

Abstract Fatherhood has a presence and a sound to it, slivers of images come to mind that evoke a collection of feelings about a father; a hard-working Mexican mechanic who allows overtime work to consume his life and health in the face of economic necessity. The precocious son is watchful and aware of the present-but-absent father who forsakes quality time for the commission the repair of cars brings in. Ever mindful, the son, now a man, is not sure he can write about his father without reducing him to a subjective, self-serving interpretation.

I
Can I write about my father?

The page seems much more open
Where I'd see a mountain converging
At the invisible spine.

D. V. Soto (✉)
Brooklyn, NY, USA

© The Author(s), under exclusive license to Springer Nature Switzerland AG 2021
A. R. Del Castillo, G. Güido (eds.), *Fathers, Fathering, and Fatherhood*, Palgrave Studies in Literary Anthropology,
https://doi.org/10.1007/978-3-030-60877-4_4

I can only recollect the face of a lion
A silly movie I'd watch every night
While hearing my father clank on an engine

Head—always bringing work home

II
My two distinct memories: father
Here at dusk, and then at dawn
with his cup of coffee, hearing
The silver scoop and pour milk into the ceramic

The heavy thud of his boots, as he puts
One foot down after tying the strings
Into a pretzeled star, the air was clear during

His mornings—unlike grandpa, who'd peer
Out into the monkey grass and elephant ears
With a cigarette in hand, mixing with
Mother's perfume and grandma's cooking

Everybody thought dad was the first to wake
But really it was I, and I could never sleep either

III
It's the kind of memory
That leaves you thinking
You're onto a poem
A new kind, new territory
Or new form

The kind that leaves you
Awakening to the empty stairs
Thinking, creating a false memory
To what end do I write my father?
Is it he I'm trying to create on the page?

IV
It was never like I really lacked for a father
If you count absence as a mark of his labor
-- and he did work hard – then he was

Just there, invisible.

        I remember every payday
        He'd come back home with a fifty-cent bag of chips
        For me and my sister. We'd watch aliens, horror
        Films of possessed dummies, and I'd hide
In the square made by his legs

V

This is still the type of mountain
That leaves me to light the candle
Of The Brave Indio's face

Whose wax has lasted for nearly
Two weeks, even though
I've let it lit overnight

              – not once

Having snuffed the damn fire out
And this is beyond the world of poetry
A more obscure reality I somehow
Observe and must note
That this flame was the entrance

VI

My father always kept it real
Telling me there are colonizers—the very
First time I heard this I was a child
And heard it again in college—he'd

Explain the French,
The Spanish, the Moors, the Arabs,
Are all also Mexican, but we are first
Coahuiltecans—a people before they arrived

VII

When dad was away, she hit
When dad was there, she'd stop
But yell at him
My mother tells an old story
Where he raised his hand
And he begged all night
To be let back in

VIII
To what end
Is this story his?
Or merely
My recount
Of something
That could be
Deftly
Subjective?

I am a rotten
Child of the US
An "American"
By birth and
Citizen

My father tells
his first meal
Was a slice of bologna
—real meat that could
Be eaten raw, with 24
Slices of meals
And an almost real
Taste of cooking—

What heaven
This country exists
He thought while
Unfolding the red
Plastic edge

IX
To what end
Am I
My grandpa's
Aberration?

A metonym
Across the
Time

My body
A material
Emptiness

Through which
He still sings
My grandmothers

Say I have his voice
My mother says
I have his eyes

And judging
By all the birds
I know

I've learned
His magic
Of flight

X
Morrison
Says it is by
Our mother's name
That we learn our destiny

But my father is Juan
The everyday Mexican
A day laborer, really

The kind who fixes
Your engines, gets
Oil and all viscous
Blackness in his nails

Digging through the metal
for white Bentleys and Buicks

XI
My father was always
Too ugly for my mother
Who was always
Too beautiful for everyone

And that's why she thought
She'd never end up with
The likes of a small-eyed
Mexican with pale skin,
Drooping face, an almost

Nagging connection to his mother
And a father that preached every Sunday

But my father was also
Too stubborn to let his love
Fleet away, and he did so oh so
Respectfully, giving her
Bouquets of freedom—real freedom
To let her live and choose

Until she chose
True transformation

XII
There was a time
When all the sprinkled
Mechanics
Filtered into father's
Lungs, into his bloodstream
And planted themselves
Right into his hip
Eating away cartilage
Like a nanobiological game
Of find and hunt

Until he became paralyzed
I watched him gather
All strength and what was left
Of our money until our sister
Took the only household job
Giving everything but twenty
Dollars for herself, and she still
Felt guilty for every last one

My father still has these stitches

On his spine, a clear line with
Perpendicular etches crossed
About nine ways
I don't remember when
He first began walking

But I do remember
Lying in his hospital bed

His hands—usually holding all
           his might in the silver hammer
           bolting down engines until
           the machine comes alive
           by his invention,
                        even the
           colossal wield of a crankshaft
               turns at his magic
           bolting into steady throws of light
now graze my head

CHAPTER 5

Unwriting the Father

R. Allen Baros

Abstract Although long committed to his marriage, a father's distancing from it as well as the writing process itself of the experience help the author understand that his straight father's refusal to reunite the family is not unlike a queer son's refusal to support traditional practices of marriage. Despite wanting to believe in the heteronormative family and expecting his father to remain loyal to its roles, commitments, and moral obligations, Baros himself must reject family tradition given his own sexuality. Ultimately, the author understands a father's promise to comply with whatever it takes to be a father may not always involve *free will* or capture the silences in the construction and telling of family narratives. Father/son ideals, Baros finds, necessitate rethinking and renewed practices and tolerances.

I ask my family to forgive me if I have poorly depicted them. Angie, Jeff, Mom, Azael, Ariadne, Dad, I love you. I've been afraid of this essay from the moment I started it. I hope you understand my fear and frustration vexed me to the point of writing.

R. A. Baros (✉)
Skagit Valley College, Seattle, WA, USA

37
A. R. Del Castillo, G. Güido (eds.), *Fathers, Fathering, and Fatherhood*, Palgrave Studies in Literary Anthropology, https://doi.org/10.1007/978-3-030-60877-4_5

I just got off the phone with my sister. I called because I was upset with my dad once again and wanted to bitch to her about it. I was angry with him for any number of reasons. Because he didn't answer when he said he would. Because he couldn't tell me what dates worked for him so I could plan a trip home to see the whole family. Because he flaked-out on my brother or sister when it came to lunch or dinner. Because he was thoughtless and did thoughtless things. I have a very low threshold for anger where he is concerned. So I called to bitch.

"Your problem is that you still expect too much of him." She tells me. "If you just stop having those expectations of him, you'll feel a lot better."

"That's not the point! Why can't he just act like he's supposed to?"

"What exactly do you want him to do?" she asks. Likely knowing that she wasn't going to get a helpful answer.

"Why the hell can't he just act like a man?" I shout. It's my usual answer. In a clever way that I've never really understood, she deflects my anger and moves on to something else. This was a common thing between the two of us, her way of reigning in my temper.

It wasn't until recently that I began to think about what I was saying when I demanded that my father act like a man. To be honest, I think somewhere in my head a great patriarch like Vito Corleone in *The Godfather* describes what it is to act like a man, "A man who doesn't spend time with his family can never be a real man." This patriarch holds abstract ideas about the family as the most important thing to being a man.

By that standard, I guess I have no reason to complain about my dad. He was always there for my brother, sister, and I when we were growing up. I remember him beaming with pride the day I graduated from college. He wasn't weak. He wasn't mean. He could be an asshole at times, but who isn't? He was there for me as a kid. So what was I mad about?

THE SHORT VERSION

He left my mom.

That might need some context. Years ago we learned that he had been cheating on my mom. They split up. He eventually moved in with his girlfriend and they had a baby. He left my mom bewildered and shocked. That is her story to tell but I remember feeling like I needed to be there for her, to help her along in ways I didn't know how, because I was her son, not her husband. I resented him for that. I resent him for that now.

We were all adults so it wasn't as though he left my mom with three kids to take care of while he went off to start another family. But we all had a hard time understanding what had happened. None so much as my mom, I'm sure. Asking us to understand what my father had done was like asking us to describe the taste of color or the smell of a feeling deep in our hearts. I rejected him, shouted at him, and reminded him each time he called me of what he had done and what I thought of it. I made every attempt he made to reach out to me a painful and contentious experience for both of us.

"That's not fair, Allen."

"Fuck you, old man! You never get to tell me about fair!"

Eventually, I allowed myself to grow distant and lose track of him. I got a call here and there and I'd check in on him on holidays, he made a point of meeting me for my birthday but for the most part, he was out of my life. Until that morning when I got a call from him letting me know he was coming to see me.

THE VISIT

Dad looks down at his hands, ignoring the coffee cup I set in front of him in my small Albuquerque apartment. It's just after six in the morning and I'm sipping my own coffee. The old man is a trucker back from an overnight run to Denver, one night up, one night back. He's not been in my apartment before. I am almost thirty and we haven't spoken much since he and mom split up a couple of years ago. I have never really forgiven him and there are times I still feel hot rage whenever I think about it. He told me he had something to tell me, something that could not wait until later when I finished teaching because he would need to sleep to get back on the road that night.

He seemed nervous. As he started telling me about his life, a life I no longer knew much about, I felt my pulse quicken and I thought, all things considered, the whiskey in the kitchen might be a good addition to my morning coffee. As he got to the point he stressed the fact that he and mom were no longer together and called it, "this thing between me and your mom." Then he began telling me about his girlfriend, something he had not done before.

"She's going to have a baby," he said.

His words took a moment to reach me. They dropped onto the coffee table with a dull thud like busted concrete and rested there before I was able to pick them up, before I was able to make sense of them. We had speculated about this, of course. My brother, sister, and I. We thought that there was a child somewhere that he had not told us about but we had dismissed this idea. My dad was almost fifty. He was done having kids. He had raised his family. All of that was over for him. New families were for young men. Only a few years ago he had told me that he was ready for grandkids and I told him to get a dog. I thought about how broke he was now, how broke all of us were. We had a family business that folded with the recession. A child didn't fit in this landscape. There was no money. There was no time! And even if he wasn't with her, he was still married to my mom. No, this didn't make sense.

"You can't…" I said before stopping. My thoughts were moving too fast to speak them, everything was moving too fast. I grabbed a thought from the whirlwind of them and forced it into a sentence, forced ideas into words so that I didn't just stammer. "Dad, you can't afford a kid. The business is gone. We've lost our house." I stared at him while he continued looking down at his hands. I noticed it because I do it too when I have to talk about something unpleasant. "Did you and…" I stopped "Fuck, dad, I don't even know her name." I resisted my urge to call her a *puta* (whore). I'd called her that before when I found out about her, when I learned that he had been with her for years before my mom found out, when I learned that he was moving in with her, when I realized the family I had always known would never be put back together again. I know it was cruel, but I was angry and wanted to hurt him.

"Mary Lu is her name," he said.

"Did you and Mary Lu plan this?"

"We talked about it."

"Not the same thing, *viejo!* (old man)" I snapped. "You're almost fifty! This kind of thing was acceptable when you had me, but you were seventeen then!"

"I'm not a kid now." He said in a way that has taken me five years to realize was the tone he uses when he's sure he's wrong in some way.

"We're supposed to have this talk, dad, but I'm the one who is supposed to say that to you!" I was beginning to shout now. Then there was silence. Not because we'd both finished talking, but because there was nothing to fill it. We were outside of a realm either of us understood. He wasn't my father, I wasn't his son, at least not in any way we two could recognize. All we could see, all we could hear in that silence was the fact that there was no definition, no script, no way of understanding how to go forward. We waited for words to come but none came. We stayed silent for a long while until I asked when the baby would be born and if they knew the sex of the kid. A month later, my baby brother was born.

Who Is He?

The man we knew was a good husband and father. He married his teenage sweetheart, stood by her, and started a family by working hard right out of high school. He got us up early on Mother's Day to get flowers and clean the house for my mom. He stood by his family and ran his own business for nearly ten years. He loved family, and fun, and board games, and dinner at Los Cuates on weekends. He liked to grill when we were all there at the house, calling for another beer after pouring most of his onto whatever he was cooking. He was proud of the house in the South Valley because we had built it, and of the house in Rio Rancho that he bought for the family when his business started doing well. He made big breakfasts for the family on special occasions with pancakes and chorizo and bacon. He liked dinner for his birthday with all of us at that Texas-style steak house I hated with the cinnamon sugar butter and the peanut shells on the floor.

This other man, the one I was getting to know, that we all were getting to know, had nothing in common with the one who we thought of as our father. At least not in my eyes. The man I wanted him to be like again— the one I knew as a kid—I wanted him to be that guy again. That father and husband from the idealized narratives about families we think of.

To be honest I had always suspected it was childish of me to expect him to be truly ideal. But it wasn't until I sat down to write this that I began to understand how foolish and unreasonable his idealization had been: ideal husband, ideal father, ideal worker, ideal provider. I don't know if it was because I was a child eager to listen to epic stories about my father or if my family simply enjoyed constructing him that way. In all likelihood it's a mixture of the two. Cultural traditions and the telling of stories offer us mixed messages and narratives about who we are, should or ought to be. They're helpful sometimes, other times they obscure memories of what was, or what we wish could have been or made sense to us.

Now I'm not saying that this image I had of my father, the ideal a child held before he understood the world, hid a bad man. Far from that. What

I'm saying is that in some way I grew to love my father as *I grew to idealize the idea of the father*. The imagined man created in culture and stories and the guy laughing at his own bad jokes because he knew it would make me laugh were one and the same for me.

A CHILDHOOD HERO

I knew as a child that my dad kept a gun and in my mind he was just as awesome as those men in the stories: the westerns and old *corridos* (folk ballads) my grandparents listened to who defended their families and their way of life. He was equal parts Gregorio Cortez and a brown-skinned John Wayne with the control and family values of a Vito Corleone, not unlike Jacob Vargas's portrayal of the father figure in *Mi Familia/My Family* and somehow still Jimmy Smits (because I really thought my dad was cool and he always had a chip on his shoulder when it came to authority).

We knew him to be the perfect son of my grandfather, and my grandfather is the man I hope to be like one day. So in the shadow of a man like that, I see my dad. I think he understood that the family saw him in this way, a chip off the old block. What's more, I think he enjoyed it. Again, that's not meant to condemn him. I think if he had possessed the will and superhuman ability to be all things to all of us, he would have done so.

What I take from this is to recognize that those idealized identities are more than just narratives. They're more than just a simple and quick way of thinking of someone. For the person who takes on those roles, those identities, and relationships associated with fatherhood, those narratives represent a kind of promise. A promise to those who are part of his family, those who call him father, son, or husband and who expect him to fulfill his cultural roles and responsibilities so that others in turn may be able to imagine and construct their own identities in relation to his. But are these impossible promises with impossible expectations? When I think about what my ideals about fatherhood imply, I find myself more and more confused about my father and my feelings about him as a father and his own performance as a son.

My dad, from what I hear from my grandparents, was always a hard worker. My grandma never said much about him being difficult. She used to joke that after his older brother Mike went through school "there wasn't any *males* (mischief) left for him to get into." He was everything that could be expected of a good son. He worked hard when he was old enough and bought himself a car with his first job—at a McDonald's, no less. He met my mom in high school. The story goes that there were lots of other girls in high school, but eventually he passed them all up for my mom. They had me, got married, and he, being a good son, was always willing to go by when his parents needed anything. He and my mom had two more kids after me and made sure that we spent lots of time with our grandparents. He bought a house; sent his kids to school, taught them the same values he had learned from his parents. Overall, he was a good son.

The problem with this narrative is that it doesn't tell the whole story or the story that goes beyond being a good son. For example, I don't know how accurate the story of my dad never getting into trouble is. He, himself, told me stories of running around and getting into trouble with his brothers, of fighting at school, of beating the crap out of a guy who called him a spic after he went home to ask my grandma what the word meant. I like to think that he and my mom found each other the best and most interesting people at Rio Grande High School and fell in love. But I often wonder, even though my parents loved each other, if they really had to marry because I was born. After all, getting married is what would have been expected of them. Did they really want something else? Would they have been allowed to want something else?

I don't know if being the perfect son, father, and husband was something he wanted. I know that it would not be something I would want, even though I feel shame and anger when I have to admit it. I could claim the same identity and hold myself to the same promise should I care to. I'm the oldest, I help my brother and sister when I can. I went to college and have earned a doctorate, first one in my family to do so. All of that makes for a lovely story about an American dream and an American boy from a Chicano background. But I will never marry a nice girl. I stand by my brother and sister but I don't know that I'm much help to them. I don't want to be the all-American boy my dad reportedly was. I don't want to be the traditional Chicano son. I don't want to make those promises, not to my family or to myself. The very idea of being the good boy or perfect son along with the cultural narratives that sustain them were things I started rejecting when I was still learning to drive. That master narrative that says to be a good son I must marry and have a family. I'm a *joto* (queer). I don't want that. As a Chicano *joto* I love my culture, but I also understand enough about my culture and the expectations it places on us to know that sometimes I can't uncritically identify with my cultural traditions. I'm a *joto*, my dad is straight, but could he have wanted something different, too? A story that went just a little queer—a little off of what was expected of him?

Even though I grew up in the same part of town my dad did, even though I went to the same high school in the South Valley of Albuquerque, and even though we both got into fights in high school, I know my experiences were different. When I fought in high school it was against boys who made fun of me for being gay. I soon learned that being the fag that fought back meant that nobody fucked with you. A masculinity propped up by homophobia never recovers from a lost fight to a faggot like me.

What Changed?

I remember a long drive up from Albuquerque, through Bernalillo, across NM 550 into the back roads of Rio Rancho. I recall pulling up to the big house my dad had bought when his concrete business started doing well and was glad to see that both my mom's car and my sister's car were not in the driveway. I didn't want them there for the talk I was going to have with my old man.

He was outside on the patio. He was expecting me and cooking something on the *disco* (disk-shaped cooker, often made from a tractor hubcap) when I walked in. He hugged me. He was excited. God damn it, he was excited and now I realize it was because I was the only one of his kids to have spoken to him in a month. Holy fuck! What did he think that meeting was going to be? He was cooking something that the guy at the *carnicería* (butcher) sold him called a "pile up" or a "train wreck" or something like that. It had chorizo, beef, *tripas* (tripe), hotdogs, and a few other things. He was excited and could not stop talking about it.

"Where's mom?" I asked him. I knew she had moved out but I wanted to hear it from him.

He blew the question off. He was excited about the meal. He wanted me to taste what he had grilled. I imagined him taking his new motorcycle to the *carnicería* to pick up this train wreck just for tonight. I hated how excited he looked. I hated how cautious he seemed. I could smell anxiety in every pressured word he spoke. I could see the cracks in his smile and I noticed that he looked older than I remembered him looking. I'd called him *viejo* for years but had never thought of him as old until I saw his eyes begging me not to press the question I had just raised.

"Why aren't you with mom?"

Still talking. He would not answer. "You're going to love this mess!" he laughed, cautiously.

I get why now. I didn't then, but now I understand what he was asking for in that laugh. The housing market was crashing around us and his business depended on people buying concrete for their homes, patios, and other projects. Looking back now I understand that he saw that and knew that eventually the business would go as would the house in Rio Rancho with its four bedrooms, huge patios, portal in the back where I had danced with my sister after I graduated college and she from high school in the same month. And amid all of that he was leaving behind a marriage that had defined him to everyone he knew for nearly thirty years. He wanted one more moment of happiness in that empty American dream house before everything came crashing down on him and our family, taking with it a life we thought we would have forever. Happiness. Like when we all went to Disney World; a surprise he sprang on us at the airport on a layover when we thought we were on our way to California. Happy like before his mom, my grandmother, lay dying and I had to be the one to tell the doctor in the presence of my dad, his brothers, and my grandfather to let her go because it was what she wanted.

He was in the kitchen. The open kitchen, which my mom had requested when they bought the house and I was standing on the other side of the breakfast bar. He reached into the refrigerator to get a pack of tortillas for dinner and when he turned around and before he could put them on the stove to warm over the open fire I started to shout.

"When are you going to work this out with mom? What the fuck are you doing?!"

"I'm not." He said.

"What in the fuck does that mean?" I demanded.

"I don't want this... marriage... anymore." The words stuck in his throat. I know they did because he pulled them out and put them in a sentence like a tired man pulls bricks from a pile at the end of the day. I don't know if he had ever said it before, I don't actually know what took place between he and my mom when she found out about the affair or when she moved out or later when she demanded to move back in. But I know he never thought he would have to tell me those words. They had no place between this father and son.

I gripped the barstool to brace myself—the world began spinning. I felt sick to my stomach, dizzy, as if untethered but I didn't know from what?

But what the fuck, dad?! There is nothing else you *could* want!

That's what I wanted to say. Those words that took me years and years to put together after replaying this night over in my head more times than a healthy person can count. But I don't remember what I actually said. I was shouting. My voice sounded harsh. Harsh like his when someone really made him angry. Harsh like his when he saw my brother and me fighting. Harsh and guttural like a bark and a roar, like his when he wanted to put the world back to rights by shouting at it. But then my voice changed. I was crying, I was screaming—my voice breaking like a child's.

The barstool was now on the floor and I can't remember if I threw it—god damn me if I did and god damn him for being my target! I must have thrown it because I needed to smash him until he did what I wanted. I wanted him to be the man I imagined him to be. I wanted the life I imagined for him and my mom. They were supposed to grow old together and years from now he and she would drink coffee on the patio in the afternoon. My brother, sister, and I would all get married and have kids and we would bring them over on the weekends for dinner and for huge Christmas parties. Never mind that none of us had those plans and that my brother and I are both gay. There was an expected role for my dad and he was walking away from it and I would beat him back into it.

I didn't fight him. I didn't hurt him with my fists though I'm sure whatever I told him hurt. My mom always said that I had a talent for saying things that left people feeling like I had beaten them. I was awful to him that night. I'm not proud of any of this. His words "I don't want this" stayed with me. They stuck to me like caked blood. Like something he pulled from deep inside of himself. They stuck to me because they fell on me when he pulled them out. He would never have planned to do that to me, leaving me stained with bloody words. But I provoked him to dig for them and stood in front of him when he pulled them from his heart, from his gut.

He did not want that marriage.

But it wasn't just the marriage. It was more. The old man wanted a new story I think. He had realized that the old one was not really what he wanted anymore. He wanted to be part of a new story, one that he wrote on his own, not one that had been written for him.

I don't mean to say I understand. I don't think I do. But I can relate. I never wanted that story either. I don't know that I'll ever forget that he hurt so many of us to write his new story, and I still question if that story went the way he wanted. But for a moment, he had something that I myself have always wanted, the freedom to choose. He made his choice, he picked what he wanted and it disrupted so much. It broke—it hurt so much and so many. I often think of how much his choice hurt. When he said the words "I don't want this" he grimaced as he pulled those meaty words away from the bone. How could anyone not be hurt by those words or what they meant?

I look at my hands now that I am older and I think of my own choices. I think about those who thought my life would fit into a narrative they understood, a story they were familiar with and I wonder what my choice felt like to them. When I made it clear to people in my life that I want only what I want, not what anyone expects me to want. Does it hurt them to hear me voice my choice? Does it throw their world into chaos? Does my choice to write my own narrative leave others dumfounded and without a part to play? I think my dad made his choices without taking into consideration what they implied for others or how his choices in the past might impact the ones he was making now as he approached fifty. I don't think my choice to live as I wanted from early on hurt as many or in as many ways, or at least I like to think that. But isn't that the point I'm trying to make here? Stories that we tell ourselves and that we make ourselves and others fit into are meant to comfort us. I may fault his choices but I can't say I don't understand his wanting to make them. I should have been able to understand more about my father that night in the kitchen. I should have been able to say something more to him that early morning in my apartment.

SOMETHING QUEER

My dad and I sit there in my small living room looking at one another across an old coffee table, across years of disagreement, anger, shame, and disappointment. It had been years since either of us took on the roles of father and son. I am now a grown man and have built a life that no longer draws a distinction between him as father and me as son. He had left my mom, started a new family, but now he was here in my home talking to me about what was happening in his life, anxious about what tomorrow might bring. But we were both out of practice at this kind of thing, off script and improvising our roles. We had to build something there, a new connection that had nothing to do with father and son. So we sat in that silence, knowing that it was the crushing silence of what should be, a longing for the world we thought we understood, even if I wasn't the son he had imagined having and even if he had stopped being the father I thought I had. At that moment I wanted to begin something new with him. I don't know if it would heal anything or if it would just make me happy to know this man who was also my dad. I wanted to try.

Since then we've begun crafting a relationship that is uneven, unstructured, and unscripted. It does not always work well; we're not always sure how we fit into each other's lives. The truth is that life is not one single narrative. I relive the past all the time and how it fits what might have been, could have been, and will not be. They all overlap and move across my imagination. That's what's queer about all this. These are all their own narratives, all part of an experience, one which I might not ever understand. But I think that is the point. We like narratives that reduce the complex to something manageable. Narratives that ignore what doesn't fit. I think that between my father and me, there may never be a narrative that we can both make sense of. We may just keep finding ways of meeting and writing each other into our days. Yes, that's exhausting, but it is also all that we have without beating each other into roles neither of us can fulfill or sitting in the void of a yawning silence between us. I don't know that I'll ever understand him and I don't know if he understands me. But maybe understanding is like being a man, just another story. Or maybe it's something different. Maybe understanding only happens when you write the story for yourself. Perhaps understanding emerges when you stop trying to write the story for someone else.

CHAPTER 6

Overall Prince, Now Father Lauren: On Becoming a Two-Spirit Butch Queen Father

Cuauhtémoc Peranda

Abstract Much of the scholarship of the House Ballroom Scene focuses on the Balls, categories, genders, and Houses—with Mothers being at the forefront of leadership for the Ballscene culture. This chapter departs from that trend and moves to illuminate the roles that Fathers play in the Ballscene. Pulling from *Paris is Burning*, and through indigenous decolonial praxis, this essay in the form of a letter to a son weaves together personal experiences of this Black, Latinx, Indigenous LGBTQ+ sub-culture, in order to make sense of the meanings and responsibilities of Fatherhood. Tender considerations of what raises one's masculinity, walking through Mexika ceremony, and evaluation of roles in a walking House builds this essay and story of the werk and call to Fatherhood a House brings.

C. Peranda (✉)
University of California, Riverside, CA, USA
e-mail: cpera001@ucr.edu

© The Author(s), under exclusive license to Springer Nature Switzerland AG 2021
A. R. Del Castillo, G. Güido (eds.), *Fathers, Fathering, and Fatherhood*, Palgrave Studies in Literary Anthropology,
https://doi.org/10.1007/978-3-030-60877-4_6

To begin this telling, this examination, this exploration, I needed to figure out a decolonial way of writing. As I read for my Ph.D. Qualifying Exams, I am struck by the decolonial method laid out in the introduction and conclusion of Shawn Wilson's in Research is Ceremony. It was not a method he used in the research for his book, but one he admired: he wished to have written his book like a letter to his son. In this way the reclamation of knowledge in the writing of a final text is not in service of the eyes of readers of western academic classic traditions, but instead this method of writing follows a more intimate sharing of understandings and unfolding—and more, a passing of knowledge from generation to generation. My task here, now, in this essay, is to write about becoming, being, remembering, revitalizing, revolutionizing, and reclaiming the role of "Father" in the House of Lauren and in my sacred, personal life. And, in a decolonial way, I write this to my son, Inky Bliss Ome'Lauren for maybe, for sure he will become a House Father one day.

Dear Inky Bliss,

My Inky, I have told you so many times to NEVER read the Father and to ALWAYS smoke the Father's weed ... and yet, my sober son, the other day, you read me with the quickness, with a word, set, placed right at the moment of question, silence, or lampoon—leading to deflation of my ego. A quick read, and a pitter patter away, you run from a wrath too slow to realize the sight you saw and told aloud ... and as I find you laughing, hiding in fear, knowing a punishment is only a simple read, or a pat against your face: one of love, without sting or trance, a pat, a mutual laugh, and a warning to never try it again, and never in public, we come to rest in a sense of family, of #Love4Lauren.

These are the memories I think of in sweet bliss of my Fatherhood—of play. Fatherhood can be too serious and often I forget that (1) the Ballroom is an extra-curricular activity, (2) play is essential to the family, and (3) OVAH (over or extreme; to be so extra and original that the world is destroyed by your greatness and reborn to be recreated in your iconic moment) creativity is vital. You, however, always seem to remind me of these things in simple yet poignant ways. Thank you, I love you my son.

Mi'jo (my son), being a Father, is more than being serious and forgetting play. It is more than raising BEAT (adj. beautiful; the result of an ovah application as in the beating of the face with a make-up brush) butch queens, femme queens, transmen, and the like. Being a Father is never chosen, it is a call—and then, of course, one responds. It is a calling, more than a choosing. Your sister Xav could confirm, I never wanted to be a Father ... but with more skills, more connections, and more children in need, somehow I fell into Fatherhood much like how I fell into the House Ballroom Scene. Two butch queens approached me and asked me to help them through the gay life and world. Because I only know how to orient myself in this queer world through Ballroom, I asked them if they wanted to learn how to "walk" (compete in a BALL/function) letting them know that I would only be able to support them in quare (a complex intersectional notion of queer) intimacy if they were my family and a part of my House (a "family" of people sharing a living space involved in the Ballroom Scene). Long story short, I asked the West Coast Regional Mother, the Overall Founding Father, the Overall Mother, the Overseers, and a few of my closest House siblings for their blessings and was given their trust and support to raise new Lauren children as their Father Lauren of California.

But helping a child through gay life or teaching a child how to walk doesn't make a Father. I have given the same offerings, mentorship, teachings, counseling, and help to young quare children as a butch queen, as an Overall Prince. Yes, the blessings and the commitment of support for me to be a Father, by the International House of Lauren, are necessary and they too alone do not make one a Father. No, a Father is made possible as long as the Father has children; the same applies to a Mother. More, Fatherhood requires more than mentorship—in some cases, the Father fills a void in a child who lost a parent, for others the Father is temporary housing for those traveling or in transition. Most centrally, the House Father teaches the arts of the Ballroom, and in the practices, a child is set-up to reach their full quare potential. Because the Father is able to speak to, understand, and guide the intimate queer feelings and experiences that need shaping and detangling—his role is unique and needed, for he has the experiences and temperament heterosexual parents often lack. The Father provides the children with skills for life that openly and outwardly proclaim one's LGTBQIA2S+ (Lesbian, Gay, Bisexual, Transgender, Queer and/or Questioning, Intersex, Asexual, Two-Spirit plus the different ways people self-identify) unique attributes and intersectionalities[1] that rest deep in ancestral knowledge. And with teaching, toward and in the mastery of oneself, gauged through the various BALL categories, but most certainly through Realness (convincing role-playing, passing, to become another person, and to redefine and create another through the

---

[1] The notion of intersectionality presents problems of its own. See Sandra K. Soto, *Reading Chican@ Like a Queer* (Austin: University of Texas Press, 2010). I thank A.R. Del Castillo for bringing this to my attention.

play of them you embody), a child will not only be self-sufficient, but will become the leader of their life and worlds. The Father does not keep a child or collective children in check but gives them broader skills for outside the House Ballroom Scene. The Father keeps the House in check, and though the whole scene is controlled by the vast matriarchy, the Fathers are present to calculate, negotiate, protect, and facilitate the Mothers-in-House-business as need be. It is the Mothers who uphold the family and the vision, they have much bigger dreams to manifest than to ensure the House can make a function or pay its dues. Fatherhood is less glorious, but more tender.

MOTHERS GET ALL THE GLORY, MOTHERS DO THE MOST WORK, BUT WHAT OF THE FATHER?

In the film, *Paris Is Burning* by Jenny Livingston, Her Ovahness (ultra-impressive and illustrious), the Legendary Iconic Mother Willi Ninja, a pioneer of vogue and Performance internationally, states that she chose to be the Mother of the House of Ninja, now The Iconic House of Ninja, because, as in any household, in any real family, "it's the Mother that works the hardest, and it's the Mother that gets the most respect [....] often the Mother is the showpiece of the House and family. The Mother is often the best walker of the House." She is the blueprint for the House in that to look at the Mother one would know the House's taste, take, and skill in art, fashion, focus, love, communication, trust, respect, affection, and care. The Mother really does look after the children and keeps them "in check." It is the Mother who confides in the children; she has the responsibility of taking care of the emotions. The Mother is also responsible for in-depth knowledge of any category, and for following Ballroom protocol and etiquette. The Mother creates, thinks, and embodies the vision of the House, which leaves a lot of other tasks for the Father.

Perhaps this is why I never wanted to be a Father. I knew the amount of administrative work required would be intense and raising butch queens is not the easiest thing to do. As a young butch queen, Overall Prince Lauren, I could really fool around and come and go as I pleased in the House of Lauren. Yes, I paid close attention to how my Father, the Founder, operated the House, but I was able to play with cuties, dance, walk, create, destroy, and be inside and outside the House Ballroom Scene. I had a lot of freedom. But I always knew what would be in store as a parent and how serious that title is. Like most things in the House Ballroom Scene, it is very serious business—it is a very serious responsibility.

As I recall, many Ballroom kids choose not to become parents. Many do not stay in a House. Most of the Ballroom Scene children do not stay in the scene for long. For many, it is a temporary stop on their way to independent adulthood so one may lose their Fatherhood or Motherhood titles when all the children leave the family—no children, no title. This is the weight of being a Ballroom parent: to keep the family, created of walkers, together. To be a parent truly means to raise kids, to help them help themselves, and help them help you attend a function together in fierce glamour—to help them help the family attend to the needs of the world, with bold direction and self-created agency. Many children in the Scene don't want to raise kids, they want to be with the kids. And I completely understand. It's easier to worry about and take care of yourself. To be the big brother or sister to others, or lend a hand when asked, is nice since there is less responsibility in such things than in having to plan and delegate, check-in and checking-up with the House family.

The Father's role, at least as I know it from the House of Lauren, is to be the butch and masculine counterpart to the Mother. But in terms of raising kids, shockingly, they are the same. Children often grow attached to their first Mother or Father and so there is always a first parent in the eye of the children. If a child should leave the House and find another Mother or Father, the first Mother or Father will stay in touch with the child in a sort of unbreakable bond beyond Houses. The Ballroom Scene is laced with these bonds and, in all honesty, it is a vital part of the cohesiveness of the House Ballroom Scene. Family then is strange and parental titles mean less in terms of what they signify and more in how the individual embodies the notion of Father and Mother. It is less about a title and more about the responsibility it carries—thereby bringing glory, honor, and status.

But to really break it down, the heteronormative kinship binary of "The Father" and "The Mother" reveals a difference in emphasis through the werking (the fineness of the work) involved in enacting these titles. As the Father, we are secondary, a foil to the vision of the House: the Mother—but should the Mother not be present, the Father is the sole standard. And so, Mother must be able to be the Father and the Father must be able to be the Mother, not in the drag of clothing and vestiture, but in the poise, the walk, and carry. The Father though will tend to focus on House dues, House-to-House relationships, transportation, 1–5-year planning, outside collaboration, and talent management. But as the Mother, he will deal more directly with the kids in more intimate relationships. The Father calls out to the whole family and reminds the family of the House goals, standards, successes, growths, expansions, and reciprocities. But in all honesty, the roles are organized per House, per regional scene, per city.

"Who's in charge of the girls? Mother is in charge of the girls! Who's in charge of the boys? Father is in charge of the boys!" (inspired by "Vogue—Dramatics—I Don't Like that Bitch" by DJ Miss Jay Kuran). To break it down, this is a way of understanding gender performativity according to parental divisions for taking care of children as well as the categories these kids themselves "walk" as a gender: the Father mentors butch queens, trade (Str8/Male-Men/Man/heterosexual/questioning cis-male), trans-men, and butches/studs. And because the Scene is made up of mostly butch queens, this responsibility tends to be a tall order, the Mother is in charge of the butch queens up in drag, femme queens (transgender women), women, and sometimes studs/butches. This calls for knowledge of make-up skills, heels, accessories, hair, among other things. And for a BALL, the fashion coordination alone can be a tall order in terms of matching without redundancy. Because a Father knows the more masculine way to approach categories, he can help the "boys" perhaps in ways the Mother cannot. That said, collective knowledge and skills are better than a single authority, because a judges' panel is just that, a panel of individual members who have the power to bestow a deadly "1 chop" (disqualification by 1 judge). So, it is best to follow experience and leave the "in charge of" idea to a simple expression of "division of labor," for general or basic tasks.

But, and I say this quite seriously, Father and butch queen relationships must be mindful of the easiest way to destroy a House—having sex with the kids—and this goes for any parent or leader in the House. I must acknowledge, it is true, there are the "Daddy & Son" homosexual fetish innuendos and rumors—and they do resonate through every House. There is always a potential for that sort of sexual relationship to take place. But it is of utmost importance for the Father and his children to resist that possibility, even in jest. Why? Because the LGTBQIA2S+ strongly comprised sexualities and those with "different than the norm" sexual practices. Moreover, a Father is often a butch queen with butch queen children, and it is quite natural for butch queens to be attracted to and experiment with each other. It is common for gays to hook up with gays. Therein lies the key of the House: with so much sex in our sexualities, the House in its practice of abstinence makes possible different sorts of relationships between homosexuals. Given this control, intimacy without sex is now possible, and diverse manifestations of this intimacy proliferate. What's more, abstinence protects a family that is already vulnerable when the folly of sexual pleasure, power, confusion, and manipulation are resisted. Father and child, instead of daddy and son, leaves room for release, escape, call, and response—it keeps the relationship open and fresh to new possibilities. And so the Father, though often forgotten in the gossip and media image of the House Ballroom Scene, provides a new idea of the Father— one that is a little more radical and revolutionary than the typical patriotic, masculine, dominant Dad.

Being a Father, Being a Good Man, Saying Goodbye, Entering the Ranks ...

In April 2016 my bio-father passed away. Joe Perez Junior was a very good da-tah to me and I learned a lot of what it takes and means to be a Father from him. My da-tah was kind, sweet, smart, sensible, quiet, and peaceful. He knew what he needed to do to make ends meet, and if he could be with family, he would be. My da-tah was the funny guy, but also the guy you go to just to be heard. I think my da-tah was a master of Zen, though he never trained in such an art.

My bio-dad's passing was hard on me, and during this period my House Father, the Founder of the House of Lauren, immediately sent his condolences and offered his open ear and heart to my hurt. My bio-father could never be replaced, but Fatherhood continued in my life. With my da-tah's passing, I hold his teaching, love, and pure sacrifice—always thinking of us, his children (my bio-brother and myself), before himself. He always wanted the best for us, even if he could not provide it. No, he had us provide it for ourselves! He nudged us toward productive and focused practices to reach our goals through study and talent. From time to time, he would clean my workspace, or tune up my car but, mostly, he did what he could to ask questions, to be involved, to try, to try... No! He cared deeply that we be involved in his life as well because he wanted us to be part of his life. My bio-brother and I have done surprising things in our lives. We have crossed the globe! Gone to places my father thought impossible to reach. His desire to be a part of our lives was only outweighed by his desire for our return with stories and pictures to share with his family and friends about what his sons do, have done, will do.

My Father was proud of my accomplishments, whatever these have been, but prouder still of his support of my reaching and seizing my goals. See, that is what I do for you, and for all your brothers and sisters, Inky Bliss. I express my joy by cheering you on and helping you to get what you need to make your life what you wish it to be. It is through pride that the gentle nudging is less a directing and more an affirmation through careful noticing. In this way, orientations and disciplines of success are built as strongly positive without the need of too much talk or avoidance or negativity—though those happen too. My bio-father used his love and pride in his children to create joy and I use it to evoke the happiness we have in the House now, and honestly, this is how to be a good man: uplift, protect, and love.

Inky Bliss, there is so much hurt in the world. There is so much abuse, domestic violence, gaslighting, and rape. Fathers, especially the "Founding Fathers of America," have desecrated this land I know as Turtle Island and created toxic methodologies in order to dominate the family unit. This is not the kind of Father I am, want to become, or wish for you. This is not the kind of Father I know how to be. A good Father is an extension of a good man, which I know to be a good warrior, a protector of space, a maker of space so that the family may thrive. A Father follows ways of love. And if abuse and neglect negate love, well then a Father should never abuse his family, and should never neglect his House. Though honest forgetting may occur from time to time.

But there are many kinds of Fathers out there. Some do think deeply about what it means to be a Father and others take other approaches to their life and Fathering praxis. As I enter the ranks of other Lauren Fathers, with their support and trust that I know what I am doing given my longevity and study of Ballroom, I am honored. As I enter the ranks of other Ballroom Fathers, I know it best to never comment on a Father's methods or strategies. It is best to let Houses run themselves. It is best to be in their ranks unaffected by others' legendary Fatherhoods or younger opinions, while also ensuring active senses primed to watch and learn, play and shade, read, prepare, and walk.

Being a Father and All My Relations

When I was thirteen, I went through the Ocelotl Ceremony. It was a year-long process that began and ended in October in Sacramento, California. The Jefe, El Chuy, was the overseer of this ceremony. In the Danza Azteca world of California, Chuy is legendary given his tireless commitment to the next generation of warriors. The Ocelotl Ceremony was known to be his production and it followed his philosophies of radical justice and decolonial practices. He was able to transform youth (from local jails, prisons, 12-step recovery groups, indigenous men's groups, and through various prevention programs) to young men through a platform from which to look into manhood critically via a traditional Aztec/Mexica praxis.

Going through the ceremony necessitated the whole Aztec Dance community to recognize that I was a "warrior in training"; it meant that they, we, had to commit to helping me learn how to be a warrior/man/ leader/healer/protector in a good way so that I could, through this process, become a good warrior. A year's duration is both an immensity and quick flash of time felt by the community and me; it's a long term of ritualized practice for uplifting men. Through the ceremony, I re-learned and was tested on my knowledge of the poetics of the four directions. I was introduced to tribal leaders, government officials, Danza leaders, and community activists. I was expected to run, lead, manage, oversee, and operate ceremonies and somehow teach the next generation of my experience as I went through it. From sweat lodge, to ceremony, to presentation, to Nahuatl language class, I was taken to indigenous communities to learn, share, and know the needs of a warrior and from where to orient and place myself. Upon completion we become honored and trusted guardians of the Danza Azteca traditions, warriors for all indigenous communities.

When my bio-father passed away, I depended on my Ocelotl trainings to help me make sense of the death ceremonies, while also supporting my families. As I walked into my Fatherhood in the House of Lauren, I depended on my understanding of reciprocity, sacrifice, giving, celebration, teaching, joy, care, and protection from the year I spent becoming an Ocelotl. My Fatherhood is not only unique because each of us is unique, but also indigenous Mexika/Aztec, Mescalero-Apache. I carry the knowledge of what it means to be a warrior, a man, into my butch queen underground House Ballroom Scene communities. And what is most amazing and warm is that the Ballroom children and parents see and acknowledge traditional forms of creating oneself, and honor is served. Because of my Ocelotl status, some Ballroom Icons and Pioneers seem to be a little more open in sharing their knowledge with me because they know, understand, and trust that I follow a sacred, ancient code of ethics that always protects the communities in which I find myself.

As I grew, so did my identities, "Ome" is the number two in Nahuatl and also represents the duality in the creator Ometeotl. I can use this prefix to help me understand my Two-Spirit identity. Two-Spirit identity is how people identify, claim, or use the term to represent themselves as both Native American and their gender/sexual orientation as non-conforming to colonial binary logics (such as Gay, Lesbian, Bisexual, Queer), I claim it as my sexuality. Because I danced with the Tlaloc-Chalchiuhtlicue Danza Azteca Group in San Jose, California, and understood my responsibility of praying for and protecting waters I at times identified as an Ometlaloque—a two-spirit warrior for the rain deity, Tlaloc-Chalchiuhtlicue (Tlaloc is the rain Spirit. Chalchiuhtlicue is the earth-bound water spirit. The name indicates the Lord/Lady duality of this ancient pre-Aztec divinity). As an Ocelotl community warrior, I also at times identify as an Omeocelotl, a jaguar warrior of the night in duality. It is then only fitting that my children are raised as Ome'Lauren: Lauren-Lauren (the double Lauren). Here, we are first Laurens committed to Family, Ballroom, and Diversity, and second, we are Laurens that check ourselves as Laurens to make sure we do not to get too lost in the materiality of colonialism and homonormative capitalism. Still, we have our only home in the House of Lauren, and we can take the classic Lauren surname whenever we need to, but the "Ome" provides space for me and my children to remember, to point to, to work with, to walk with the indigenous peoples of this land (an often forgotten history of continual contributions to the House Ballroom Scene). We take on an extra responsibility.

Ome'Lauren is less a claim of my own space in Ballroom within the House of Lauren, and much more the plain truth. It is the fucking TEA (truth, knowledge, gossip) that I am Native American and I walk Ball, and Ome'Lauren helps me praise fashion, play with a label, but also remember that we need to decolonize America through our walking. We are not capitalist hungry lovers of Ralph Lauren, but walkers, moving, shaking critics of the world, pushing for, YES, a better tomorrow together.

THE CALL TO BE A FATHER

Inky Bliss, you do not decide to be a Father. Someone does not give you the title of Father. You are called to be a Father and you decide how to respond. It is a gift given by children who need a role model, who need tenderness, who lust to walk a ball, who may not be able to make it through the night without you because the world doesn't quite understand their intersectional hella (super) gay ways. These bonds are more permanent than one might think. A House is not a team, it is not a club, it is not a fraternity, and it is not a gay street gang (well sometimes it may smell like one). A House is a family; it is made, chosen, bonded by, and committed to. Though there is no blood, no biological ties, the House tends to find itself just as strong.

I am thankful the LGTBQIA2S+ are more accepted in broader American society today than in decades past. But there are still plenty of children being told they are an abomination and are kicked out of their homes. HIV infection rates are on the rise while domestic violence among queer groups fueled by rampant alcoholism and drug use are still issues we must reckon with, resist, refuse, walk, rewalk, and revolutionize! We must think harder and dancer stronger if we are to decolonize our capitalist consumption and promote ecologically sustainable, healing-sharing in queer reaching, gesturing to ovah, extra, excess, and utopian futurities.

I was given a call and I am learning my response when we walk as a House.

I love you Inky Bliss Ome'Lauren.

I hope this helps in your future figurines of Fatherhood.

Ometeotl

A'HO

#Love4Lauren

#OvahOmeLauren

#L4L

Father Don'Té Ome'Lauren

PART II

Fathers, Father Figures, and the Family

Introduction to Section

Presentations of the interplay of parenting, fathers, father figures, and gay sons and wards among different family formations.

Owning It

CHAPTER 7

Tommy Paved the Way

Robert Jude Frausto

Abstract When Corky's mother passed, his father, cousin Cayo, and great uncle Tommy raise him. The sensitive, precocious boy is perceived as hopelessly effeminate and his father won't have it. Cayo, who moves in to nurse the dying mother, mentors Corky's intellectual growth, then becomes a Minnesota farmer transforming Corky into a farmhand. When his father dies, Corky goes to live with his Tía Tacha and her flamboyant brother, Tommy, whose friend is Colonel Frank Dixon. Both, now openly queer, served courageously during World War II. Corky loves and admires Tommy for his fearless approach to life, camp humor, and honest acceptance of his sexuality. His father, Cayo, and Tommy each taught Corky something—to act like a man, think rationally, and be true to his gay self.

R. J. Frausto (✉)
Albuquerque, NM, USA
e-mail: corque@me.com

A. R. Del Castillo, G. Güido (eds.), *Fathers, Fathering, and
Fatherhood*, Palgrave Studies in Literary Anthropology,
https://doi.org/10.1007/978-3-030-60877-4_7

I grew up in a small town in South Texas, Eagle Pass, a dusty border town across the Rio Grande from Piedras Negras. My family had lived in that part of Texas since the 1870s when my great-great-grandfather and his sons joined the US Army, recruited from Torreón, Mexico, as Indian scouts. I was born in the mid 1950s, when Juan Crow (anti-Mexican Jim Crow laws) was still in effect in Texas, but dad was the County Attorney and mom was a grade schoolteacher. We were country-club kids and were shielded from the worst of it.

I realized I was different when as a child I pretended I couldn't swim so the lifeguard who was teaching me to swim would hold me. But I didn't know I was gay, others did. That knowledge settled the way I was treated, and the demands and expectations that were placed on me through much of my early life.

Like many small towns, "town queers" in Eagle Pass were the target of ridicule and an example of what a real man should not be. Ovidio, a thirty-something, slightly heavy man was a flamboyant and effeminate queer and you didn't want to be told you were acting like Obie. Kids would stare and point when they saw him walking down the street. Once when he was leaving a shop and we were walking in my dad clapped him on the back and bellowed out: Be a man, Obie! I couldn't believe my dad humiliated Obie that way. I can't imagine the way he must have felt. There was also Oscar, a skinny effeminate man, known as *Oscar La Flaca* (Oscar, the Skinny (Female)). He ran political errands for my dad, was active in the party, and served as a campaign volunteer. I also recall the grocer's trans-gender brother who lived in the shadows of the marketplace. Dad had helped a drag queen get out of prison. It was done as a favor for the local grocer, the man's brother. Perhaps it was a shared connection between the grocer and my father: each had a gay brother. The grocer felt he owed my dad so once a month we would stop by the market and the grocer would give us a crate of fresh vegetables and fruit. We would take half to the convent and keep the rest. We would often see the grocer's brother through the curtain that separated the shop from the living quarters in the back. She would peek shyly through the curtain with her hair made up and wearing a robe. We children would wave politely as we ran to get the box of fruit and play on the dolly.

It appeared to me then that one's sexuality was not as wrong as male effeminacy and the perception of weakness, which was thought unnatural by the town folk. Effeminacy carried the stigma of being powerless, of being inconsequential, it was a stigma which I bore and which my dad had to purge from me.

DAD

I was the gay kid, the middle child of three boys, born sickly so the family story goes. Because I nearly died, my parents prayed to St Jude and if I lived they would name me after him. I did and they did. My name is Robert Jude. Corky is a nickname from birth. It's ironic that I'm named after Saint Jude. The epistle attributed to him in the New Testament warns against and condemns profane men and their perverted lusts. All the prayers and novenas to Saint Jude to make me straight failed, which is also ironic since he is the patron saint of hopeless cases, I must have been too hopeless a case for even him, his own namesake. We were a very Catholic family; my supplications should have worked.

I was a sensitive, artistic, bookish, and effeminate child. But while my mom was alive I was allowed to be me because I was my mom's *consentido*, her favorite, and for the first seven years of my life she protected me from my dad. After she died my world changed and surviving the next five years became my crucible. I have discovered that before her death, my mother asked several friends and relatives—a cousin, my godparents, a former teacher, the neighbors, a couple of aunts—to watch over me. It seems she knew what was in store for me. I can't imagine how my dad held back his disdain while she was alive because after she died he let loose. The mantra of my life became "Be a man, God damn it!" usually accompanied by a smack upside the head. I had to learn to walk, talk, throw, run, eat, drink, and act like a MAN. I was not sure what my dad meant by "a MAN", but I knew it wasn't me. I was a *vieja*, a woman, and an old woman at that. Apparently, I walked like one, talked like one, and acted like one. And that's what I was called daily by my father, brothers, and the kids in the neighborhood. They also called me queer, *joto*, *maricón*, and *mariposa* (all derogatory Mexican Spanish terms for faggot). *¡Eres uno de los cuarenta y uno!* (You're one of the 41! This refers to a scandal involving 41 queer men in Mexico City in the early twentieth century).

What must have rankled my dad most was my lack of athleticism, in particular, my complete inability to play baseball. He had played during the war, in Alaska, was All-Alaskan shortstop. He had also played semi-pro before he went to law school. We were a baseball family and I hated the game. He forced me to play little league. So I was banished to right field where I played with ants and other bugs until a left-handed batter came up. Then they would call a time out and move me to left field. After I played the requisite two innings I sat on the bench. At bat I was worse. I was called Arnold Palmer because my swing was something akin to a golf swing. According to my dad I swung like a "rusty gate and couldn't hit a watermelon with a guitar." I also committed the greatest sin in batting. I stepped in the bucket. I must have had a good sense of self-preservation, if someone is chunking a ball at me I'm getting out of the way.

Then dad tried to cure me of that affliction. It was a Sunday and we were playing ball in the yard. He had already kicked me out of the house with the usual, "Get outside and play some ball, be a man, god damn it!" I guess he saw me step out of the way of a pitch because the next thing I know he was shouting at me that baseballs don't hurt. He made me stand about fifteen yards in front of him and threw baseballs at me. I was supposed to let them hit my chest. I tried but it hurt and I was scared and cried. It was humiliating. I was trying to stand and take the hit but I just couldn't. The balls hit me just not on my chest. A neighbor came over and scolded my dad. They yelled at each other, he never treated me like that in public again. At home it was different.

After that event I became used to being asked, "Your dad treating you right, you ok?" by my godparents, our neighbor, my aunts. And what a spot they put me in. As if I would narc on my dad knowing they weren't going to be there when he came after me for complaining. My answer was always, I'm good, no problems, everything is ok.

GI Joe came out as a toy at Christmas in 1964 or so. I asked Santa for one and got it. I played with it for a while and then I took it to the neighbor's house to play GI Joe and Barbie. I must have been playing with it wrong because Dad took it and threw it in the trash shouting: "No son of mine is going to play with dolls!"

Once we were driving between Del Rio and Eagle Pass when he noticed a kitten by the side of the road. We begged him to stop and rescue it. He did and I was holding it in the back seat talking to it. He must not have liked what I was saying because he suddenly stopped the car and said that if I was going to act like a damn queer with the cat he was going to leave it there. I started to cry and he gave me something to cry about. He took the cat from my hands put it back on the road and drove off. I never did own a cat until I left home in my twenties. I've owned at least one ever since.

The summer my mom died was traumatic in other ways also. My older brother Skip suffered from shock due to a traumatic incident. It was in August of 1963; we had been at baseball practice and left the field to get a drink of water from the neighbors water hose. Skip and I were standing in the yard when a car pulled up to the curb and a man jumped out of the car and ran up the steps and into the house. He and the man in the house started to argue. Then the owner of the house pulled out a gun and shot the man. We watched it happen through the living room window. The man staggered out of the house and down the walk. He fell across the hood of the car and rolled to the ground. He died there. I ran across the street and pounded on the door shouting: "Call the cops, call the cops!" But Skip froze. *Se quedó bien picado* (He was planted in place; stunned).

There was no trial. The shooter copped a plea and we didn't have to testify. But Skip was in bad shape, he wouldn't eat and was having nightmares. He became depressed and most likely had PTSD. The adults decided he had *susto*, a Mexican folk malady resulting from fright that causes the soul to leave the body. He needed a *limpieza* (cleansing) from a *curandera* (Mexican healer), so dad set up the ritual. The healer put Skip in the bathtub and half filled it with water. She lit candles and sprinkled holy ashes on him. She rubbed a *huevo* (egg) on his head and prayed and chanted. Cayo, an older cousin who was staying with us, didn't have any patience for magic rituals and grabbed me and said come on. We pulled sheets over our heads and ran around the house and yard pretending to be ghosts shouting "Woooo, woooo!" The *curandera* got pissed and left shouting that the energy was all wrong and we didn't respect her art. Dad chewed us out but we kept laughing and he finally gave up. Skip and I have had our issues over the years, his fuck ups are probably my fault. I messed up his healing. If souls are real, his is still missing.

My dad tried to teach us the value of honesty and the consequences of lying and stealing. His methods were unconventional. We had been visiting Tía Teta's convenience store in Del Rio. It was an obligatory stop on our way out of Del Rio, heading home to Eagle Pass after visiting Tía Maria. My cousin Cayo who had come to live with us when mom died was with us. He was in his twenties, about seventeen years older than me, and had dropped out of college to come help my dad out. He encouraged us to shoplift comic books from the rack. A few miles out of town dad noticed we had the comic books and asked where we got them. We told him and he chewed us out and turned the car around to drive back and return them. He made us go in the store and fess up. He wasn't raising thieves.

Years later when I was working as a caseworker with teens with disabilities one of my clients showed up at my office with a bag of stuff. The poor kid had no filter and told me he and his girlfriend had shoplifted it from different stores the night before. I knew exactly what to do. I took the stuff, put the kid in the car and drove from store to store to return the merchandise. I walked in with the kid and made him take the stuff to the manager and confess and return the stolen goods. Every manager we met was shocked I made him do that. You have to make amends, do the right thing, and face the consequences. No questions.

We were not supposed to take money from anyone. At all. Period. My older brother Skip and I wore the same size pants. One day I found a quarter in his pants pocket and went to the store and bought candy. Dad asked where I got the money and I told him. Then he asked Skip and he lied; said he had found it. Dad kept challenging the story we both stuck to ours. The situation kept escalating. He took us to talk to the parish priest, I told my story and Skip stuck to his. Dad still insisted that one of us was lying. The next stop was the County Jail, my dad was the County Attorney and had pull. He had us locked up until we told the truth. We were in the holding cell, with some drunk guy in the cell next to us. I was bawling to Skip "Tell him the truth!" He finally 'fessed up. A local lawyer had given Skip the quarter and he left it in the pants pocket. We drove home in silence. I was stunned. It was the first time I ended up in jail, but not the last due to DWI's (driving while intoxicated) and stuff like that before I stopped drinking and got clean. Historically, I was in good company but I don't recommend it.

Despite the way he treated me I loved and trusted my father. One of his maxims was "You can tell me anything…" I believed him and he didn't let me down. After mom died I was pretty messed up. I would lie in bed at night and count all the people I knew who had died. Then I would start to count the people I knew that were going to die and I'd cry myself to asleep. I would also worry about anything my troubled mind would come up with. Once it was my dick size. I was eight and had started worrying that my dick was too small. I'd pull down my pajamas and look at that erect little stub and worry. I finally worked up the courage to ask my dad, at two in the morning. So I walked down the hall into his room, woke him up, pulled down my pj's, and showed him my dick. I told him it was too small. He shook his head told me it would grow and sent me back to bed. That was it, never mentioned it, and never teased me about it. It grew but I'm still waiting for it to grow bigger.

A few years later when I was ten and a Boy Scout, I was at a camp out and sharing a pup tent with a classmate. We started talking about different girls in my class and talking about how we would like to kiss them. That led to us kissing each other. The older campers heard us and started teasing us and calling us names. Eventually, the Scout Masters came over and settled them down and we all went to sleep. The next day I was sure they were going to tell my dad what had happened. I had to beat them to the punch so when I got home I told him I had gotten caught kissing another boy and he just shook his head and asked why I did shit like that. Then he told me to be careful and sent me to bed. That was it.

Dad was aware that I was a fragile kid. I was very attached to our dog Bullet and Bullet was old and fading fast. Dad didn't want me around when they had to put him down so he sent me to stay with Tía Maria and my grandfather in Del Rio for a week. Papa Tutui was old, ninety-three, he had been born in 1869 and he was still active. Every morning he would walk out to his workshop and spent the day tending the goats, completing projects, and smoking hand-rolled cigarettes.

The week I was there he was making a fly whisk out of strips of leather. I spent the day chattering to him about whatever came to mind and getting into his stuff. Finally, when I let the goats loose and we had to chase them back into the pen he sat me down with a piece of flannel, a needle and thread, and taught me how to sew. He had me make pillows while he cut leather strips for his fly whisk. That was a great time. We had long conversations in English and Spanish about God knows what. I learned I could be creative, I could be myself and no one was telling me how to act, what to be.

We moved to El Paso in 1967, by then I was twelve years old and I had come to accept they were right all along: I was gay. I had looked it up in the Bible, in my dad's law books, at the library. I was gay and I was trying desperately not to be. Dad had loosened up a little, he had stopped hitting me, but I was sure I was still a disappointment to him. I wasn't becoming the man he wanted me to be.

Then I caught the flu, bad, two weeks in bed, I felt like I was going to die. At the same time dad had an attack of malaria. He had caught it during World War II (WWII) and his drinking caused it to flare-up. We were stuck at home together for a week. So we talked. He on the couch, me on the floor next to him. And we watched re-runs on TV. One movie we watched was *Inherit the Wind* with Spencer Tracy as Clarence Darrow. We talked about the movie, about the bigotry and narrow-mindedness of the townsfolk. That conversation shaped my attitudes toward freedom and religion to this day. And we became friends, he started to understand me and I started to forgive him.

It was a cold and cloudy day in March 1968. We were still living in El Paso and dad was driving to San Antonio. The road out of the neighborhood went behind the middle school. That day I didn't go in when the bell rang, for some reason I stayed by the back fence. I watched our white Buick come around the curve and past the school. I waved as the car went by, he didn't wave back, I don't think he saw me. It was the last time I saw him alive. He was killed in a car wreck that night.

Recently, a friend at work mentioned that I don't act stereotypically gay. I agreed and replied that my dad beat it out of me. That he did, but he also taught me to be a man of my word, to do the right thing even when it hurt, to stand and fight for my political convictions. He was flawed, he did the best he could with the strange gay kid that fate dropped in his lap. He never tried to make me not gay, he just didn't want me to be girly. In the end, I was his son and I knew he loved me.

CAYO

Cayo was my older cousin. Tía Maria's eldest son. My dad had taken care of him when he was a kid and he worshipped my dad. He helped while my mom was dying and he was one of the people my mom had asked to take care of me. He did. He lived with us for a year or so after she died. After that he joined the Peace Corps and was stationed in Colombia and later Nicaragua. I named one of his sons, Robert, after me. Cayo was loud, outrageous, and blasphemous. He valued logical thinking and was quick to challenge beliefs and superstitions. He was an iconoclast; every belief, every tenet was subject to ridicule. In conversations and discussions he would challenge your ideas and opinions relentlessly. He forced you to define your terms and clarify your thoughts. He forced you to think, to use your brain as a tool. To him the value of a man was in his ability to think, to be rational and logical. When we would ask him to drive us to confession he would challenge the power of priests to forgive sins. He would say: "I'll sit on the toilet, you sit in the shower, we'll close the curtain, you give me a quarter and I'll forgive your sins." I never took him up on the offer.

While he was in the Peace Corps, Cayo met Joan, another volunteer. She was from Minnesota. They married and settled in Rochester to work the family farm. That happened around the time that dad died. He became an active part of the community in Rochester. He fought for Native American rights, a liberal Democrat with a conservative Libertarian streak.

I spent several summers working his farm during high school. It was always an adventure. Cayo worked me like any other farmhand. I baled hay, ran fence, castrated calves. I worked hard and finally developed some muscle. It was like something out of Tom Sawyer. Cayo's nephews and I rode horses, went shooting, and camped out. We raided apple orchards and snuck up on couples making out on the back roads around the farm. It was an idyllic time. I loved those visits.

Cayo looked and acted like John Wayne. He was certainly flawed, he was a braggart, he was anti-Semitic and denied his Mexican heritage. He claimed we were from a branch of the Chiricahua Apache tribe. We aren't, the Fraustos are from Mexico, near Torreón. I've never been able to figure out why he hated being Mexican so much that he would make up a history for himself. I have had the sad job of telling his children that their dad lied to them all their lives. It hurt me when I discovered the truth. But he also taught me that you go where the truth takes you.

The pretense lasted through his funeral. He had a native ceremony, there was drumming and chanting much like at a powwow. One important moment during the memorial service was when a trans woman spoke about the unconditional acceptance she had received from Cayo. That exemplified Cayo, he lived what he believed. With Cayo my sexuality was never questioned or an issue. He took me as I was and nurtured and loved me. He valued my thoughts and opinions and I knew it. His love was unconditional.

When my younger brother, Johnny, was dying several years ago I didn't think twice about leaving home and spending a month nursing him while he battled leukemia. Cayo had taught me that you sacrificed to take care of family. He taught me to question and to train my brain to think. And despite his apparent cynicism he taught me to fight for the poor and the oppressed. He taught me to fight for social justice.

Tommy

When my dad died in 1968 my brothers and I were left to Tacha, Tommy was part of the package. Tacha was my dad's half-sister, she never married. She was practical and responsible. My dad trusted us with her. She didn't let him down.

Tommy was my dad's oldest brother, from my grandfather's first marriage. He was twenty-three years older than my dad. He was born in 1900. He was the best guncle (gay uncle) a kid could hope for. He lived in

California, with Tía Tacha, his younger sister. They lived together all their lives. When Tommy came to visit, life became an adventure. There were hikes in the woods behind the house, games and music, and jokes and stories. Tommy would put a bathrobe on over his clothes and dance to David Rose and his Orchestra playing The Stripper. Tommy was a riot and we loved him dearly.

It wasn't till years later that I figured out that Tommy was a product of a *Sin Preguntas, Sin Decir* (Don't Ask, Don't Tell) policy. Everyone knew he was gay, but no one really talked about it. I learned to understand euphemism and innuendo early on. Little by little I pieced together his story. I learned that he had attempted suicide at twenty-one. He started to talk about it when he, Tacha, and I returned home from the hospital after my younger brother, Johnny, OD'd (overdosed). He mentioned it once and Tacha shut him down. I think that was the way he came out.

After my brother Johnny died a few years ago I ended up with Tommy's old photo album. It is tattered, worn and falling apart, and full of yellowed, faded snapshots of men. A few shirtless, usually posed, more often in couples or groups. A great many of them government or general issues (GIs), sailors, and service men. There are two pages with Tommy and a group of GIs at the beach, all of them shirtless and in swimming trunks. And there is a cryptic photo of a GI with the inscription *Con todo mi amor, Sgt. E. Long* (With all my love, Sgt. E. Long) scribbled over. There is a picture of Tommy hugging a man from behind, they are standing on a front porch, Tacha is smiling in the background. Each of those photos tells a story, each story is lost forever.

I think Tommy dated a cop for a while when they lived in San Antonio in the late 1930s and 1940s. The adults in the family would talk about Tommy and Casey the Cop. Never said anything bad about him just that he was always around. Apparently he was a fun guy.

Once Tommy mentioned to me that during Prohibition he would steal grain alcohol from the hospital he was working in. (He was a surgical scrub nurse in the army.) Then he would mix it with orange juice so he could get the GIs drunk and take them to the parade grounds. That must have been a euphemism.

He used to laugh when he retold the story of the time a guy at the bar asked him if he wanted to go under the nearby bridge for "Some good times." Tommy went eagerly but was disappointed when the man pulled a bottle of Good Times whiskey from his pocket. Not the good times he was expecting.

He told the story about the time he was being harassed on the street in Del Rio. It was evening and a car full of men were following him down the street and calling him names. He finally got tired of it and told them that if they didn't leave him alone he was going to flag down an approaching police car, and that the cop was his friend. Someone in the group challenged him to call the cop by name. Of course he didn't know the cop's name, so as the patrol car passed by Tommy threw his arm up in a wild wave and called out in his best Mexican drag queen voice, *¡Adios, policía!* (Farewell, police officer!). They all busted out laughing and left him alone. *¡Adios, policía!* became a family catch phrase.

And there was the time he took us to the Battle of Flowers Parade in San Antonio. When we got home he realized that he had been pickpocketed. Tía Maria was visiting and asked him if he hadn't felt it. He replied, *Pos pensé que mi 'staban agarrando las nalgas, 'stava chulo y lo dejé.* (Well, I thought someone was grabbing my ass; he was good lookin' so I let him.) Tommy was about seventy at the time.

Tommy was quick with a comeback. In Acuña across the river from Del Rio, there are men that will watch your car and feed the meter for a fee. We had parked when a man came running up offering his services. Tommy asked him how much and the price was too high so he turned him down. The man cautioned: *Bueno pues les van a quitar las placas!* (Well then, you're going to lose your plates!) He was referring to the license plates. Without missing a beat Tommy popped out his upper plate and said: *¡Pos a comer atole!* (So be it, we'll have to eat gruel!) That became the family catch phrase for dealing with the inevitable. When something can't be helped, *¡Pos a comer atole!*

Tommy and Tacha had many friends. Tommy's friends were over more often. There was Blake Fontaine, Benny, Talerico, and Frank Dixon. They would come over weekly to drink with Tommy, play cards, tell jokes and stories, and listen to music.

Sitting in the living room while they were around the kitchen table I was able to hear stories of tea dances in apartments and houses in the 1930s and 1940s. They would all bring food and drink and dance and party. One quote from Tommy about the parties that I still remember: Fig Newtons and scotch, its best if you dunk them! I tried that a few times during my drinking days, they aren't bad. I overheard Tacha teasing Benny and Talerico about cruising on opposite corners of Santa Rosa Park and asking why they just didn't go home with each other? She didn't seem to understand that they were looking for something more than sex.

I teach a unit on gay Chicano subculture in my Chicano Studies class at the high school where I work. We read a research paper on a "witch hunt" that occurred in New Spain, in the 1640s. By the end of it a group of twenty or so gay men were thrown into the bon fire. There are documents describing the men and the lives they led. I am struck by the similarities between those men 400 years ago, the men I knew growing up, and the man I was until a few years ago. The parties, the nicknames, the petty jealousies, living our lives on the margins of society only wanting to be left alone, to love who we choose, as many as we choose, when and how we choose. There isn't much difference, some things never change.

Blake rented us half his duplex when we moved to San Antonio. His real name was Blas Garza. He called himself Blake Fontaine. We called him Blakey Wakey Darling. His was nelly as all get out. He had a series of boyfriends all younger than he was, all trade. As he grew older so did the "boys." The last one I met was in his late forties, Blake was pushing seventy-five or so. Blake told fortunes and read tea leaves. He was flamboyant and dramatic. For some reason we called him when my dog was having trouble delivering her pups. He dashed over in his pajamas with a stethoscope around his neck. I'm not sure what he intended to do with it but it looked pretty funny. He showed me a photo album of his porn once, mostly straight, some gay, I looked at a few and left pretty quickly. I was thirteen, it was mostly harmless, I was ok.

Benny and Talerico were less of a presence. But they helped when they could. Neither Tommy or Tacha drove, so they took us places and lent Tacha money when it was late in the month, before *los cheques* arrived. We were living on Tommy's pension and Social Security, Tacha's Social Security and our survivor benefits. Tacha made sure we got a good education; we were sent to Catholic military school. There wasn't much money left after tuition, we were poor. In any case, Benny and Talerico were reliable friends we could depend on.

Frank Dixon was an enigma. Loud and flamboyant, he wore bright plaid pants and a toupee. He was an "Oooh, girlfriend!" kind of guy. Like Tommy he had been a nurse in the army. He had been made colonel by the time he retired. But there was much more to his story.

I was in high school, a sophomore and read history books just for fun. I was upstairs reading a book about the Bataan Death March when there in the middle of the page is a sentence about Major Frank Dixon. Frank just happened to be over and I dashed downstairs and asked him if that was him in my book. He just kind of nodded and said, Yep, there are other books that mention me, want to borrow them? Of course I did and the next time he visited he brought me four or five books. They all dealt with the Japanese attack on the Philippines at the beginning of WWII. Frank was stationed in Manila and went to Corregidor when the war started. He worked in the hospital there. He made it through the siege of the island and after the surrender was forced into the Bataan Death March. He was tortured while he was in the POW (prisoner of war) camp and was also on the Death Ships. His experience on the Death Ship was horrible. The Japanese were about to lose the Philippines so they were moving the prisoners to Korea and Japan. The Japanese put a few hundred POW's in a hold meant to hold about forty-five men. Then they shut the hatches. The men panicked and started to kill each other and drink each other's blood. In the middle of the melee Frank and a group of about four to five men climbed up on a platform and back to back fought off the mob. The American bombers then came in and sank the ship. Frank learned to swim that day. He swam back to the Luzon and was promptly recaptured. He was then shipped to Korea and was there when the war ended.

The last book I read told the story of his return to the States. During the war one of the American prisoners had become the lover of the Japanese Commander of the prison camp. There was a Congressional investigation underway and Frank was called to testify. I can't remember the results of the investigation, it certainly was treason, but it also showed that gay men could also serve their country with honor. In some cases they did so openly. I viewed Frank in a different light after that. He showed me that an effeminate man was not weak, he could be brave, he could overcome insurmountable obstacles. Frank truly is an American hero.

Tacha made our daily meals, but Tommy made the big productions: menudo and tamales, Thanksgiving and Christmas dinner. He would start drinking about the time he started cooking and usually would be too drunk to eat when the meal was done. We would put him to bed and continue with the meal. I still use his recipes and look forward to making tamales at Christmas.

I have fond memories of sitting across the bed from Tommy spending the long summer afternoons playing Chinese Checkers, Gin Rummy, and Crazy Eights. Even though I dated girls through high school, Tommy would tease me about the obvious crushes I would get on my classmates. They were mostly one-sided bromances but they were obvious and I got teased over them. It wasn't malicious: I got the same sort of teasing over my girlfriends. They accepted my friends then, just like they accepted my lovers later. That was never a problem.

Tommy was the life of the party. When the *tías* (aunts) would visit we would play *Lotería* (a form of bingo where cards with pictures are called instead of numbers) and *pirinola* (slang for penis; a small, six-sided spinning top). He would call the *Lotería* cards and had a different name or joke for each card. Of course, I was *El Negrito, por ser prieto (because I am dark)*. He was *Tomás, el Borracho (the drunkard)*, Tío Mundo became *el Mundo (the globe; also a pun on Mundo, the diminutive of Edmundo)*, and Tía Maria became *María, la chichona (the large breasted), just like La Sirena (the mermaid)*, they were pretty hefty, like the prow of a battleship. When we played *pirinola*, Tommy would be the first to shout out "And don't play with *pirinola*" when one of us had to take a piss break. This was usually followed by the *carcajadas* (bursts of laughter, guffaws) that followed us down the hall to the bathroom. If one of us took too long we would be teased with "*Ya deja la pirinola (Quit playing with yourself)*, hurry up, we're waiting." It was a raw and earthy humor and you had to be able to dish it out and take it. No hurt feelings, no crying when you lose. *Porque el que juega aguanta o si no se atiranta (If you are going to play you have to take it, or else get out)*.

Tommy was generous to a fault; he was of the school that if someone admired an object you gave it to them. One gained power in the giving. The lesson is not to get attached to things, they are temporary, we are temporary. Tommy was hyper Catholic in a Mexican sort of way. He had an altar in his bedroom, a shelf covered with statues and photos of saints. It was crowded with photos of dead relatives and holy cards of saints with prayers on the back. There was always a candle burning, usually a San Judas Tadeo (St. Jude Thaddeus) votive candle. He traded prayers with his sisters and cousins as if they were baseball trading cards or maybe more like Pokémon.

Every morning he would tie a surgical cap tight around his head and down some Maalox, then he would take his prayer book and cards and start praying. He would take the broom from the *San Martin de Porres* (St. Martin of Porres) statue and brush his head with it to get rid of his hangover. He beat his breast and prayed for forgiveness for his sins, the sin of drunkenness the night before and the sin of drunkenness the night to come. In the end Tommy drank himself to death. His liver couldn't keep up with the drinking and when he finally stopped it was too late. His nephews served as pall bearers. He was buried at Fort Sam Houston National Cemetery. He had served his country proudly, it was his request, his right.

Tommy taught me how to be gay. He taught me to appreciate camp humor, show tunes and musicals. He taught me to be flamboyant when the occasion called for it. He was an expert at self-deprecating humor and I learned from watching him. He always had a joke or a story at hand and so do I. He showed me how to be a guncle, to invent games and play with my nieces and nephews, take them on adventures, support them, mentor them, cry, celebrate, and laugh with them. I've tried to be to my nieces and nephews what he had been to me. Watching Tommy and his friends I learned the value of cultivating relationships with relatives from the next generation. We don't usually have children and often must rely on our nieces and nephews. We have to teach and strengthen those relationships by example. That is what I have tried to do.

I never had to come out to my family. They knew before I did. They accepted me and my boyfriends and now my husband. A couple of times I even brought home guys I met at the bar. Once I guess we were too noisy and Tacha came upstairs and made me tell the guy to leave. Other times we would come downstairs in the morning and she would make us breakfast.

It was Tommy that led the way for me. He showed the family that there was a place for a gay family member and to their credit they accepted him and loved him, just as they have accepted and loved me. I am not the only one Tommy paved the way for. I have cousins with gay sons and daughters, not one of them has been disowned or shunned. They have all been accepted and loved because of Tommy.

As I go through my daily life sometimes I become my dad, sometimes I am Cayo, and often I am Tommy. That is the role I play best, it's the most fun, it's a reflection of myself. Dad taught me to act like a man, Cayo taught me how to think, Tommy taught me to be gay, to be myself. Years ago a friend in a bar asked me what I wanted to come back as in my next lifetime. Without missing a beat, without even thinking, I said, I don't care as long as I'm gay. That was Tommy speaking, that's the one that matters most, that is the man I should strive to be.

CHAPTER 8

Todo sobre mi madre/All About My Mother

Carlos Manuel

Abstract A secret photograph portrays the author as a frightened boy standing with his mother and an unknown man. With time, the child's quest for his paternal origins is eclipsed by his mother's strength and steadfast devotion to him and his siblings. Still the youth longs for and wonders if a father would have prevented his homosexuality. To complicate matters even more, after coming out to his brother, the author eventually realizes his brother's conditional acceptance of his sexuality is dehumanizing and unacceptable. After much reflection and after the writing process itself, the author concludes that meaningful guidance and support is what really distinguishes parenthood and he now understands his mother has been more than a father figure; she's been both a female and male guide.

"It's alright, bro. I don't care if you're gay. Just don't be a fag or I myself will beat you up."

These are the words that came out of the mouth of one of my brothers when I told him I was gay. Apparently, he didn't care if I was gay as long

C. Manuel (✉)
Drama Department, Contra Costa College, San Pablo, CA, USA

© The Author(s), under exclusive license to Springer Nature Switzerland AG 2021
A. R. Del Castillo, G. Güido (eds.), *Fathers, Fathering, and Fatherhood*, Palgrave Studies in Literary Anthropology, https://doi.org/10.1007/978-3-030-60877-4_8

as I didn't act like a flaming queen, something I truly did not think about until many years later. At the time of this conversation, I didn't think anything about what he had said. All I heard was "I don't care if you're gay." The rest was overshadowed by the fact that he was accepting me as a homosexual man, and that made me happy. Back then, in the 1990s I was slowly coming out of the closet to college friends and my immediate family.

The process of coming out, as many gay people know, is not an easy one. Some of us experience an incredible struggle while others have it easier. I personally lived a very difficult internal struggle, but once I accepted myself as a gay man, I created a very meticulous plan when coming out to friends and family.

But what does the experience of coming out to one of my brothers, my coming out to others, and my personal challenges have to do with fathering and fatherhood?

I think back to that moment when I discovered a photograph of my mamá, in a white dress, standing next to a man in a suit. Common sense told me this was a wedding and that the man standing next to my mamá was the groom. There was nothing special about the photograph; I had seen wedding photos before, but never one of my mamá.

I was eight years old when I discovered that photo, and again, it wasn't the picture itself that caught my attention nor the man standing next to my mamá, but rather the small frightened boy standing in front of them, wearing a light blue jacket and tie, and light blue shorts with shiny black shoes. I was that boy.

And it was then, at that moment, when I, at the age of eight, discovered something that would turn my innocent, simple world upside down and full of mystery, distrust, fear, and a great deal of doubt. I was too young to understand many things but I was old enough to consider the implications of that wedding picture. The moment I saw myself in that photograph two questions came to mind: How can I be in that picture if they just got married? Am I really their son?

These two questions haunted me for a long time. Because my mamá wasn't around at the time of my discovery, she was working out of town and I was living with my maternal *abuelos* (grandparents), I had no other choice but to come up with my own explanations as to why I was in my mamá's wedding picture.

The first thing I concluded was that it was not possible for me to have been born of that marriage. At my young age I had already learned that children came from marriage and it had never occurred to me that grown-ups engaged in sexual activities outside their marriage vows. So, it didn't make sense for me to appear in that photograph because I couldn't have been born yet. The only other explanation that came to my innocent mind was that I was not the son of the couple in the photograph.

For weeks I lived in fear of everyone around me and kept my thoughts and suppositions to myself. I tried to be the boy I was before, but I often asked myself if the parents coming to pick up other kids at school were actually my parents, or worse, if the actors on TV shows I watched were really my mother and/or father.

I always had a vivid imagination, and at age eight I started to create an alternative life where the people around me—uncles, aunts, grandparents, cousins, brothers, sisters—were not really my family. They all knew it and had come together to conspire against my true life and real identity. I held on to this view of my family until my mamá came back home, which was months after my discovery of the photograph. Once home, the first thing I did was to pull out the photo from my super-secret stash of life evidence and present it to mamá asking her to explain the puzzle of my existence.

¿En dónde ancontraste eso? (Where did you find that?), she quickly asked.

"Not important, mamá." I replied. "What's most important is an answer to why I'm in this wedding picture." I was very direct and my voice was firm just like Velma Dinkley from the TV show *Scooby-Doo*; cartoon watching was not wasted on me.

I remember she sat me down and with a soft voice she started to explain everything to me. It turns out the man in the photograph was in fact her husband but not my father. That man, the husband in the picture, was the man who had agreed to marry my mamá even though she was no longer a virgin. The man promised to love her forever, or at least until someone younger came along, and someone did. He left her even though my mamá was seven months pregnant and had already nursed two children by the man in the photograph. My mamá's explanation helped me make sense of things. I now understood why her husband had treated me so badly even though I had called him father more than once.

¿Ahora entiendes, Carlos-Manuel? (Do you understand, Carlos-Manuel?), she asked.

"But if that man is not my father, who is?"

For forty years my mamá still has not answered that question; I no longer have the desire to find out who my father is or was because to me my mamá has become both parents. But for a very long time I did wonder how I would have turned out if I had lived with and/or known my real father. I recall, when still a boy, of overhearing talk about how a boy without a father and with only a mother would turn out to be a sissy, an effeminate boy, or worse still, *todo un joto* (a true faggot) because as the Mexican saying goes, *Dime con quién andas y te diré quién eres* (Tell me who you befriend and I shall tell you who you are). Back then, at the age of ten, when I heard those adults talking, I was just a boy trying to be a boy; my biggest worries were whether I could remember my timetables or explain what a diphthong was. Yet, hearing those adults talking about how great an influence a "father" has on a child, suddenly made me worry that my life would not be a perfect one. And so, my fear of being a gay boy began.

So here I am today, still thinking about what it would have been like to have had a father as a role model, or someone I could have counted on in troubled times, or gone to when needing an adviser, or someone I could have played sports with once in a while because, although I'm gay and artistic, I've always been inclined toward sports.

Of course these questions are based on the assumption that my real father would have been a perfect man: caring for my mother and me, working to bring food to the table, and making my mamá the happiest woman in the world, while rearing his *only* son as a well-educated, caring, accepting, understanding, and responsible man.

But life didn't turn out that way. I grew up under, first, a stepfather who I remember for his frequent kicking of me because I liked playing with my girlfriends, for beating my mother, and for leaving her for someone else. Yes, that man is the man in her wedding photograph. Second, I grew up under the influence of my maternal *abuelo* (grandfather) who became my official "father" and that of all my stepbrothers and stepsisters, and under *abuelo's* care were the many uncles (brothers to my mamá), who also became father figures in our lives.

Yet, it is necessary to make something very clear. It may sound as if I was exposed to years and years of great fatherly advice when actually the years of counsel and guidance were few. I'm not saying this to complain, or to have you feeling sorry for me, or even to infuse a melodramatic effect into this personal narrative. No, I'm only saying this to make clear how—since discovering that wedding photograph and speaking to my mamá about it—my life changed: doubt, fear, uncertainty, shame, guilt, self-mutilation, internalized homophobia, and denial became part of my attitude, behavior, and personal beliefs.

Thirty-five years later I still wonder how my life would have been if I had grown up with both my mamá and my father. I'm sure things would have been different. How different? There is no way to tell, but that doesn't stop me from often asking myself hypothetical questions. For example, would my father have taken me to soccer games, to swimming lessons, or encouraged my desire for gymnastics? Would he have gone running in the mornings with me? Would he have helped me with my homework or to learn how to ride a bicycle? Would he have cheered me on when I prepared for debate competitions? Would he have taught me to defend myself against bullies (because there were many bullies who took pleasure in making my childhood and teenage years hell)? Would he have taught me to dance, sing, and appreciate music?

At the same time, I also ask myself many hypothetical questions that concern my sexuality or my *joto* (gay/queer) life. For example, would my father have accepted me when I finally came out, or better yet, would I have dared to come out to him? And if so, would I have done it with as much ease as I did with my mamá and the rest of my family members? And if he had accepted me, would he have supported me? And if he had not accepted me, would he have stopped talking to me, would he have disowned me as other fathers have done? Would he have forced me to speak in a deeper voice? To walk a little stiffer rather than swing side-to-side as many of my friends often say I do? Would he have forced me to become a more masculine male? Would he have accepted my boyfriends, my music style, my fashion choices, or my desire for musical theatre? Would he have been ashamed of me? Would he have allowed me to be around his "drinking buddies" or would he have ignored me and chosen someone else to be his child? All these questions have been with me for many years. They do not overwhelm my life and are not present at all times but they are, without a doubt, part of my psyche and subconscious mind.

This brings me back to the beginning of this essay, to the exchange I had with one of my brothers when I came out to him. "It's alright, bro. I don't care if you're gay. Just don't be a fag or I myself will beat you up." For many years I did not think about what he actually said. I was just happy he had accepted me. But as I became more comfortable in my own skin, I came to the conclusion that my brother's acceptance of me was a conditional acceptance, an acceptance that is similar to the once unconstitutional military "Don't Ask, Don't Tell" policy. I still remember when President Bill Clinton signed such blatant discrimination against sexuality into law on November 30, 1993. It made it legal for gay people to be part of the military as long as they kept their sexuality hidden; otherwise they could be discharged. For me this law quite simply meant: "If you don't tell me you're gay, I won't have to beat you." I'm not alone in making such an interpretation. In the play *The Laramie Project* (written in 2000), which addresses the unfortunate events surrounding the death of Matthew Shepard, a character explains the significance of conditional acceptance as "'You leave me alone; I leave you alone,' which is such crap." Basically, what it boils down to is: "If I don't tell you I'm a fag, you won't beat the crap out of me." What's so great about that? How is that representative of social justice? Another thing I thought about after hearing the Laramie Project character's opinion of conditional acceptance was what my brother had said to me, "Just don't be a fag," which today I interpret as his acceptance of me as a gay man as long as I am not a sissy, wear a dress, put on makeup, speak in a high-pitched voice, and/or be effeminate. I'm sure I have disappointed him throughout the years because I have done and been all of the above at one time or another in my life.

But what does my brother's conditional acceptance of my sexuality have to do with the notion of fathering? To me, a lot.

Like me none of my stepbrothers and stepsisters had a father. Our father figures were our many uncles and our *abuelo,* who, except for me, my brothers and sisters call "Pa José." My *abuelo* was a respected man in the community because he kept his word. He was also a man to fear because if anyone in town crossed him, he would settle things in violent ways. My *abuelo* was after all a child born during the Mexican Revolution of 1910. He was only five years old when the revolution ended in 1920. He lived a good deal of his life during periods of political and economic upheaval during which, according to many accounts, personal business was not settled with words but with guns. In fact, as a child, when visiting my *abuelos* in their little town in Michoacán (and later living there for a period of time) I still remember two things about my *abuelo*: the gun he carried in the inside packet of his jacket or under his shirt and the many guns and ammunition he hung on the walls of the house "for protection." It is safe to say that my *abuelo* was a tough man who raised his children, both male and female, but especially his boys, to be as tough as he. In taking over the role of father figure for many of my cousins, brothers, sisters, and me, he was no different.

This is the root of the toughness, and at times, stubborn close-mindedness in some of my brothers and even me. We all lived with adults who didn't have a formal education but honored and respected the land, and knew how to protect themselves, their properties, and families with their fists, feuds, and firearms. Needless to say, my brothers, cousins, and I grew up in a harsh and dangerous environment. We obeyed the adults, never questioning their commands, decisions, or guidance; never disobeying their orders and always learning from and accepting their worldview and opinions as God's own truth. We were all fatherless children, reared by father figures who took that role not because they wanted to, but because it was their familial duty to help their unfortunate daughters and sisters who ended up separated, divorced, or widowed after a few years of marriage. This was true of my mamá who had a child out of wedlock (me) and later married a man who promised her the moon but left her and his four children, on this earth, to fend for themselves.

Throughout the years, I questioned how my life would have turned out if my real father had raised me because, believe it or not, at some point in my life, I blamed my homosexuality on the absence of a real father. Yes, that child who at age ten overheard kin-related adults and their acquaintances talking about how a boy without a father would turn out to be a *joto*, soon after discovered his own homosexual feelings and became an incredibly scared boy, afraid to even look at other boys for fear of being discovered. He became ashamed of expressing himself personally and artistically for fear of being taunted by other boys—which did not help because he was already being bullied on a daily basis. That boy, who at age ten eavesdropped on those adults, kept their biased and unfounded opinions to himself and later used them against himself. Those adults were, among many others, my older cousins, uncles, and male neighbors who gathered together almost every Sunday at my *abuelo's* house because that house was the center of *la familia Anaya* (the Anaya family). Anaya should have been my last name, but instead I ironically carry the last name of the man in the wedding photograph, a man my half-brothers and half-sisters never met and I vaguely remember.

Now that I think about my brother's response to my coming out, it truly doesn't surprise me nor does it anger or sadden me because I understand where his "sensitivity" (or lack thereof) comes from. Instead his response empowers me since he has had to witness me behaving like a sissy: wearing makeup and dresses, speaking in a high-pitched voice, and being effeminate. He knows I live a happy and fulfilling *joto* life having married the man I love and with whom I have shared a loving relationship for the past sixteen years. Also, as a professional, my art has been defined in part by my queer identity.

So perhaps I was never in need of a real father, but rather I was in need of positive, strong, open-minded, educated, artistic, inclusive guidance that could have turned me into a better person than the man I am today, no matter who or where it came from. Perhaps I was never in need of a father because, although it is important to have a father, it isn't necessary. My mamá after all was able to bring up seven children (two were take-ins), provide a roof over our heads, and put food on the table. She worked in this country as an undocumented immigrant for many years, met another man whom she married, and thereby obtained US legal residency. Later she would bring us, her children, to the United States. Even today, after all her children have grown and now have husbands, wives, and children of their own, my mamá continues to be both mother and father to us all as if to defy the heteronormative family and social structure. More significantly, my mamá became a strong, independent, open-minded, and accepting *luchadora* (fighter); a woman who, as Anzaldúa has written, had "the guts to break out of bondage."

"To break out of bondage" is exactly what I feel I've done in regards to wanting to know who my father was and wondering what my life would have been like if I had had a real father. I have not thought about these matters in years. If I'm thinking about it today it is because I am writing about it presently and for no other reason. The realization about not caring to know and/or wishing to have a real father came to me some time ago when a brother-in-law and I had a confrontation because he would not accept my gay sexuality and decided to keep my nephews away from me until my sister convinced him otherwise. "Being a man doesn't mean you can sleep with my sister and get her pregnant," I told him once. "Being a man means being able to take care of my sister and the children; being a husband to her and a father to them instead of getting drunk all the time and making her work so you all can have a roof over your head." These words came out of me in anger and frustration because my brother-in-law was an abusive husband and a bad father, not because he didn't accept me as gay. Days later, as I tried to make sense of the situation, I started thinking about the meaning of fatherhood and came to realize that my desire for knowing who my real father was and the life I could have had with him was pointless because I had been nurtured by a great woman, a woman full of courage and compassion, love and understanding; a resilient woman who never gave up on her children. Yet, it is not until now, through the writing of this narrative, that I'm able to confirm such a realization. That makes me happy, as does the realization that my mamá has been the adult and parental figure I have always needed and had in my life.

Today, whenever I look at my mamá's wedding picture, now framed and atop the mantel in the living room, I see a woman in a white wedding dress smiling at an uncertain but hopeful future. I see *her*, the person worthy of the respect, honor, and acknowledgment she deserves. My mamá is more than a father figure—she is a female/male guide who has contributed to the life I now have. She is my Tonantzin (Aztec earth mother and goddess), standing tall, strong, and proud, right behind her little frightened boy. That boy who one day would come to understand the meaning of her wedding photograph and of having *una madre* (a mother) who is the embodiment of empowerment.

CHAPTER 9

Tito—A Remembrance of My Father

Larry T. Baza

Abstract Tito Cepeda Baza, the author's father, left Guam, arrived in San Diego having joined the US Navy, and married into a Mexican American matriarchy. He attained the rank of Chief Petty Officer despite the Navy's segregation of Pacific islanders—Guamanians and Filipinos—as Stewards, virtually menial servants. Tito's first-born son, Larry Tito Baza, delicate and effeminate as a boy, was loved. As Baza grew older, he "butch[ed] it up," married a wonderful woman, then divorced to embrace gay sexuality, but found the mainstream LGBT movement generally insensitive to race and class issues. When Baza participated in this country's civil rights, Chicano, and anti-war causes, Tito was proud. When Baza came out to him, Tito loved him still, and bonded with Baza's partner through gardening.

After joining the US Navy, Tito Cepeda Baza, first-born son, left his family and island village in Guam, located on that small chain of islands in Micronesia, named "Las Marianas" by its Spanish colonizers. The

L. T. Baza (✉)
California Arts Council, Sacramento, CA, USA
e-mail: larrybaza@cox.net

A. R. Del Castillo, G. Güido (eds.), *Fathers, Fathering, and Fatherhood*, Palgrave Studies in Literary Anthropology, https://doi.org/10.1007/978-3-030-60877-4_9

United States acquired both the island and governance over the Chamorro people as a result of the Spanish American War. It made it a "territory" due to its strategic location in the Pacific Ocean en route to the Philippines and Asia. I am Tito's first-born son, Larry Tito Baza. As a teenager I asked my father why he had joined the Navy and left his homeland. He said he wanted to see the mainland (United States) and other parts of the world.

The Navy assigned and trained uneducated young men, especially Filipinos and Guamanians to be "Stewards." In the strict stratified class system of the military this meant they were relegated to perform menial work on the ships and work as cooks for the other enlisted men (non-officers) or for the Officers' Quarters. The same was true on naval bases where the Bachelor Officers' Quarters were separate and of higher quality than the barracks for single enlisted men. If the Stewards were skilled and subservient enough they could be assigned, as was my father, to an Admiral's home where they would basically serve as kitchen servants. This was supposed to be an honor but in my mind a servant is a servant. My father was reluctant to share with me and my brother his dissatisfaction or abuse during his more than twenty-two-year military service until later in life when his sons became activists in the civil rights movements of the 1960s. My father maintained a quiet pride in providing for our family and in the patriotic values he learned in the US Navy.

The Navy brought Tito to San Diego, California, for boot camp at the Naval Training Center. Like most young straight men who complete boot camp he wanted to go off base to see his new home base, San Diego, and especially meet young women since he'd only been with his fellow Navy recruits. Chamorro and Filipino boys hung out together because they were brown Pacific islanders, Catholics, and had been segregated as Navy Stewards. In preparation for their "Liberty," or time off from boot camp, my father's buddies gave him a nickname. They told him no one in the States had a name like "Tito" and if he wanted to meet girls he should have an American name, so he became "Larry." I asked why Larry? He laughed and said he couldn't remember why but if it worked and made him more appealing to girls, why not?

These boys frequented a few pool and dance halls and a bar that catered to them in downtown San Diego just south of Market Street adjacent to Chinatown. Local girls attended these dances, some were Mexican American, my mother was one of them. Her name was Hortensia Celaya. Her family called her Tencha and her girlfriends called her Jean, a version of her middle name, which was Jenny. Tencha and Tito met at a Halloween dance but she had noticed him before then. She told me she was attracted to him because he was very handsome. And indeed he was with cold black hair, high cheekbones, a charming smile, and a black mole below his lip on the right side of his face. I have the same mole but on the left side of my face. He told me he thought she was the most beautiful woman he'd ever seen. So Larry and Jean fell in love, got married, and began a fifty-four-year life together as Tito and Tencha. World War II began and Tencha gave birth to their first child, Marian, who would only live for sixteen weeks. Following the tragic loss of their first child, I was born while my father was at sea. I was born into a matriarchy consisting of Granma, Mama, and my aunts but headed by my powerful Mexican grandmother, Eloisa. Granma ruled the family and in turn my mother would rule ours. Marian's death caused the matriarchy to overprotect me. Aunt Millie once told me they were bound and determined that I would live after the loss of Marian. I was nearly two years old, walking and talking, before my father came home from the war. The only man I'd known was my step-grandfather, Ernest, Granma's second husband, an African American man. I'm told that I was at first reluctant and shy when I first met my father because Grampa had been my father figure. Grampa cared for me as he did his own blood grandchildren, my cousins. I adored him my whole life and the feeling was mutual.

From birth through childhood I was bonded to the powerful women of this matriarchy. I was an effeminate boy not unlike many gay men with stereotypically close relationships with their mothers. Amazingly, my father accepted me as I was and loved me despite the fact that in any other family I might have been called a sissy, but never in our family. I had asthma and my health was always an issue for the matriarchy. I had little interest in boy's activities and was more interested in the things girls do. Daddy, Grampa, and my uncles never berated or chastised me into being more of a masculine boy as I would later learn other gay men had been forced to do. My Uncle Dooney would tease me a little when I was a teenager, imitating me with a limp wrist but never in a mean or hurtful way. My behavior would change as a teenager; maybe Uncle Dooney's teasing resulted in such a change. Just as many teenagers struggle to fit in, I struggled as well. First, I was a racial minority within a minority. I was one of the first post-war generations of new mestizos of Mexican and Chamorro ethnicity. Second, I had that inner feeling that many gay, lesbian, bisexual, and transgender people have, I felt different but didn't yet know what that meant. I would deeply suppress sexual arousal that surfaced at age fourteen when I would see images of men in swimming trunks or boys changing in the ninth-grade locker room. I would try to change my behavior and take on the gestures, walk, talk, and masculine mannerisms of my peers. I would learn later from gay men that I should "butch it up," that feminine or soft behavior was not acceptable even among gays. That continues to this very day; personal ads for sexual hook ups seek other "straight acting" men and no fems! There is also the issue of race in the LGBTQ community—a microcosm of the larger society where race remains an unresolved issue that is not honestly addressed. For all of our advances as an LGBTQ civil rights movement, we remain segregated by race and class.

In high school I would "fit in," through my relationships with girlfriends, which included sexual relations. I also had two straight boys as my closest friends. I would have my first gay sex with an older man I met through my annual summer job. Also, there would be the occasional anonymous sexual encounter with men but I remained in the closet. Then along came the sexual revolution and I conveniently decided that I must be a bisexual who had relationships with both men and women. I would marry a wonderful woman I had met through a man I dated. I discussed none of this with my father or mother. Somehow, though, I knew my mother suspected what was going on by certain comments she made but there was never a confrontation. Through all this my father never questioned my life. Dad was actually very proud of me and both my brothers' assimilation into mainstream culture. He loved our command of American English because he didn't have a high school education and spoke with an accent all his life. We, on the other hand, were ecstatic with pride when he achieved the Navy rank of Chief Petty Officer before he retired from the service. That rank had been his goal since the very beginning of his military career. Even so, he understood why we had embraced the Civil Rights, Chicano, and anti-war movements. He was proud of us and supported our political activism but he would never take part in any of it. Both my parents accepted the friends I brought to their home whether straight or gay. Of course the gay ones weren't introduced as gay so my denial continued.

My marriage ended through mutual consent and it was a sad turning point because my wife and I knew we had to pursue our own lives apart from one another. We have remained friends all these years and we share a special love and respect beyond that which drew us together. The end of our marriage crushed my father because he'd grown very fond of his daughter-in-law who was such a young, strong, independent, and beautiful woman. But then he had married a beautiful woman whom he loved for her strong will and power. He was a man so sure of his own masculinity that he accepted the strength of these Mexican American women in their roles as matriarchs, not unlike my Grampa. My mother accepted the end of my marriage, though her knowing looks questioned the changes in my life. My father was sad we had not given him grandchildren. He let me know this was a sad turn of events he didn't understand; divorce was not common in his culture. Nonetheless, he handled this news as he had every difficult event in my life, without judgment and with encouraging words for me to move on with my life. His assurances and calm dignity served him and our family well.

I did move on and began the long overdue process of coming out at age thirty. I went to therapy, which was an unsatisfactory experience because the white, gay, male therapist had no experience working with a gay, mixed race man of working-class background. Therapy did encourage me, however, to come out to my mother because of our close relationship. Still, I was surprised and hurt by her response. She dismissed my revelation by saying "I think you are confused and you should see a therapist, after all you've had girlfriends and you were married." I replied I was not confused, had been seeing a therapist, and that my sexuality was part of who I am. But she insisted I was confused and told me I should not speak to my father about this matter. I said I would consider her request but would not guarantee I wouldn't come out to my father and the conversation ended. I was deeply troubled by her comments, especially regarding my father. I decided to ask my brother's advice since he had a very close relationship with our father and because I had come out to my brother first. My sexual identity came as no surprise to my brother and it has never affected our relationship. In retrospect he likely knew that I was gay before I could accept it myself. His advice to me was that I should tell Dad because he loved me and he was sure he would understand, never mind what Mama said. I did tell my father in a private moment between us. He paused for a few moments, which seemed like an eternity, and then he simply said, "You are my son and I will always love you. Now I understand some things about you better." He'd said this with a particular tone, then there was silence indicating the topic of the conversation was finished. I was filled with mixed emotions of relief, joy, and happiness but I wanted to continue the talk. I asked him if he had any questions or other comments and he simply said no and the conversation ended. I couldn't understand why he wouldn't discuss the matter further so I went back to my brother to ask him what he thought of Dad's reaction. My brother said what should have been obvious to me and that was that I told my father the truth about my sexual identity, he'd accepted it, and assured me of his love and approval. So what more was to be said? He asked me if I thought he should have asked me about the physical mechanics of gay sex, which was preposterous because Dad was proper and never told dirty jokes or engaged in sexual innuendo. My brother suggested I drop the subject, continue to be myself, and enjoy my father's love and acceptance. He was absolutely right, of course. A few weeks later my mother let me know she had heard my father and I had had "a little talk," and with a knowing look, she said, "That's good, I'm glad."

Time passed and boyfriends came and went but when Tom, the man that would become my life partner for twenty-nine years, was brought to the family, he was welcomed by everyone. Tom and Tito developed a special friendship because they both enjoyed gardening. At family gatherings at my parent's home I would go to the kitchen to help mom and the women prepare the meal and catch up on family gossip. Tito and Tom would always be found in the backyard discussing Tito's vegetable garden, his roses, or gardening in general. The image of the two in that backyard is one of my fondest memories.

Regrettably, my father passed away suddenly following major surgery. I was filled with sadness but consoled by the love, acceptance, and guidance he gave me. If in my life I exhibit any semblance of calm and dignity, it's because of his example.

CHAPTER 10

Deddy

José Héctor Cadena

Abstract Having complied with many of his family's expectations by becoming a good son, attending university, and growing self-sufficient, the author has developed a strong bond with his father. Cadena speaks of his love and respect for his father and of how much he has benefited from his father's regard and mentorship. When the author departs from his family home in Tijuana to reside in San Diego, he tells his father of his gay sexuality. But Cadena is surprised to find his father does not really know him or understand his commitment to self and identity. In time, however, the father reaches out to his son and finds new ways of being with him that no longer privilege gender binaries or homophobically insensitive ways of being.

My father will arrive tomorrow sometime between seven or eight in the morning. He will wake me up with a warning call: "I'm fifteen minutes away" which means I have to be ready. Unsure of myself in the darkness, I jump into the shower where the rush of water does away with any remnants of my most recent dream. I will be ready for him. My father lives in

J. H. Cadena (✉)
University of Kansas, Lawrence, KS, USA

© The Author(s), under exclusive license to Springer Nature Switzerland AG 2021
A. R. Del Castillo, G. Güido (eds.), *Fathers, Fathering, and Fatherhood*, Palgrave Studies in Literary Anthropology,
https://doi.org/10.1007/978-3-030-60877-4_10

Tijuana and to avoid the long wait at the border, he crosses early to visit me in San Diego on a Saturday. I know when he is near, when to step out into the morning light before he arrives. We will go to the swap meet or the thrift store after a fast-food breakfast.

I've learned lots of things because of my father. Deddy taught me how to fly a kite, how to bargain at the swap meet, and because of him, I once had dinner with five nuns. The list goes on and on so every time I get into his white car and he accelerates, I know he loves me for who I am. I used to fear he would no longer love me. I was afraid that he would stop giving me advice. Deddy's words have at times been hurtful, but to him his words are like a shield for the protection of his children. I was afraid to lose that protection. I thought Deddy would disown me. In my twisted imagination, I had envisioned turning the other cheek to him. All I knew was that I couldn't go on without knowing his love for me was unconditional. So I told him on the night I was moving out of his house.

Deddy, soy queer (Dad, I'm queer). The truth is, I don't quite remember how I said it. Deddy understood I had made some reference to sexuality about me liking men. But he must have understood something else as well.

¿Qué (What)? he replied. His eyes tracing an imaginary map from left to right then in all directions as if in search of a point in space where I went wrong. I had nothing more to say. If it had been as easy as when I told my mother, my brother, and my sisters, I would not have felt so small or cold that night.

Dónde quedó tu educación (What became of your upbringing)? he finally blurted out. Did he imagine my common sense had left my body? I wondered for weeks after my confession if I had had a worthy upbringing. I felt thirteen again, doubting my future and forgetting about the size of my body.

"I am the same, Deddy," I assured him.

"Who have you told about this?" Deddy asked without making eye contact.

"Just my mother" I lied. I felt lying would mitigate the pain he was in. I thought briefly of the time I stood on the Golden Gate Bridge the day after I kissed a man. How my mother's voice rolled in with the fog: "there is another way *mi'jo* (my son), there is another way out of this, not like this …" Deddy was the last person to find out.

No le digas a nadie más. No se lo andes contando a nadie (Don't tell another soul. Don't go around telling people). He wanted to keep me hidden.

Here it was. The man—who took pictures of me when I was a-year-old toddler wearing his giant shoes—was shaken. Is this what it took to destabilize my strong and steady father? Is this what becomes of love—his love? Do fathers love their sons with hidden stipulations? I felt cheated as if Deddy had somehow seen me for the first time. I was surprised to realize that I did not know this man who wanted to keep me a secret. Before he stood up, he left me with one last task as if we were repairing a fence: "Fix this!"

After living in Deddy's home for five months, I had thought it would be a great gesture to open myself up to him, but I left that night with all of my belongings to a new residence in San Diego. As I drove to the border and across it, I kept thinking about his last words to me: "Fix this!" Fix this? But there was nothing to fix. I had done everything that was expected of me. I respect my parents, I stayed in school, I'm a good son, and I'm self-sufficient.

Nothing has been "fixed," and the world didn't come to an end. A few weeks later Deddy was calling me again.

Now during breakfast or while in search of a new toolbox at the swap meet, Deddy no longer tells homophobic jokes. He no longer asks if I have a girlfriend or brings up ex-girlfriends. Could it be that he loves me still? I notice that now he asks about my work and my writing ....

CHAPTER 11

My Two Boys

Gustavo V. Segade

Abstract A father writes of his two sons, Alex and Mateo, both of different temperaments and talents, and once thought to be of different sexualities—one gay, the other straight—until it became clear the boys were gay. Both artistically inclined, Alex becomes an actor and playwright, Mateo a dancer and musician. They collaborate in artistic ventures. The boys grow apart as adolescents and come together as men.

I have written two prose/poems about Alexandro and Mateo, my two sons. They are middle-aged men. Alex is 45; Mateo is 43. They are different people, that is why there are two poems. The poems are about them, but also about Irina and me, and the people who form our lives.

G. V. Segade (✉)
Emeritus, Spanish, San Diego State University, San Diego, CA, USA
e-mail: gsegade@sdsu.edu

ALEXANDRO

Alexandro was born on April Fool's Day 1973
when the Chicano Movement
was in its cultural nationalist vs. marxist stage
when the Feminist Movement started to really happen
computers were things of the future
the internet hadn't appeared
there were no iPhones
LGBT was not even in the cards
Viet Nam was a killing ground

Alex cried for 18 months
Irene and I saw *The Exorcist*
We were horrified when Alex cried in the night
He had a Dracula widow's peak
We got scared of our sleepy boy
Irene and I had met a year before
We got married after 5 weeks of courtship
now we had this screaming kid
and my Movement was almost ending
I was kinda nuts

At age two, Alex was a real person
By age four, he was showing real smarts
By age six, he could read and almost write
By now he knew about the ancient Greeks,
the ancient Mexicans, other Native Americans
and the tales of their gods and heroes
which made for many hours of Dungeons and Dragons
into teen age with other nerds.
I had a judge friend who cautioned against this game
This game became our whole lives
We went to San Francisco on vacation
Alex and Mateo heard the music and saw the sights
in that glorious way-out Kaleidoscopic town
our kids, Alex and Mateo,
decided they were going to be artists.
The four of us have been since then
consciously dedicated to the humanities and culture
and of course
to the arts.

Alex could dance like his muse
the goddess Terpsichore
I took him to ballet classes on Saturdays
I didn't know for sure that Alex was gay
Until he graduated from high school
I was at that moment
recovering from a heart attack.
I never was against guys I knew were gay
but I didn't want anything to do with gay life.
Irene told me, *Your son Alex is gay*
At that time AIDS meant horrible meaningless death
My colleagues at SDSC were dying.
I went to see a Kaiser shrink
She let me cry my eyes out
I recovered, and life went on.
Alex has had to work his way
Bus boy, library clerk, yahoo computer guy
Hounded by two Chinese roommates
who thought Alex would rape them
in their sleep
He got a B.A. in English at UCLA
Where he met, at 18, the love of his life
His husband, Malik Gaines:
African American father and White German mother.
Charles Gaines, now married to Roxanna,
Barbara Rosato, now married to Joe,
famous artist and art teacher.
All these people form,
along with Mateo and David,
our family

Alex and Malik had to do a lot of college classes
At USC Alex attempted to get an MA
He failed and the program failed
It was too Hollywood-oriented to please Alex
And me, I have never trusted that institution
The failed MA cost $40,000 in student loans
Back at UCLA Alex worked on an MFA
in Performing Arts under Mary Kelly
Malik worked on a Ph.D. in drama history

Then they went to New York
Malik as assistant professor at Hunter College

Alex as lecturer at Parsons School of Design
They lived in a second story tenement in Brooklyn
Alex got another part-time job at Bard College
Two new teachers, teaching art, in New York City.

In 1994 they began the group My Barbarian:
Jade Gordon, Malik Gaines, Alexandro Segade.
Jade can act, leading-lady act
She sings, she makes masks
and, like Malik and Alex,
she has, they all have, creativity
The future was on them.

They performed in raunchy bars at 2 a.m.
And the REDCAT
in the Walt Disney Concert Hall complex in LA
They have performed in Spain, Italy, France, Germany,
Egypt, Israel, Canada, and Mexico, from Tijuana to Mexico City.

Greek tragedies are somber plays
Women were permitted to see Medea murder her children
Greek comedies are raunchy plays
Women were prohibited from attending
The actors often used large penises as props.
My Barbarian offered a play in which
Alex and Malik had penises three feet long
Jade had six breasts all dangling out.
Irene's aunt and uncle left when they saw those appendages
Saying the music was too noisy for their ears
Irene's brother, Ira, was heard to have said
If you're going to have penises, make them long long penises.
My Barbarian had all those years of Greek mythology
and all those years of Dungeons and Dragons
My Barbarian made mythic future
out of the classical past.

Now Alex has a seven-year contract at Hunter College
Now he is Co-chair of the MA summer program at Bard College.
My Barbarian has received accolades including
being part of the Whitney Biennial in 2014
My Barbarian, real artists in New York
The Mother and Other Plays starring
Barbara Gaines, Victoria Gordon, and Irene Segade,
featuring performances by Eleanor Austin and Mary Kelly
Irene, Barbara, Joe and I went to NY to see the whole thing

It was great
My mother Luisa/Louise always wanted me to be an artist
The fates turned against me on that one
My son is an artist in New York City, New York
That's more than enough for me.

Alex is constantly working on his drawing.
He is creating a graphic novel that has a lot of style
Alex creates style.
He is learning Spanish
He recently commented on my biography
Which shows he can read Spanish

He knows and opposes
what the current U.S. president
is doing to destroy our nation:
malevolent idiot incompetent nazi crazy person
whom we have to stop, before he stops us.

Alex and Mateo get along now
In LA they worked together on a play, *Future St.*
Alex wrote, directed, and was the lead actor
Mateo did the music
Mateo is a leading disc jockey
all over the country
The cast of *Future St.* were students of Alex
all the way from NY
The play was published in *Theater,*
Yale School of Drama, Volume 48. Number 1

This writing is about
our family's history and myths
It is not about our tragic flaws
It is about our successes and achievements
It is about our lives
Life doesn't end with a big bang
It doesn't end with a whimper
It ends period

Alexandro Abraham Segade
is trying to be a good man
Good to his spouse, his parents, his brother,
his friends, and his society.

MATEO

Mateo was born on April 22, 1975
Vietnam was still killing people.
At first we thought that Mateo couldn't hear
He was so silent compared to screaming Alex
Alex had two years of relating to himself
Mateo has always had a brother
to be compared to and against

Matt is constantly on stage
Sometimes he is Madonna
Sometimes he is Tori Amos
Sometimes he is Melanie
Mateo is the surreal element in our family
He is always out there, not in space
but certainly way out of your mind
He learned that if people laughed
they could not hurt you
that was his *l'chaim*
Mateo was the kid with his underwear
on his head that made you laugh
and laughing often brings you to tears
tragic and comic masks, but they are only masks
What is behind them?

Mateo could act
He and Alex took parts in Junior Theater at Balboa Park
At 7 Mateo auditioned and got the part of Rumpelstiltskin
He was a great Rumpelstiltskin
In high school Mateo and Alex acted as brothers in a play

When Alex came out, Irina and I celebrated
We had one gay son and one straight son
Boy, did we get that wrong
Irene and I knew nothing about gay life.
Irene has had to research and study LGBT life
Now she is co-chair of education on gay life
in San Diego County
She and Dennis Nicely give workshops for GLSEN.
She uses her and my mistake:
We thought we had one gay son and one straight son
to introduce herself to the teachers and students
when she begins to educate them about LGBT life

Mateo has had so many jobs
He made money drawing pogs
He wrote articles for now extinct magazines
He starred in incidents on San Diego bus lines
He worked in a funeral parlor
He attended the School of Performing Arts
where they tried to drown his creativity
At one time in grammar school
Mateo took some Barbie dolls to class
The bilingual, Mexican-American christian teachers
were trying to put Mateo and Alex
into social concentration camps
because Irene and I were raising queers
We had to get them out of that school
The teachers and we knew nothing
If that happened today
Irina would have sued those teachers.

Mateo tried not to be gay
In high school Mateo became friends
with Alex's worst enemy
Soon Alex was Mateo's worst enemy

Music became Mateo's life
Mateo studied the songwriters, and their histories
He corresponded with super-star music groups.
Mateo became a night club dancer
He was only 17, but somehow he danced on stage
where he tore a Bible up in a frenzied song and dance
Drum-Drum-Drum-Drum-Drum

Mateo got hired by a music company that did not
count your hours on the job
They wanted your whole life
all your hours
And if you needed a bit of stimulation
there were chemicals that could perk you up
all the way to hell
Mateo went to drug hell
Mateo took Irina and me and smeared us
into the drug culture
Mateo went to fix up in Tijuana
Buy at a certain *farmacia*
go into the alley

and shoot up
almost caught by a border guard
with a needle on the floor of the car.
Irene would stalk Mateo at work
to get a glimpse of him
He was forever in a bad mood
He and Alex stopped talking
This went on for years

In 2002 I had a stroke
It left me unable to talk
I had to learn English,
my Spanish pronunciation was gone.
Mateo came to rehab to visit me one time
He couldn't handle my being sick

Mateo met David
things began to change
David was not out yet
His father who was over 80 did not
know that David was gay
David owns a business
His employees did not know they had a queer boss.
Mateo started taking methadone
At least that is a legal drug
Mateo had been to rehab at Stepping Stone
He clashed with them
They did not approve of methadone
David finally came out to his father and to his friends
I sense that David's life has improved
since he met Mateo
I sense that Mateo's life has improved
since he met David
That is called love

Mateo and David are the people
Irina and I count upon to get our electronics fixed
We go to lunch and holiday dinners
Mateo and David, and Irene and I
went to New York at Xmas 2016
We had brunch at Alex and Malik's apartment
in Greenwich Village
We saw Stephen Colbert in person
We had a wonderful time

Mateo loves animals
Everywhere he goes he meets a cat
They become friends.
One of Mateo's life-long interests is
The Serial Killer
He has read all about them
Wrote to one recently and the killer wrote back
Mateo does not want to be one of them
His love of cats would not let him be a serial killer

Mateo is now a D.J.
Turn turn turn the disc goes on turning
Mateo travels constantly
San Marcos to LA and back
San Francisco, Miami, Portland, Atlanta
The Bearracuda Heretic Cruise, out of Ft. Lauderdale, Fla.
Mateo works well with the drag queens
LA's Queen Kong, Gamer Night at Precinct DTLA
He works mostly for the Boulet Brothers
Who are drag queens and owners
of most of the places where Mateo performs

This writing is about
our family's history and myths
It is not about our tragic flaws
It is about our successes and achievements
It is about our lives
Life does not end with a big bang
It does not end with a whimper
It ends period

Mateo David Segade
is trying to be a good man
Good to his partner, his parents, his brother,
his friends, and his society.
July 17, 2018

CHAPTER 12

Punched in the Stomach

Marcus H. Fisher

Abstract His father dreamt of him before his birth and knew the author was stronger than he thought himself to be. The universe and father received the boy completely, but at school the kids bullied him and called the child names even though they needed him during classroom activities. As a preventive measure to bullying, his father enrolled them both in karate classes, but Marcus did not like its severe approach to training and had to leave. In high school, Marcus joined the Drama Club, became a thespian and joyfully wrote and performed in plays. Now the young man wonders had he completed karate training and withstood the pain, would he now be a different kind of survivor, a tougher one with great command over feelings?

There are lots of situations where my dad has done well and not so well in his role as the first man to love me. He often told me when I was a little boy that he dreamed of me before I was born. His dream took place in heaven, where he was sitting around and I was standing in a doorway and said, "Hi, I'm your son," and then I walked away through the door with

M. H. Fisher (✉)
PATH, Seattle, WA, USA

© The Author(s), under exclusive license to Springer Nature
Switzerland AG 2021
A. R. Del Castillo, G. Güido (eds.), *Fathers, Fathering, and
Fatherhood*, Palgrave Studies in Literary Anthropology,
https://doi.org/10.1007/978-3-030-60877-4_12

a little girl. A few months later I was born to my parents, who already had two girls of their own. From then on my dad and I always talked about our dreams, it was something we shared as men and as healers. It was reassuring to know I was meant to be here for a reason. No matter how the universe planned to mold me, my dad was given a preview of who I was yet to be.

By age nine I knew I was different because I knew I liked boys and because I knew that I wasn't like other boys. I wanted to read all the books in our class and make all the art projects I could with paint and crayons. I finished my class assignments on time and other boys would ask me for help with class work but would not ask me to hang out with them or come over to play with me. My dad never played sports with me, so when the other boys found out I didn't know how to toss a ball they'd throw it at my face. I didn't know most of the dirty words they yelled at each other, so every time they said "joto" (faggot) and looked at me, I just thought it was a nickname. If I was ever to be in a fight, and thank God I never really was in one, I was told to fight for my life even if I hadn't started it. I didn't even know how to ride a bike because my dad stopped teaching me; I fell so many times and was scared to fall again and be hurt by the black top and gravel on the ground. My dad was a hardworking guy at NASCO, a major manufacturing company in San Diego. He would come home late at night when I was already in bed and I was not able to tell him how much I hated being in school.

When the Mighty Morphin Power Rangers came out on television, I found my purpose in life at age nine—I was to become the next youngest Power Ranger! They were cool, smart, and the guys were very handsome; they knew karate, fought against evil and bullies, and everyone loved them. Who wouldn't want to be a Power Ranger? My dad saw my enthusiasm for these heroes and signed us both up for Kenpo Karate at a recreation center close to our neighborhood. We both had matching uniforms and got to meet other people. I met other kids and was having a blast running and jumping with them on the blue mat. What I really wanted was to be strong, and my dad was there with me to help from far away in the adult's class. The instructor I had was different from the teachers at school and different from my parents. When I fell and asked him to help me up he would tell me to do it myself. I would look for my dad to help me, but the instructor (who looked like the singer Meatloaf) kept telling me to stop being a wimp. I wanted my dad to help me, but because of my age I had to remain with the other kids and the asshole instructor who kept telling me I wasn't doing anything right because I didn't want to get sweaty or punch him harder.

At the end of certain classes, they had what was called "Circle Time." I joined everyone in the Horse Stance (I thought it was called a Horse Dance but I copied everyone else's stance so I wouldn't get in trouble). The lead instructor went inside of the circle, bowed in front of one of the students, whipped his arm around, and punched the student in the stomach. Did he do something bad? You're only supposed to hit bad people, right? But the instructor went around the circle to each student and delivered a punch to his or her stomach. Each student was punched, including my dad who took the punch to the stomach like nothing. I thought it must not have hurt if he took it so well, I should be fine. It was my turn; the instructor bowed, and then punched me in the stomach. All I remember was being on the floor and crying; it hurt so much. I was confused. Why was I getting punched by an adult and everyone else seemed okay with it? Why did he punch me in the stomach? Did I do something wrong? Was I a bad student? Was I bad?

My dad explained to me later, after taking me to McDonalds, that it was to discipline us, to get us used to being punched so if I was ever attacked by someone I would get back up fast and attack. I then started to think, "Who's going to attack me? The Putties? Rita Repulsa?" At my age, discipline meant you get hit with the *chancla* (slipper) for doing something bad. We were only supposed to hit bad people or hit back when defending ourselves. But if we were learning how to block and maneuver ourselves around being hit, why couldn't we also block a hit from the instructor?

I attended two more class sessions, and each time I still didn't know how to take a punch. I cried each time expecting the instructor would hit me. I cried hard thinking: "how could I be so bad? Why was he supposed to hurt me?" He saw how devastated I was and he gently delivered his fist with no force to my stomach. My dad finally saw I wasn't having fun and wasn't advancing in class like the other kids. He saw I didn't like being punched and didn't understand why I was being hurt. He chose to take us both out of class and I put my dreams of being a fighting hero on hold for a while. But a year later when the Power Rangers movie came out, I entered a contest and drew my favorite Power Ranger in action and I won advanced screening tickets to see the film before it came out. I won something for the first time in my life! I was so excited I told my dad we should go together, and he happily agreed. We saw it very early in the morning at one of the fancy theatres in La Jolla and dad bought us both popcorn and soda.

Years later dad allowed me to participate in high school theatre. I liked being someone else and writing stories I could act out on stage in front of people. He and my mom encouraged me to continue with that because they both saw it made me happy. From the very first theatre class I took I was hooked. I went from Introduction to Theatre all the way to Drama Club and eventually became an honorary Thespian. Dad would pick me up from school and ask me how rehearsals were going and when the next show would take place. He even has a floppy disk of a copy of one of the playbooks from a performance.

One year while I was still in high school, my dad and I went on one of our little trips to the swap meet on a weekend. Amongst all the *chingade-ras* (cheap things) and carnival food, there was a medieval medallion stamper making pendants. I only had $20 in my pocket and to make a silver pendant, which I wanted, cost $80. I walked away and lost my dad for a while, but I knew I'd find him later. I found him walking up to me with a small fuzzy bag and said he made a medallion for me. I opened the bag and found a silver medallion: on one side was the theatre masks "Comedy & Tragedy" and on the other side the face of a man playing the panpipes. The theatre show my dad enjoyed the most was A Midsummer Night's Dream when I played Puck, a fairy who magically made people fall in love with one another. He said, "I chose it because this is you. I see who you are, and I love you."

Some people may say that staying in that karate class could have been the opportunity for me to grow and that my dad took that away from me. By learning to take a punch or be hit by others, I could have learned to expect an attack, hold back an opponent, and defend myself when I needed to. Learning how to fight could have helped me face fears in the future and control my emotions. I could have been a fighting machine instead of the cubby guy I am today. But ultimately my dad wanted me to be a kid, living without the fear of being hurt by others. He wanted me to study and be good in school, not pick fights because I knew a fighting move or two. Regardless of my lack of training in fighting or weightlifting, my dad was the one to tell me "You're stronger than you look, Marcus."

PART III

Fatherhood, Queer Consciousness, and Neurodiversity

INTRODUCTION TO SECTION

Mental health issues such as depression, bi-polar disorder, and schizophrenia are shared with clarity and resolve and with particular attention to queer consciousness, masculinities, sexuality, family relations, and loss.

Fuerte Fierce (Strong and Fierce)

CHAPTER 13

¿Cómo estás, mi niño? (How Are You, My Boy?): Memories of Father and Fatherhood— Mental Illness, Enforced Masculinity, and Loss

Eddy Francisco Álvarez Jr.

Abstract Álvarez Jr. recalls a childhood among strong-willed women and a father with whom he shares a name but who suffers from schizophrenia. Macho hypermasculinity is imposed by the family's matriarchs as if to police the author's emergent boyhood queer sexuality. In contrast, the father accepts his queer child perhaps because "schizophrenia [has also] queered him." As the family's eldest son, Álvarez must perform as the patriarch during and after his father's demis. Publicly, a stoical Álvarez avoids grieving his father's passing or calling attention to his own emotional needs. Privately, he is at a loss. The night of his father's death, Álvarez, is given power-of-attorney over whether or not to resuscitate his parent, he does not.

E. F. Álvarez Jr. (✉)
CCS at CSU Fullerton, Fullerton, CA, USA

A. R. Del Castillo, G. Güido (eds.), *Fathers, Fathering, and Fatherhood*, Palgrave Studies in Literary Anthropology, https://doi.org/10.1007/978-3-030-60877-4_13

HAVING TO BE

My dad, Eddy Francisco Álvarez Sr., is buried in Riverside, California, at the Riverside National Cemetery. He rests among hundreds of other patriots, which one finds by the little plaques sticking out of the well-manicured lawn against the distant mountain range that hugs the Inland Empire. His death marked the end of his short but brutal battle with cancer and a lifetime of dealing with the demons of schizophrenia. Because I am a junior, whenever I visit my father's grave and see my own name on the tomb it is a bit surreal.

To stand before my father's grave is to see into the future—*my own burial site*—and I am reminded of my mortality. In the end, we represent a collection of memories that hopefully won't be forgotten. I sometimes wonder if my life was marked the day my father named me after him—if the stories I share here were already written.

On May 8, 2002, at 11:20 pm my father passed at the Veteran's Affairs hospice care in West Los Angeles as recorded in his death certificate. Earlier that day, my sisters, mother, and grandmother, all of the women in my family, huddled around him on his last day. His organs were failing and we attended as his spirit left, little by little, and his body shut down. I stood apart from the women looking out the window and around the room, trying to avoid looking at him. But I couldn't. This was the end. My insides turned and my eyes swelled up from holding back my tears. I shouldn't cry, *porque los hombres no lloran* (because men don't cry). I felt a knot around my throat so tight I could hardly breathe, but I stood strong like the pillar I was socialized to be. That evening I morphed into *un hombre* (a macho) as the event of my father's death unfolded before us. Nearly numb, I stood by in that hospital room divided by three curtains for patient privacy and watched the women of my family cry for him. I witnessed their strength in this moment of grief. My father's inert eyes seemed to be watching me. But perhaps he was already seeing the light that would take him elsewhere. Maybe the voices in his head had already made their final pleas for redemption. Who knows? Perhaps he was not looking at me at all, but rather holding on to whatever strength he had left to communicate, to protect, to love others as was his way. My thoughts were interrupted by the muffled conversations out in the hallway and the occasional screams of other patients.

I held my father's hands and found them very cold, still with the little strength left in them he grasped mine, his last brave attempt at communicating his love for us. His hands were as soft as always. They didn't show the signs of wear that marked the hands of poor or working-class men. With those hands he prayed often for his own salvation and that of his family. Remnants of these prayers could be found in his Mead Notebook journals, which he filled with rows and rows of lists of his sins, prayers, and questions he had for God. His gentle hands held mine—this is one of the most vivid, tactile memories I have of him, of the last few days before he left us. His left hand pressed mine as if telling me, "It's gonna be ok, take care of them for me" as he would often ask me when I was growing up. "Take care of your grandmother and your sisters, especially your little sister, Patty." Little did he and I know it was *they* who would take care of me.

The doctors told us his organs were shutting down: he couldn't speak, couldn't move, and could barely breathe. We had decided not to connect him to any life support system. That was my father's decision, a request he asked me to execute by signing the power of attorney over to me. In consultation with my sisters, I asked that they not resuscitate him. But even though it was what he had wanted, to this day I wonder if I made the right decision. Often I sit with regret and terror at the thought of having had to make that decision.

Mental Illness

It was his way to repeatedly warn us to be careful, in part, because he was being a parent and a Catholic, but also because he suffered from paranoia caused by his schizophrenia. When we were in high school he told us not to drink water from the drinking fountains because Fidel Castro had poisoned the water. He asked us not to look into the eyes of others because they would steal your soul. He warned us not to talk about politics or they would kill us. It was as if he harbored every Cold War suspicion a Cuban refugee could imagine. When he still lived with us, and I was a teenager, whenever I'd get ready to go out he'd warn me to be careful about catching diseases. *Cuidado con las enfermedades* (Be careful with the STDs), he cautioned. I always wondered if he actually meant, "Be careful with AIDS because I know you're gay." This was the nineties and AIDS was killing Latinos and other people of color at high rates.

Back in the hospice room, I realized that I would now be "the man of the house." My grandfather was gone, and now so was my dad. This role, which I hadn't wanted or asked for, was being forced on me due to tragic circumstances. At twenty-four, it seemed to me as if I now had to be the protector, keeper, and guardian of my family. I resented it. It was hard to see my mom there, still my father's wife even though they had been separated for many years. She cried for her husband although no longer in love with him. She cared for the kind man that he was and the good father he had been to their children. When I was sixteen, they separated, but he'd ask her to come back to him. *¡Estás loco!* (You're crazy), my mother replied, not actually referring to his illness, but to the farfetched notion of becoming a couple once again. But the sad truth is that he *was* considered "crazy." He had been diagnosed with schizophrenia when he was eighteen and discharged from the US Army Reserve in 1974 for having visual and auditory hallucinations. The doctor who wrote his discharge letter indicated, "Mr. Álvarez is permanently and totally incapacitated to work or study." And so it was that for as long as I can remember my father never had a job. He wanted a part-time job, but no one ever took him seriously. He stayed home and helped my mother take care of us even though he was the one that mostly needed looking after. He was "incapacitated to work or study" and perhaps to have children, but he had three of them. And though he was not the perfect father, overprotective to the point of suffocation, he did his best. Our education and well-being were his number-one priority and that included making sure our souls were saved because he was a devout Catholic. His religion served to sustain him through his illness.

As I look down on his grave I think of my childhood with him. I recall when I would come home from school he would ask me how school went and what I had learned that day. *¿Cómo estás, mi niño?* (How are you, my boy)? *¿Que aprendiste hoy en la escuela?* (What did you learn in school today)? As a child I would tell him, gladly sharing with him what I had learned. However, he would ask me the same questions when I was in college and I often shrugged in response. As I got older his questions annoyed me, in part, because for many years, I was angry with him, angry that he was "crazy." I called him *un loco* (madman) and was embarrassed by him. It pains me to admit these things, but I must write them down to expel the pain they cause me. The Chicana author, Ana Castillo, asks that one "write what's tearing at your heart, what you need to resolve" (Masad 2016). It also pains me because I know my father loved me deeply and I did not always feel the same toward him—or at least I didn't show it. In her book, *A Life on Hold: Living with Schizophrenia*, Josie Méndez-Negrete writes about her family's own struggle with schizophrenia and acknowledges the challenges posed by mental illness, but she reminds us "the disease does not deplete our loved ones of their ability to feel and love" (2015: 4). My father did so much for me, big and small things, always making sure I was ok, *me consentía* (he spoiled me). He bought me a typewriter, a record player from Radio Shack, and placed me in Catholic private school the first two years of my education even though we couldn't afford it. That is why when he was dying I knew that performing as "the man of the house" would be my way of making up to him and acknowledging his thoughtfulness and everything he did for me. But even so it wasn't enough; he died and I felt responsible. As his executor, I had to make life and death decisions that were not easy. I don't know if we did the right thing. I have often felt like I caused his death.

I have since learned that people with schizophrenia need to have a stress-free environment. They need to be listened to and helped throughout their illness. I don't know if we were of much help to him because we knew very little about the illness and were not attentive to his needs. Unlike Méndez-Negrete who made an effort to listen to her schizophrenic son, often we would not listen to my father, we would tell him to be quiet, and we didn't understand that allowing him to tell his stories no matter how delusional could help him cope with his illness.

MY FREEDOMS AND HIS RESTRICTIONS

During my childhood my parents, for the most part, allowed me to be myself, have a voice, and a sense of individuality. I am so thankful to them for that. My mother allowed my participation in adult conversations and validated what I said. She witnessed me unfold into the queer kid I became and only occasionally policed me. On several occasions, she told my sisters and her friends that she knew I was queer. But, in retrospect, she upheld patriarchal values more so than did my father. He just wanted me to do well in school and he wanted my soul to be saved. He allowed me to be who I was, never censoring my gender performance or the games and activities I was involved in that could have been perceived as a threat to normative gender roles. He was not like other fathers invested in turning their boys into machos. He never called me names or made me feel like an outcast. He loved me unconditionally. I want to believe that this was due, in part, to his thoughts and mental dilemmas that wouldn't allow him to recognize or enforce the norms, that his schizophrenia queered him in some way. We were both queer. Perhaps he didn't see me the way my mother did. Mothers know when their sons are different, or so they say. My dad was more worried about evil spirits taking my soul or a car running over me than he was about my sexuality. Or maybe he was and I just don't remember, maybe I've blocked it out.

While I am happy that my father didn't try to make me into a hypermasculine male, his general over protectiveness annoyed me. His hovering over me led me to call him names. I was both ashamed of him *and* loved him. It was so confusing and despite suggestions from my dad's psychiatrist, my mother would not take us to family therapy. She didn't want to expose us to that, but I believe it would have helped us. As Méndez-Negrete writes there is so much we don't know about the illness and we know even less about the topic and Latinos.

Although my father accepted me there was one thing he would not let me do that I desired greatly and that was to play Little League baseball. I hadn't played much baseball but I knew that's what little boys did. Some of my friends at school especially the white boys were joining teams. They'd hop into cars with their families on Saturday mornings with snacks and lawn chairs and begin their initiation into this American institution—one of the many training grounds for sport-loving, ball-beating boys. *Papí, quiero meterme a Little League.* (Dad, I want to join Little League). My dad's answer was a resounding "No!" I begged and begged, but he said no. I asked my mom and she'd send me to him. She even advocated on my behalf, but his answer was still no. *Papí, ¿puedo jugar beisbol?* (Dad, may I play baseball)? *¡No! ¡Es peligroso! ¡Te puede pegar un batazo o una pelota y te mata! ¡Es muy peligroso!* (No! It's dangerous! You could get hit by a bat or ball and be killed! It's very dangerous)! This was his stock answer for the many things I wanted to do. He had a mortal fear of the most mundane and otherwise safe activities my sister and I wanted to be a part of. Danger lurked everywhere, the voices in his head said so. He had been hearing voices since he was eighteen, which may have been triggered by his army boot camp experience, being away from home, and possibly a mental breakdown that wasn't registered as one. By the time I was born in 1977, he had been hospitalized several times and been to several psychiatrists. *Lo llevamos con psiquiatras Cubanos*, we took him to Cuban psychiatrists my grandma used to say believing a Cuban doctor could save him. By the time I was asking to sign up for Little League, he was taking over eleven pills a day to control his depression, anxiety, and the voices that told him I'd be smashed to bits by a baseball or knocked out forever with a deadly concussion. He must not have cared that in the eyes of society, his little queer boy could have used a dose of masculinity training. This boy who sat for hours creating fashion designs and cutting them out to display to his mom, the boy who staged music videos with his sister pretending to be Daniela Romo or Laura Leon, *La Tesorito* (the Little Treasure). I still remember pretending to be Laura singing on the beach in her video for *La Abusadora* (The Abuser)—*yo no soy abusadora, yo no soy abusadora* (I am not an abuser, I am not an abuser), we would sing or play at being the gorgeous ladies of wrestling from the show GLOW. But I *also* wanted to play Little League—throw a ball, make home runs, win medals. *¡Es peligroso!* was dad's mantra as was his ritual iteration of Our Father's prayer or the recitation of a litany of Hail Mary's to offset his running list of sins. After a few months, I stopped wanting to join Little League and asked for a typewriter, which he bought for me. That typewriter was the beginning of my journey as a writer.

THE CULTURAL BURDEN OF MANHOOD

I avoided crying at the hospice where my father lay dying and I contained my tears at his funeral. I remember watching family, friends, and acquaintances at the funeral. The women in my family, stronger than I will ever be, and dressed in black, were crying again as they had when he passed away at the hospice. My grandmother wailed lamenting the death of her only child. She had outlived her husband and now she had outlived her boy, *su niño*. As if a scene out of García Lorca's *House of Bernarda Alba* or a Mexican *telenovela* (soap opera), I looked on with my mother and grandmother as my dad lay catatonically among us and was laid to rest. But I wouldn't cry in my efforts to appear strong. Upon reflection, I realize now that I didn't cry because I feared my family would think I was weak. I was convinced that in order to help them and be the protector my father asked me to be, I could not let them see me cry. A therapist in training once told me that I was "parentified" at a young age meaning I was the parent to my parents yet I never quite saw it that way until now. As my father lay in his casket, the young psychology intern's words had a particular truth to them. For the service that day, I had written a few words for my father but I couldn't read them, afraid I would break down in front of everyone, I asked the priest to read them for me.

Another reason why I wouldn't cry at the funeral was because I didn't want to confirm that I was *el maricón que todos sabían que yo era* (the fag everyone took me for). False notions of masculinity were burning inside of me like the poison that prevents boys from playing with dolls, show emotion, or allow for caresses between them. Such affection is demonized preventing expressions of public affection that forces us to police our preferences for and performances of love and desire. In doing so we are teaching our boys that in the rawest moments of a life crisis event—death, illness, joy, and desire—we must suppress our vulnerabilities for the sake of heteronormativity and hypermasculinity—preventing us from expressing our emotions.

Today, eighteen years after my father's death, I am openly queer, but I'm still learning about masculinity and the impact patriarchy has had on my family relationships and me. I didn't know it then but I know now that my masculinity is intricately tied to my sense of family and that I'm still burdened by what it means to be a man in this society and among my kin relations. I'm still processing the pain of growing up with a dad who was schizophrenic and of my having to take "charge" when he was dying. The pain of that burden still haunts me and I want to better understand why I felt the need to have to perform as a stoical self.

I believe there were several reasons why I felt it was necessary for me to posture as an emotionally distant individual during the death of my father. Were I to express my heartfelt emotions, I would allow others to see the pain and madness I had been living with all my life and not only during the months my father was dying. I didn't cry in order to protect myself and my new role *como el hombre de la casa, lo que se espera del hijo mayor* (as the man of the house, which is what is expected of the eldest son), the role *abuela* (grandmother) placed me in when she would ask me to sit at the head of the table, and then expect my sisters to serve me as if I were the *pater familias* of the family and home. I was not asked but expected to sanction and enact time-honored patriarchal conditioning anticipated for the eldest son in traditional Latino culture. I didn't cry because my *llanto* (cry) would have been more of a howl of anguish than sobs. But in the solitude of my car on trips back home from the hospice, on the crowded lanes of the 405, I cried like a child, cried uncontrollably as if releasing a deep hurt, anger, fear, and confusion when just minutes before I was signing paperwork on life crisis decisions concerning my dad and playing the part of the responsible adult. I was so angry with him, grandmother, and the Christian God I still believed in for putting me in that situation. *I needed and wanted to be taken care of* after having taken care of my parents for so long. I needed to heal. I wanted my dad to die quickly so the fear and pain I was feeling would go away. But these thoughts would only make me feel worse. I was evil. I deserved to suffer. These thoughts occupied my mind. But there in the privacy of my car with only the stereo on and the buzz of cars whizzing by, I howled relentlessly, *lloraba*.

REFERENCES

Masad, I. (2016). 'Write What's Tearing at Your Heart': Feminist Ana Castillo on Writing Her Rape. Retrieved from https://broadly.vice.com/en_us/article/write-whats-tearing-at-your-heart-feminist-ana-castillo-on-writing-her-rape.

Méndez-Negrete, J. (2015). *A Life on Hold: Living with Schizophrenia*. Albuquerque: University of New Mexico.

CHAPTER 14

My Dead Father

Miguel Garcia Jr.

Abstract Having survived a difficult birth, the author's victory over an early death appears foiled by bipolar disorder, the experience of which Garcia compares to "rehearsing for the process of dying." Life as he knew it is gone; institutionalization, loss of authority over the self, and neuro changes seem to predict slow death routs life in the present. Even the author's attempt at engaging in queer "romance and intimacy" are deemed ill-fated. Garcia's abusive father is himself "dead" and domestic violence at his hands is the likely cause of his mother's dangerously premature delivery. Yet recollection of the author's grandmother and her commonsense approach to gardening reveals that even the undesirable has value and purpose in life, and that healing may take place given time.

Recently I casually mentioned my dad to a mentor and she apologized for assuming that he had "passed." Because I haven't found the words to explain our relationship neatly, I shrugged it off and said that we're just not very close.

M. Garcia Jr. (✉)
Harvard, Cambridge, MA, USA
e-mail: miguelgarcia@gse.harvard.edu

© The Author(s), under exclusive license to Springer Nature
Switzerland AG 2021
A. R. Del Castillo, G. Güido (eds.), *Fathers, Fathering, and
Fatherhood*, Palgrave Studies in Literary Anthropology,
https://doi.org/10.1007/978-3-030-60877-4_14

125

Father's Day was last week and I thought very hard about to whom I would say "Happy Father's Day." I suppose it felt ungrateful of me to let the day pass unrecognized. Because no male figure stood out for me, I smugly settled on thanking my mother. She chuckled and shook her head, knowing that I'd never say those words to Miguel Sr. She knows as well as I know that I've never had a father. Not in the traditional sense at least.

My name is Miguel Jr. and I'm named after a man who is dead to me.

COMING UP FOR AIR

No one is born a fighter; we are forced to become one. I weighed 2 pounds when I was born. I came into this world with a cord around my neck and a mother who had braced herself for my death. When I turned 25 my mother sent me a text message saying that she believed I could make it through what turned out to be my worst bout of depression because she saw me fight for my life right out of the womb. I'm a fighter, she said. I learned to be early on.

The thing about family secrets is that there are winners and losers. The losers suffocate from the forced silence and are left to make do with less air. Everyone else breathes easy.

What my mother leaves out is that while she was pregnant my dad was a raging alcoholic who would hit her for saying hello to other men and spend grocery money on liquor and other women. Though my mother describes this time of her life as the most difficult, I don't think she understands how our bodies are still marked by his blows.

My aunt told me that before I was my born, my mom had been experiencing severe pain and bleeding and that she dragged her to the hospital. My mother had learned that pain was routine and that being strong meant surviving. Pain had become so routine that she couldn't even sense that something, me, was dying inside of her. By the time she reached Hutzel Hospital, the physician had all but told her to prepare for the funeral. The umbilical cord had taken hold of my neck and the effects of the oxygen deprivation were still unclear. Developmental disabilities were to be expected.

I was subject to experimental surgeries for premature babies and my chance of survival slowly increased from the initial estimation of 10 percent. I know my mother wanted me to live. But this doesn't change the fact that I had to be removed from her body to survive on my own.

So when she says I'm a survivor, the secret is that my father's abuse reached me before I was even born. His hands made their way from her body onto my neck. I survived both him and her.

I read an interview of James Baldwin one time in which he stated that he became a writer because he believed he was too ugly for people to listen to when he spoke. For me, writing has been the most effective way to give words to that which I've been forbidden to speak, to loosen the grip others have had on my throat.

This Body and Boys

A few months ago, my very incisive therapist ended our weekly session by comparing my bipolar recovery experience to that of an elderly person coming to terms with the inevitable degeneration of the body. I remember considering her point as both really stupid and painfully accurate. While I appreciated her candor, it wasn't clear to me if her motivation for sharing this was rooted in a belief in its therapeutic value or rather a more egotistical desire to say something clever. I suppose the difference is inconsequential because the only thing that has stayed with me is the observation's accuracy. Her interpretation provided words to my experience in a more disrobing way than even my mother could. The truth is that restarting my life after being diagnosed as bipolar has often felt like rehearsing for the process of dying.

This, I understand, sounds melodramatic. After all, I am an able-bodied, moderately self-sufficient adult who has never had to experience ageism or things like elderly abuse the way my grandmother has. But, I have been institutionalized due to cognitive incapacitation, had important decisions made for me without my consent by family members, and have also been led to believe on various occasions that my life as I knew it was gone. And while I'm not literally dying, my illness has forced me to prematurely grapple with the existential questions of life duration and life purpose. Because of characters like Carrie Mathison from "Homeland" or Andre Lyons from "Empire," most Americans have come to assume an easily digestible version of the disorder usually marked by mood swings, impulsivity, and erratic behavior. For the unlucky 3 percent of us who have come to know bipolar disorder intimately, however, these are but the more satisfying aspects of being bipolar. These "symptoms" feel like highs, a million synapses in the brain reacting to unprecedented stimuli; restless limbs and fingertips intent on re-introducing themselves to a newly kalei-doscopic world. More than a bizarre dream, though, for me, bipolar epi-sodes have been periods governed by an insatiable desire to feel deeply and to dare significantly.

Bipolar disorder is a disease of the brain that kills gray matter and requires medication that changes your behavior and makes you feel old. For me, this cruelty of circumstance is compounded by constant remind-ers of how "smart" or "in-shape" I used to be, which occur when I'm unable to recall a close friend's name or when I come across old pictures of myself twenty-five pounds lighter—all before the hospitalizations and Lithium. Maybe I am not dying, but moving forward has been a master tutorial in letting go and starting over. And yet, I am still a twenty-something single person overly concerned about how this reality will impact me in what often feels like the most critical area of all: romance and intimacy.

Since my brain and body are deteriorating prematurely, my dating life has resembled an extended speed-dating event, fueled by a sense of urgency and desire for stability. I've made concessions in all the key areas: looks, availability, and compatibility. As often is the case with rushed actions and underdeveloped plans, I've ended up with less than ideal out-comes. My most recent rendezvous began almost idyllically with an unex-pected connection with a handsome waiter and ended with the realization that a cocaine-addicted, recent stabbing victim was bound to come up short in the "stability" category.

I know very well that my mental illness colors the way I love and how I search for love. But I'd be lying to myself if I maintained that these inse-curities about my "lovability" and my damaged self-esteem existed only after my diagnosis. The truth is that I carried these fears with me well before the first time I was asked to strip out of my clothes and into a psy-chiatric hospital gown. I can't trace their origins exactly but I recognize the same instincts in my "neurotypical" girlfriends who stress about find-ing "the one" during medical school or my gay male friends who silence these thoughts with late encounters filled with moans and slapping skin. In many ways, I must admit I am both of these people. But I do believe there is something distinct about my relationship with my brain. It has betrayed, lied, and manipulated me into false realities and dream-like trances. It demands medication, vigilance, and constant re-assessment. It has also required my forgiveness and compassion. Somewhere along the line, my brain went haywire and I've been making amends with it ever since. And I always wonder if the boys in my life will be half as forgiving toward it as I've come to be. After all, this life, this body along with this ill-behaved brain, is what I have to work with.

I hope someone will find it beautiful and worth the trouble. Most of all, I hope I will, too.

Lessons from My Grandmother's Garden

To her benefit, the same therapist who compared my mental illness with an age-related dimming of the faculties also encouraged me to confront the lingering shame I carry and bring with me into relationships. Over the years, I have wanted to do away with the bipolar symptoms, to flush the strong medications down the toilet, and to reject that this life now will never be as it was. The mainstream, pop-psychology version of acceptance might seem fitting for other circumstances, but it is enraging to those of us who have dropped out of college, been homeless, and have been abandoned as a result of our brain's premature decay. Our acceptance requires not only a reckoning of the past but also, to some degree, a letting go of the future.

I imagine my grandmother, Juanita, has had to contend with a kindred experience with the progression of her dementia. Only she has done it without my PhD-level therapist, Amelia. I don't mean to compare the severity of our brain-related ailments, but I do think about how her value on this earth is not diminished by an uncooperative brain. I know deeply and with certainty that her presence on this earth is sacred, even when she mistakes me for an uncle or fails to alert others when she soils her pants.

When I was younger, I would spend summers in Mexico with my grandmother where I served as something like her botany intern. Mornings and afternoons would routinely slip away from us as we pruned, potted, and planted vegetation in the enclosed garden of her home. Part of the reason I have resisted the yearning to visit my grandmother's home is the knowledge that our once lavish and sprawling garden has been reduced to a small number of pots now maintained by a home-care attendant. Because the memories of us in the garden have survived the psychotic episodes and Lithium, I want them to remain intact. I often think about how our gardening produced more than the plants and food which she cultivated with ritual precision. I didn't know then that she would influence my views toward mental illness and serve as a recurring voice in my head, reminding me that healing takes time and that even the things that appear ugly to us have value.

For all of her strengths, my grandmother was not known to be a soft or affectionate woman. I witnessed her coarseness of character soften when we talked in the garden. On one occasion, when I was eleven years old, I recall being scolded for mistakenly plucking out weeds that had appeared in a corner of her garden lot. Having noticed an unusual stock of green sprouts, I set out to remove them as to not interfere with the otherwise neatly manicured patch of beautiful flowers and shrubbery. In response, my grandmother rather righteously imparted to me that, "not everything wild must be killed." Later that day, she explained to me that the new species of plants were being grown as special ingredients for a medicinal tea. Comprised of *manzanilla, flor de manita*, and laurel, the tea would be sent to a cousin of mine who was suffering from "madness" and "melancholy." A few years later I learned that this cousin had experienced an onset of manic symptoms very similar to my own and was subsequently sent away to a prison-like facility for the mentally ill in a nearby town. His locking away became the biggest thorn in my grandmother's side. She never stopped talking about it.

I recall my grandmother secretly housing him in one of her many rooms and devising plans to get him out without his parent's consent. I never asked if the remedies made it to him but I recall poignantly my grandmother's words on madness and human dignity: "The flowers you like so much may be pretty but are useless in my remedy without the weeds you so quickly pulled out." She reminded me that just like the wild weeds, my cousin served a purpose in our family; and though he was ill, he could recover and blossom into something beautiful and purposeful.

Even though I haven't spoken to my grandmother about my illness, she somehow knew to send a special concoction of herbs to Detroit from Mexico when I was initially hospitalized in 2011. I drank the tea daily and religiously. Thinking back at these experiences, I wish I would have questioned her about an antidote for the lonely and heartbroken. Perhaps she would have wise words to share or instructions for a herbal remedy to prepare. In lieu of these, I make do with therapy, journaling, and the invaluable counsel of close friends. I know now that just like the weeds I sought to kill, we are all parts of a larger ecosystem, at times clashing with one another and at times cooperating to give life to small miracles made possible through unlikely synergies. Even though I haven't benefited from my grandmother's dating advice, with her dementia serving as a barrier and all, her approach to my cousin's mental illness has shaped my own. I imagine that continuing to deal with my bipolar diagnosis will in turn influence how I approach my so-called love life.

In my twenties, the hardest part about finding love has been distinguishing between the kind of weeds that invade gardens and the kind that contribute to their bounties. And being bipolar doesn't make the discernment any easier. Perhaps a visit to my grandmother's house is overdue. I'll just have to wait around for one of her "good days." I wonder if she'd consider revisiting the garden with me.

After all, she's sick and a "little wild," not dead.

CHAPTER 15

Alchemistas (Alchemists)

Christian Emmañuel

Abstract The author compares the legal and economic power of the father over his children and their home to a kind of domestic postcoloniality. The state facilitates the father's power to select a child's name and identity, challenge a mother's custody, take possession (assisted by police forces) of unwilling children, as well as undermine the economic stability of the home by withholding child support payments. During his youth, homeless shelters offer help as Christian's family sinks into poverty and his mother's mental health deteriorates. But the love and care of the author's grandmother allows him to understand the power of agency, self-determination, and value of queer masculinity and identity and to see that birth only begins "the everyday struggle to become."

C. Emmañuel (✉)
San Francisco, CA, USA

A. R. Del Castillo, G. Güido (eds.), *Fathers, Fathering, and Fatherhood*, Palgrave Studies in Literary Anthropology,
https://doi.org/10.1007/978-3-030-60877-4_15

133

When the police entered our home, my sister and I—both of an age where showering together wasn't unusual—froze. From behind the plastic shower curtain we could hear raised voices, the sounds of crackly transmissions from an officer's radio, and our mother's body being knocked into the furniture. Paralyzed, my sister and I looked into each other's eyes hoping for a miracle that never came. As the chaos drew closer, we stopped breathing altogether. Something unthinkable was going to take place, our lives were about to change and there would be little we could do to stop it. I prayed to dissolve into nothingness.

I cannot tell you if I screamed when the shower curtain was wrenched back. Or what thoughts ran through my mind as we were forced into pajamas and carried out of our home. What I do recall is how the neighbors gathered outside to watch the spectacle of our lives, of shampoo dripping from our hair as we were placed in the backseat of a car, and my mother's terrible screams. This was my experience of fatherhood as it was enforced by the state of California. I never stopped dreaming of an escape from it.

Let me be frank, this is not just another *Mother v. Father* custody case, neither is it a matter of favoring one parent over the other. This is something of a domestic postcolonial story.

*   *   *

Christopher and Estella met in their teenage years as car-culture lowriders, partying it up on Broadway and drinking on the San Francisco piers. Their love was blind retaliation, bent upon rebelling against their strict immigrant parents, and defying assimilation into a culture they felt alienated by—fenced in, they chose each other. My sister, Vanessia, was born in 1989 at the height of my parents' devotion to each other. By the time I was born in 1992, Estella and Christopher had separated. It was once useful for me to believe that my parents may have been a happy couple and that my birth was only a matter of bad timing. Despite the fantasies I had of living in a happy Mexican-Puerto Rican nuclear family, my father would claim dominion over me in name alone. I came to know him as part of an aesthetic for absence and turmoil. He was not there for us and an unrelenting force complemented his belief that money is intrinsic to manhood.

Unable to persuade my mother into aborting me, Christopher turned up at the hospital where I was born to name me after him. As if a postcolonial agent, Christopher's signature on my birth certificate confirmed symbolic ownership over me, then he left to make a new life and establish a family on whiter shores. My mother altered the birth certificate so that I became Christian rather than Christopher and gave me the middle name Emmañuel, the only thing on the document disassociated from my father. But I would be left with my father's last name, a Castaing among Oropezas and Garcias, unsure of where and with whom I belonged, surrounded by faces and features similar to my own. Once the christening ritual was completed I was more spatial territory than human being—something my father could lay claim to and mark as an extension of his own biological will. In this initial act of naming, fatherhood took hold of more than my identity and resolve without having to care for, engage with, or invest time with me or my well-being. It was only after child-support payments increased that my father returned to lay physical claim to me and my sister with the help of the state's police force.

In my father's eyes it is irrelevant that single female-headed households are three times more likely to struggle with poverty. He viewed child-support payments as a personal affront that threatened the economic ease of his life in the suburbs. Not wanting custody over us, nor wanting to be forced into paying more child support, my father orchestrated a state dog-and-pony show. Whether he retaliated against my mother for her poverty or her decision to date Black men, Christopher used the police to drive home his claim that she was a depraved woman who kept his children away from him. The fatherhood that Christopher performed for the courts included scheduling visits with us he wouldn't keep, leaving us in the care of his mother, and attempting to placate our terror with gifts every time the police took us from our mother. Once in his care, Vanessia and I would be parked in front of a television and ignored. When it became clear to Christopher that child-support payments would not be dropped, he disappeared altogether. He would bide his time until Vanessia and I aged out of child support law. As the years went by, my father's presence was in the gifts he would send; tokens of his absence, stand-ins for a fatherly relationship. My resentment and hatred of him haunted me as I grew to become an effeminate, bookish, and soft-spoken young man. I stopped relishing the ways in which a man pronounced "*mijo* (my son)." What remained with me over the years, in spite of my rage and the conviction that there was no such thing as a savior, was hope in a mythological father figure similar to those I so often watched on the silver screen. But my decline into homelessness as a teenager rid me of such romantic notions.

*   *   *

As hard as my mother tried to be both mother and father to us, work three jobs, and ensure we got an education, we fell deeper into poverty and came to depend upon homeless shelters and motels. When the child support stopped so did the gift-giving. I wouldn't see Christopher again. I began to observe that fatherlessness was not rare nor something to be ashamed of. The fantasies I harbored of a hero-father coming to save the day were a distraction from the real heroes surrounding me. The shelter housed incredibly resilient women who confronted their addictions and took their lives into their own hands. As my mother's mental health deteriorated, my grandmother, Esther, took up the mantle of raising me.

Esther proved to me that unconditional love and self-determination are the highest powers in one's life. Her parenting helped to sustain me through love and understanding.

I confided in her my true sensibilities and disillusionments in life as well as the fear of never having a sense of belonging. Her response continues to be the foundation of my understanding of masculinity. She told me that my queerness is evidence of god's love, and that the pain I was born into was simply a matter of turning lead into gold. *Es mi alchemista, con agencia puede transformar cualquieres* (You are my alchemist, with agency you can transform anything you want). I considered how and why my life came about and the meaning of the nickname she gave me; I began to interrogate others' assessments of my being. But my entity was not for someone else to define—this would have to be up to me. Experiencing homelessness led me to conclude that one's birth isn't a passive event marking the beginning of one's life. It is not something that happens to you rather life is the everyday *struggle to become*. Without further guidance I began the slow grueling rise to self-actualization, an ongoing journey in transforming the self and manifesting goodness from what already exists.

*   *   *

My freedom would not be dependent on my hatred of Christopher or the state that enabled him to terrorize my childhood. Through trauma, loss, and rage I crafted my own mosaic of what fatherhood is and is not. I divested myself of those fictions of masculinity my peers subscribed to, I observed the frailties of alpha-males, and learned to laugh in the face of western masculinity. I couldn't bring myself to be shaped by a masculinity based upon acquiring wealth, sexual conquests, or social status. Instead I use my queer masculinity to shape my landscape, valuing personhood that expands human agency and dignity even when these are systemically denied or stripped away.

I have chosen not to seek out a relationship with my father. Fatherlessness became my greatest blessing for I was untethered to any one way of being a man. When I consider concepts such as fathers, acts of fathering, and fatherhood, I am greeted by a group of men and women who contributed their humanity to me on my journey. Even though I may resemble Christopher physically, I could never be like him. To me this is the true alchemy that queerness presents—we are not recreations of our parents, damned to living in circular patterns determined by the contexts of our birth. We are catalysts refining tradition and molding new sensibilities. We reshape trauma and violence against us into unconditional love for ourselves and for others. Terrified children become the leaders of their communities; never to be seized by the state, rather they set out to transform it.

CHAPTER 16

Coming Home to Myself

Luis A. Chavez Rodriguez

Abstract Hospitalized for symptoms of depression, in part, resulting from having to process consciousness of his gay sexuality, the author describes how depression robs him of his sense of place, awareness of the here and now, and the will to live. As he heals, Chavez Rodriguez comes to understand that his depression and anxiety as well as his transborder identity and queer consciousness are all part of him and help enrich his understanding of the world, his place in it, together with the decisive power of agency. What is more, although his father has been punishing and distant in the past given his own battle with bipolar disorder, the author understands that "[r]eaching out for mental health [also signifies] reaching out for a father/son relationship."

In 2014 my father was detained and deported in the following year causing us emotional, social, economic, and academic turmoil. As a result, my family moved from San Diego, California, to Tijuana, Baja California, where I live now. At this time, I also faced the bewildering process of creating and using language to understand and articulate my identity as a

L. A. Chavez Rodriguez (✉)
University of San Diego, San Diego, CA, USA

A. R. Del Castillo, G. Güido (eds.), *Fathers, Fathering, and Fatherhood*, Palgrave Studies in Literary Anthropology, https://doi.org/10.1007/978-3-030-60877-4_16

queer male. Language shapes our experience, and the way we understand and make sense of experience. But language can be a double-edged sword because the meaning of particular discourses, their implications, and specific association with language use is telling. For me, growing up bullied and marked by words such as "faggot" and "gay" embedded negative feelings in me. As I grew in understanding and came to own my sexuality I had to transform these negative feelings and come to terms with the fact that, yes, I am a "faggot" and, yes, I am "gay" but not see these attributes as necessarily a bad thing.

I do like and I am sexually attracted to men. Identifying as a gay male, at first, was difficult because I felt a bit pressured to fit the stereotypical portrayals of the gay male in popular media and society as a whole. Eventually, I understood that just because I was a gay male didn't mean I had to change who I was to fit a category. Fitting the category of a gay male or any category, for that matter, is not the only way to make sense out of life.

Transnational Identity

Given my personal experience in the context of Tijuana's queer community, I would have to say that being queer is bittersweet and complex. The queer community in Tijuana is small enough that people know each other or know of each other. There is rivalry between queer males, which is partly due to class status, looks and appearance, and the competition for the attention of men, or a combination of all of these factors simultaneously. This is not to say all queer men in Tijuana perpetuate or are subject to these dynamics. On the contrary, there are queer males in Tijuana who are committed to social justice issues and uplifting the quality of life of other queers. Nonetheless, there seems to be a history of tension between queer males and the rest of the queer community. This includes lesbians and the trans community as if there were a caste system where bisexual and straight-passing males are privileged over other queers who are discriminated against. We see this especially in the case of femme queer males by straight-passing queer males. Being a queer male in Tijuana means experiencing anxiety when holding your partner's hand in public, being afraid of nasty looks from the public, and being subjected to acts of discrimination in public places such as being kicked out of a commercial center. Queer people need to restrict themselves and behave in certain ways to "survive" environments that are homophobic.

I do feel much more at ease when I am in San Diego when it comes to being queer. I feel afraid in Mexico because sexism is more prevalent in Mexico and gender norms are stricter. There have been cases of extreme intolerance where gay/queers have been kicked out of clubs through the use of force. I feel that despite the need for greater changes, homophobic incidents occur less in San Diego than in Tijuana. Moreover, the entitled attitudes of queer people in San Diego are encouraging and have allowed me to stand up for myself in homophobic places like Tijuana and at home. I resist by painting my nails and bringing my partners home even though my parents may not be comfortable with it. My biggest form of resistance is bringing the men I love home.

Being transborder informs my queer identity and my queer identity informs my transborder identity. Transborder queer identity allows me to understand that attitudes and beliefs about queer people are socially constructed, vary according to geographical location, and result in diverse lived experiences and realities. I've been able to appreciate how individuals experience the world differently and still remain connected through difference and the exchange of ideas. Being transborder has given me a sense of global citizenship and responsibility in uplifting not just those in my community but all those around the world since they also form, shape, and influence my community, a community without boundaries.

MENTAL ILLNESS

My father and I were diagnosed with a mental illness; he with bipolar disorder and I with depression. At seventeen I was dealing with the pressures of applying and being accepted to college, deciding what I wanted to do in life, and coming to terms with my sexual orientation as a gay male. It all felt overwhelming and my mom had to take me to the hospital because I was having suicidal thoughts. My experience with mental health is complex. Part of me believes that mental illness can be caused by emotional trauma. However, in my case, my mental illness is both a result of emotional trauma and genetics, but it was not until recently that I grew certain my mental illness was partly genetic. My father would cope with his mental illness by saying "Estoy loco" (I'm crazy) and laughed nervously because deep down we both knew it was true. He did not know how to process his mental illness and accepted the stigma associated with it. My brother also experiences symptoms of depression and anxiety.

I came out to my friends, my mom, and brother the following year. Before coming out to my mother I went for walks in the park, I sat in front of a lake, and I tried to speak the words "I am gay" but the words got caught in my throat. It was difficult to say out loud "I am gay." I wanted to come out to my mother because I told her everything and consider her my best friend. I did not want to hide my sexual orientation from her. I also wanted to stay true to myself. When I finally came out to my mother, we were in her car; she in the driver's seat and I in the back seat. I could not face her and never specifically told her I was gay. She had to ask me, "Hijo (my son), are you telling me that you are gay?" I responded yes. I begged her to have mercy on me, that my sexuality was not something I could control. At this time in my life, if I could I would not be gay. I think my mom did not know how to process the fact that her first-born child was gay. She later told me I was confused. I was so disappointed with my mother. Of all the people I knew, I thought she would be the most accepting of my sexual orientation. I was also angry with her; how would she know if I was gay or not? It took some time, but she eventually accepted my sexuality. She did so because she told me I'm her son and she loves me. I think she understands that she doesn't need to justify her love for me. Even when I speak of the experience, my mom loves me in all her defiance although she may not believe I think she loves me because I'm gay. My mom is my everything.

She now accepts my sexual orientation as a part of who I am. I also remember wanting to come out to my brother so that I did not have to hide my relationship with my ex-partner. We were both in my room and after I told him, he said to me, "You must be really frustrated not being able to be yourself." I did not expect my brother to respond this way. I underestimated my brother's maturity. I felt relieved that my brother had at least a slight idea of the difficulties I faced being gay. With regards to my father, I did not come out to him until I turned twenty-one. When I told him, I was already in a state of emotional distress. My ex-partner had broken up with me and I cared more about that than what my father thought about me and my sexuality. I dropped the "bomb" and told him *soy gay* (I'm gay). I hugged my father and my father hugged and said *Te quiero* (I love you). But his response may have been more ambivalent than he gave me to understand because he would later ask my mother if I needed therapy or hormones. Looking back, this does not surprise me. I once asked my father when I was trying to understand my own distrust of my ex-partner, why he was so suspicious of my mother's devotion to him. During the course of the conversation, my father told me I could not move out and live with another man because this was not God's way. I felt so frustrated and broken all at once. How was it possible my father could be so ignorant?

LOSING SELF

When I was doing research for one of my SDSU Chicana and Chicano Studies courses on the school to prison pipeline in the context of mental health, I discovered that an indicator of depression in children can be linked to a child's fear of losing one or both parents. I remember telling my mom I was afraid she was going to die. I also remember telling the playground staff in elementary school that I wanted to die. I have no idea where this came from at such a young age. Growing up I had to see a therapist and started taking medication as if to deal with a temporary medical crisis. My mother kept dismissing the possibility that I needed medication, so I made little of it. I paid most attention to my disability when I was going through difficult times, which led me to believe that it was only when I was experiencing difficult circumstances that I felt depressed. However, there came a time when I was depressed for more than a year, I had no future aspirations for life and lost the will to live. I literally just went through the motions of being alive. Getting up in the morning was difficult, taking a shower was difficult, changing in and out of clothes was difficult. I tried reading books on mental health. I did guided meditations and still did not improve my emotional well-being. I was in this consistent state of not knowing what was happening to me or what was going on around me. It was as if I did not understand the world as I once had. I lost interest in my personal hobbies. I lost myself.

Depression and anxiety form part of who I am, but are not entirely who I am. I was asked if my mental health informs or contributes to my sexual identity. I think my mental health and sexual identity complement each other in the sense that they are both two different identities yet are somehow intertwined that allow me, along with my transborder identity, to see and understand the world and my place in it in a more complex, deeper, and meaningful way. These identities have and continue to force me to seek ways to transcend boundaries and it is in the process of seeking ways, and actually transcending boundaries, that I have learned the most. I personally believe the most valuable things I have learned have to do with myself. For it is through me and my understanding that I am able to understand and connect with others in a meaningful and profound manner. However, that my father and I share mental health issues does not make me feel any closer to him, but it does allow me to feel some form of compassion for him. Even so it makes me want to blame him for everything that has gone wrong in my life given his emotional abuse of me and my genetic mental illness. I feel like he damned me. However, I know I cannot blame him for my mental illness nor any subconscious behavior I may have picked up from him. I am responsible for myself and my actions, no one else is. When I was forced to move to Tijuana with my family because of my father, it was I who decided what to do in my new surroundings and with the circumstances I encountered there. With the help of my community behind me, I embraced a transborder identity and its lifestyle. I decided to learn from this experience to let it teach me. I create my identity and I decide what to make of things.

Finding My Way

I sought out counseling to confront emotional pain. In Tijuana mental health resources are sparse. To access psychological counseling meant waiting two to three months for a thirty-minute appointment. I experienced first-hand the consequences of not having access to mental health services. So I sought out resources in San Diego. I went to the South Bay Guidance Center where there was a waitlist due to limited space. Such experiences opened my eyes to the lack of accessibility to mental health resources for queer people of color and/or working-class folks. My lack of access to mental health resources discouraged me from seeking any more help. It was not until a year later when I had a crisis breakdown that I sought psychiatric help. I was so desperate for help.

In Tijuana I started seeing a psychiatrist who claimed to have psychic abilities and did not think that I needed medication, she may not be certified to prescribe medication. Anyway, it was all about her and her alleged ability to help me instead of actually helping me. In our last session she was going on and on about irrelevant things like my getting a masters or a PhD as a motive to keep going on. I responded, *¡Me vale verga la maestría, me vale verga el PhD!* (I don't give a fuck about a master's; I don't give a fuck about a PhD!). She then asked me to tell her how she had been helpful to me to which I responded, *En nada* (You haven't). This was not the first time things escalated between us and she warned me she would no longer tolerate such disrespect and that she had the option of rejecting me as a client. I walked out of her office in a fury.

I sought another physiatrist although it isn't easy finding an affordable physiatrist in Tijuana. Fortunately, my mother is studying to be a nurse and has contacts. I finally got medicated and to be honest the medication changed my life. It has and continues to help me. I am me again. I sang growing up but I stopped singing throughout my depression. Now I sing again. I have goals. Once again, I am excited about life, there is so much I want to do. I know who I am and what I want. Part of knowing who you are is not knowing who you are completely and being okay with that. I am not saying that I do not have my moments of depression and anxiety. I do but not like before. Tajsha Lewis explains in her interviews from the book *The Color of Hope: People of Color Mental Health Narratives* that not being happy and not being positive is sometimes just a part of us and that is okay: "I've been hospitalized twice [because of my mental illness] … Since then, I've begun to recognize that the illness is a part of me" (Lewis 2015, p. 6). This means being aware of the realities of your life and accepting them or making peace with them. Also, sadness and negativity serve as a way of knowing and perceiving the world. I am not encouraging this state of being in the world, but I also don't discourage it, especially when it cannot be resolved through counseling, medication, and a genuine effort to try to be okay. Furthermore, this allows me to question beliefs and practices about human behavior and mental health that are seen as or are understood as normal. Depression and anxiety form part of who I am, but they are not who I am. They inform me and, in a way, make me empathetic. I decide what to make of this depression and anxiety. I cannot decide how they make me feel and how they actually affect me, but I can decide my perspective on it and I decided that I am much more than my depression and anxiety. I also feel that my depression and anxiety are a call or a constant reminder that I need to take care of my mind, body, and soul. I thought of what Nayyirah Waheed wrote in *Salt,* her book of poetry: "i did not make the long hard journey through and across the spirit world" for any part of me to belong to another "unless i decide" it be so (Waheed 2013, p. 125).

MY FATHER'S FATHERING

Reaching out for mental health resources in part was reaching out in search of my father. My soul was looking for a relationship with my father. I tried having a constructive conversation with my father once. At the time I was dealing with trust issues in my romantic relationships. I asked him why he did not trust my mother. He told me he did. He ignored the many occasions he accused her of being a whore, forever interrogating her about where she had been and what she was up to. I ran away from home for the first time when my father punched me in the face for defending my mother during one of his countless arguments. He accused my mother of being a tramp. He would monitor my mother to the point of obsession. It felt as though my brother and I did not exist. My mother, brother, and I left home one day after my father lashed out at her. I had hopes for a new start without him. We spent the night at a shelter, but the following morning my mother returned to him. I told her to leave him, but she would not for fear my brother and I would end up drug addicted or become criminals. I came to hate my father. The cultural theorist, bell hooks, talks about this kind of hatred in her book, *The Will to Change: Men, Masculinity, and Love*. She expressed how her "… longing for [her] father's death began in childhood. It was the way [she] responded to his rage, his violence. [She] used to dream him gone, dead and gone" (hooks 2004, p. xv). Like hooks, I also wanted my father gone, dead and gone. How then was I supposed to have a conversation with someone who did not realize or assume responsibility for his behavior? This refusal on his part discouraged me from continuing any kind of relationship with my father.

HAVING TO HEAL

My father, however, serves as a mirror. I use my father as a reference of unconscious behavior I might embody. This allows me to make the subconscious conscious. What does this mean? This means that at times we engage in behavior we are not aware of. This can be positive, negative, or a combination of both. For instance, in my relationship with my first partner I was insecure, jealous, possessive, and untrusting of his honesty. I also exhibited a similar type of violent behavior my father inflicted on my mother. I learned to confuse violence for love and practiced it as such. Through the art of mindful meditation, I realized that I learned this from my father in a subconscious way. Once I realized this, this subconscious behavior became conscious. Reality, however, is much more complex because I also picked up what I consider positive traits from my father like discipline, which I believe plays a pivotal role in how I conduct myself and see the world. My mother, too, comes into this sphere of influence, I may have subconsciously picked up an inferiority complex from her. Growing up I always felt like I was not good enough, it seemed as if I was always trying to prove myself, trying to convince others that I was worth their time, nearly begging them to believe in me. When in reality my soul was begging me to believe in myself. It was not until one day when I sat with my mother in the backyard and we asked each other personal questions. In this space of intimacy, my mother broke down in tears, telling me how she never felt good enough, no matter what she always feels inadequate. She told me that growing up she was never encouraged to be herself. My mother lived with different relatives throughout her life because her mother was a drug addict. Going from one family to another, she lost her essence. She lost her dreams. Most importantly she lost herself. It then occurred to me that this feeling, this energy of not feeling good enough, might have come from my mother. However, I am now doing the excruciatingly hard work to change.

Sometimes healing means making peace with pain. Pain is, after all, a way of knowing that deepens one's understanding of the complexities of the world. As a transborder person I have been allowed to see that I embody both my mom and dad's good and bad qualities. Yes, my parents—my father, my mother—are my first exposure to the world. But I am mine and only mine. I am not theirs and I decide how and what to make of this energy I inherited. Energy cannot be made nor destroyed, it only changes form. I choose to embrace it, make peace with it, and learn from it. After all, this energy is ancestral and with it comes knowledge. It is a part of me, but it is not who I am. I am transmutation, a continuation, I am a bridge and a vehicle for change, healing, and empowerment. I embody my ancestors, past, present, and future. My impact on and in this world, like that of many others, cannot and will not be erased.

In my first long-term relationship I faced many challenges. I did not trust my partner, I did not want him to go out with his friends, and I got jealous for the most absurd things. One time my partner told me *Eres como tu papá* (You're like your father) but I denied this immediately. I tried so hard not to be like my father that I denied the possibility of being like him. After the end of my first relationship, I went through a painful process of grief and healing. Through this process I learned I did resemble my father by being distrustful, jealous, and possessive to say the least. I grew up with and lived with my father until I was eighteen. I had been exposed to his way of being for some time. Through this process of grief and healing I read several books in search of answers. In one of these books, David Richo, author of *When the Past is Present: Healing the Emotional Wounds that Sabotage our Relationships*, explains that people look for things in their present relationships they may not have received as children from their parent/s or guardian/s. I projected standards onto my partner of all the things he ought to be. Subconsciously, I made him responsible for healing the hurt I carried from childhood due to my father's lack of emotional guidance and support. When my partner failed to meet these expectations, I felt conflicted and manifested that conflict in the relationship. I learned that no one else is responsible for my father's doings and no one is responsible for my healing, security, or happiness. I am responsible for all that. A partner can bring you joy, but healing work is on you. When we come to terms with this reality, we take ownership of our responsibilities while growing in a way that is empowering. I learned to practice the art of accepting people as they are. Richo writes, "[Allow him] to be who [he] is in that moment rather than making any attempts to control [him]. We are open to perceiving him for who [he] is, what [he] is saying, and what [he] is feeling. This is how someone feels truly loved by us" (Richo 2008, p. 51). Through this understanding of acceptance, one can engage in what bell hooks calls true love: "True love is unconditional, but to truly flourish it requires an ongoing commitment to struggle and change" (hooks 2000, p. 185). I call this authentic love.

My cry for love, although I did not know it at the time, was and still is looking for my father's love. I searched in other people for the love I did not receive as a child from my father, especially in romantic relationships. My cry for love had me chasing after my ex-partner long after it was clear that he did not want to get back together with me. My cry for love prevented me from putting myself first, loving myself, respecting myself, instead I lost myself to be with someone. Feeling lonely and desperate for affection, I allowed someone to mistreat me. My cry for love resulted in random hook-ups with strangers just to feel some form of being wanted. My cry for love resulted in endless overthinking, breakdowns, and a desperate search for answers as to why I felt so empty. Today my cry for love is me trying to be at peace with myself by trying to find ways to heal, and not lose myself, self-sabotage, or let my insecurities take over me.

Healing is an ongoing process. Like any process, healing is not linear. I know I am healing because I am learning from my mistakes, but most importantly I am learning about myself in deep complex ways that make me more and more complete. I am aware that I engage in healing processes my father might not have had the opportunity to engage in. This makes me privileged.

My father, the person who inflicted violence on me, is still my father. He made me battle and revolt. He taught me the truth early. My father is a lost child who did not have the love he longed for. Still he has so much to offer. No one taught him other ways of being or thinking. No one taught him how to love or what love looks like. Whenever I try to create a relationship with my father, one that goes beyond a simple greeting or a routine "I love you," he shies away from it. As though he fears to be loved. Like a lost scared child who shies away from strangers and if you get too close, he loses control and cries because these feelings are so foreign to him. How, then, do I approach my father? Should I hold him as I would hold a terrified child? How do I explain to my father that all I want is to love him and for him to love me, whatever that looks like for us? How do I let my father know or understand that there is no need to engage in a relationship of rivalry, pain, disappointment, or discouragement? How do I tell him that we can cherish each other in the moment and that that is enough, that we can collectively imagine ways to accept and respect our differences? How do I communicate to him that love is more complex than joy and happiness, that pain is constructive and can possibly allow for personal growth in a healthy way? How do I tell him that forgiveness is not something that only god is capable of? How do I let you know that despite all the pain you have caused I yearn for your love? That I want to know you? That I see your hardship? I see the human in you, the inner child in need of love. I came here to touch your pain, to heal it. This pain has passed from one generation to the next. The world is changing. I like many others came here to make a change. Hate is real and powerful but hate itself makes love more powerful. If you allow it, hate can be a vehicle, too, and evolve into a love that is complex, multifaceted, and embodied by us. *My father is still capable of so much. It is not too late for my father and me. It is not too late.*

REFERENCES

hooks, b. (2000). *All about Love*. Washington Square Press.

hooks, b. (2004). *The Will to Change: Men, Masculinity, and Love*. Washington Square Press.

Lewis, T. (2015). Interview with Tajsha Lewis. In V. Hazzard & I. Picot (Eds.), *The Color of Hope: People of Color Mental Health Narratives* (pp. 6–7). CreateSpace Independent Publishing Platform.

Richo, D. (2008). *When the Past Is Present: Healing the Emotional Wounds that Sabotage Our Relationships*. Shambhala.

Waheed, N. (2013). *Salt*. CreateSpace Independent Publishing Platform.

CHAPTER 17

The Best

Fredy Caballero

Abstract After a decade of self-imposed exile, the author returns to and reunites with his family and father. A new immigrant in Los Angeles, far from his homeland in Honduras, Caballero pursues higher education at the University of California, Los Angeles, and gets involved in campus and community advocacy for immigrant youth rights and social justice issues. The work is exhilarating, fast-paced, and demanding; downtime often involves social drinking that leads Caballero to alcohol dependence, depression, and loneliness. He now understands his father's frustration with mental illness, alcoholism as self-medication, and its affect on the family. Caballero reaches out to his father, not to blame or scold him, but to love, listen, and protect him, and allow his father's voice to be heard as empowered.

Dad said, "I'll be right back. Gotta visit uncle Toño and aunt Clara. We're going to stop for a bit to say hi. Feel free to listen to my music in the glove compartment." He parked his blue Ford 4x4 and I waited in the front passenger side.

F. Caballero (✉)
UCLA, Los Angeles, CA, USA

© The Author(s), under exclusive license to Springer Nature
Switzerland AG 2021
A. R. Del Castillo, G. Güido (eds.), *Fathers, Fathering, and Fatherhood*, Palgrave Studies in Literary Anthropology,
https://doi.org/10.1007/978-3-030-60877-4_17

I opened the glove compartment and pulled out a CD case of Tina Turner. I had never listened to her music before. Some thirty minutes later, I noticed time flew by and made a mental note that "The Best" was by far my favorite as I raised the volume. In the distance Dad said his goodbyes to his uncle and aunt, smiled at me, and proceeded to walk toward me.

"Tina Turner is one of my favorites, specially the song playing now," Dad said to me.

As I grew older, I listened to this song over and over again. This truly was the first real musical connection and bonding moment I had with my father.

During most of our time together, my father and I had a very difficult relationship. It was not only that he knew I was gay, but all the trauma he had undergone as a child and adult complicated what he understood about me being gay with his own emotional pain. But my story here is not about blaming others or placing blame on older generations. This story is about how dad and I changed over time to become closer and understand each other better.

The first cornerstone to such a bond was music. Music helped my father and I develop a connection that is now a deeply rooted understanding of love in our hearts, body, mind, and soul. Music became our respite from life and its chaos. Music muted out the white noise of the world's social pressures, discrimination, and pain.

Dad enjoyed when we all went to the beaches of Tela and Puerto Cortes in Honduras. He would put on blast music from artists such as Tina Turner, Bob Marley, Vicente Fernandez, Alejandra Guzman, José José, and others. He would drink a lot, too. Danced like a goofball. Teared up and hugged us all. He became as uninhibited and free as a child. But he didn't share much of his past or pain. He didn't share what he felt. He didn't talk about his depression. He only danced, drank, and joked out loud making us all laugh.

He just wanted to feel validated. He wanted to feel his love for us was real and validated by us all, and music was his medium. Music allowed him to exist for us, to connect and show love to the world. Dad knew there were things in life you couldn't control, but music wasn't one of them. Music liberated and empowered him and he loved sharing it with family, especially with me—his only son.

Dad never meant to be angry at the world; he never meant to harm anyone either.

We have a lot in common. We both had a rough childhood having been physically and mentally abused. But Dad had no real support network. No professional counseling or its culture. I, at least, had a support network of friends and access to counseling. Dad did not. He endured disapproval and disregard from family and friends. And it took a toll on his mental health. A toll from which he is still recovering. Now that I am back I try to understand how the pain of his past has caused his mental health to suffer by listening to him, being a voice for him, empowering him with words of appreciation, and by sharing this story.

I also had a drinking problem—though it began for me as recreational. I realize that having lived alone without family relations for almost a decade isolated me, ironically, in a world of accelerated energy and activity, but even so it lacked the touch and affection of a family.

It is true. Alcohol is a depressant. It makes us feel good for the moment, but it does not solve our trauma. It does not empower our mind. It only makes us feel free and liberated momentarily.

Unfortunately, alcohol was not only a venue for self-expression for dad and me, it became possessive. My dad became dependent on it and could not let a week go by without taking a drink. Eventually, I became a victim of alcohol abuse myself—there were dark moments when I felt depressed and alone, cornered, and against the wall. There is nothing worse than alcohol combined with depression. I felt as if all I accomplished didn't matter. I tried to serve society through corporate business by trying to change practices of inequality and inequity. But I realized I wanted to heal the world when I couldn't even heal myself. I had so much on my plate and no easy access to a hug or kiss from members of my family being alone and an immigrant in Los Angeles facing many challenges. Only then did it dawn on me that this was how dad must have felt as well.

Having experienced the darkness of isolation and the loss of immediate family support for nearly ten years, I realized I, too, was self-righteous in my disapproval of my dad's behavior.

We all told him he needed to change his ways, but no one asked how we might help him. Instead we told him what he should do. We sanctioned him. We told him the only way was this or that. We did not empower him as an autonomous and sovereign agent, as an individual, or human being. During these encounters he often cried out, "No one loves me. No one understands me."

I now understand. Society expects us to be self-sufficient and to obey the rule of law. As a family, we did what society expected of us. But some rules dehumanize and suck the soul out of a person instead of empowering them to seek help. We pressured dad, which took a toll on his mental health and impacted him physically.

Here I am.

I just want to listen. Dad needs to be validated as a person who is also vulnerable like all of us. I have promised myself to be there for him whenever and wherever he needs a friend. I will listen to my dad even though it may not change much or erase the past.

Dad needs me.

The other day, I spoke with dad over the phone and told him "I don't want to yell at you anymore. I don't want to scold you for things in the past. Our past is over, but we have the present, which is what matters. We are both in charge of who we are, of our own character, and have time to love and respect each other and that's all that matters."

He listened as I said that. Then, I said, "Dad, I'm here for you and with you. I am here to listen to you and not yell at you. Feel free to call or text me anytime. I love you."

Then later that day, he texted me, *Feliz noche.* (Good night).

And I replied, *Te amo. Buenas noches, Papi.* (I love you. Good night, dear dad).

As I sat in my room that evening, there were tears of happiness on my face after years of pain and confusion. I thanked God for my renewed relationship with my father because, in the words of Tina Turner, "It's simply the best."

PART IV

Desire, Daddy Issues, and Taboos

INTRODUCTION TO SECTION

The content, sensibilities, and practices of the essays in this section may be described as erotic, incestuous, unsafe, or even dangerous. The disclosure of some of this content did not come easy.

Fragmentos Taboo (Fragments of the Taboo)

CHAPTER 18

Border Crossings

Omar O. González

Abstract In this erotic and ironically humorous narrative, the author relates a coming-of-age sexual encounter with a father figure. Since the boyhood banishment of his enlisted biological father, the author quests for "paternal love," a term González uses to encode various kinds of sexual pursuit, especially one that elicits the familial endearment for boys as *mi'jo* (my son). Given the author's self-described hypersexuality, this may involve sex with men that crosses legal and normative boundaries of sexual activity such as man-boy sex and sex with kin relations. Through this work, González expands notions of sexuality, object of desire, and sexual drive in pre-adolescent queer boys in Chicano/Mexicano culture.

My father slams the front door carrying the last of his boxes. My mother, now reduced to a torrent of tears, commanded that I help her pack my father's belongings. My sister, clearly my Dad's favorite, was begging my father not to leave. Although I did not express my grief, I, too, would miss the warmth of my father's bear hug embraces, made all the better after he developed his biceps serving in the armed forces. He frequently kissed me

O. O. González (✉)
California State University, Northridge, CA, USA
e-mail: xicano73@ucla.edu

© The Author(s), under exclusive license to Springer Nature
Switzerland AG 2021
A. R. Del Castillo, G. Güido (eds.), *Fathers, Fathering, and Fatherhood*, Palgrave Studies in Literary Anthropology,
https://doi.org/10.1007/978-3-030-60877-4_18

and told me that he loved me. I felt loved by my father until that day. My mother went on a rampage after he left. She tore every family picture to shreds. She began to condition us to hate our father and being small children, we could only acquiesce. My sister and I visited my father weekly, but the warmth had cooled to a polite estrangement. Where would I find the masculine warmth that I craved?

Several years later…

The beautiful *conjunto* (*ensemble*) music fills the crisp desert air of the summer nights of my youth. I am a pre-adolescent attending a wedding reception perhaps or just a summer barbecue at my *tia's* (aunt's) house in Ysleta, Texas. As I was wont to do, I am reading in the dim light coming from the kitchen that spills out into the backyard. I take a book everywhere I go. My extended family had stopped questioning my parents long ago about my incessant need to read. At that age, I was probably reading something by Madeline L'Engle (the author of the *Time Quintet* series that includes *A Wrinkle in Time*) or one of the books of *The Great Brain* series by John Dennis Fitzgerald.

The only thing that rivaled my obsession for reading was my erotic desire for other men. I had already had sexual relations with a man, but they were against my will. Those traumatic experiences did not stop me from desiring other men. Rather, they reinforced my desire for a different type of love—the one that my father withdrew. The forced sex by my Anglo stepfather was coldly mechanical with little warmth. I was his receptacle. I longed for the warmth of a Chicano who drank and laughed and danced. My stepfather was stoic and reserved. I desired the affection that my *tíos* (uncles) granted their wives and girlfriends. I longed to be held in their arms with my head buried in their barrel-chested fur, inhaling their manly scents of physical, manual labor, as they danced to the *conjunto* music that fill my adolescent memories.

As I would read, I noticed the men's bodies as they danced with their women. The thighs bulged through their tight Levis. The thick mat of hair protruded from the top of their Western style shirts matching their moustaches. I could see the outline of genitalia on my favorite *tío's* (uncle's) jeans and the rising and falling of his erections. This *tío* (uncle) exuded masculinity (he installed water heaters and repaired air conditioners), and I melted every time he would utter his nickname for me, *¡Orale, ya vino el Homer!* (Alright, Homer has arrived!). He was very generous with his hugs, and his hands would often linger on my body. He was and still is an alcoholic, but at the time I just thought he was a heavy drinker.

I always stayed within his vicinity when he was intoxicated. The mix of his body odor, his Stetson cologne, and the alcohol coming from his pores was *intoxicating* to me.

I have one memory of his getting drunk after his girlfriend left him for drinking too much and spending too much time at the local country western bar right off I-10 and Zaragosa. He was at the usual congregating spot, his mother's house (my mother's *tía*), sitting alone at the fire pit with a couple of empty cartons of beer. He gave me a huge bear hug when he saw me. I inhaled him as deeply as I could when I was pressed up against his chest. I seized this opportunity to rub his back. My hand went further down toward his belt line. His shirt, Western style of course, was no longer tucked inside his jeans. I rubbed the base of his back slowly, running my fingers through the *pelos* (hairs) sprouting there. He responded in kind. He stroked my hair and lifted my shirt to rub the smooth skin of my back. I was still pressed up against his chest and slightly opened my mouth wanting to taste his salty, drunken Chicano working-class essence. His throbbing erection threatened to split the tough denim at the seams. This was not my first experience with another man's erection pressed against me, but it was the first one with which I exerted my agency. He felt me moving my stomach on his erection. He didn't say anything. He just tilted my chin up toward his dark Chicano indigenous face and kissed me lightly on the lips. He pulled away and asked me with an intense look in his eyes, "Do you love me, *mi'jo* (son)?" I replied, "A lot, *tío*." He gave me his big toothy smile and said, "Let's go to the store. I'm outta beer."

I ran to tell my mother that I was going with her cousin (her favorite dancing partner since my parents' divorce) to the local Good Time Store. I made sure to adjust my erection before I went inside the house. She didn't even look at me when I told her. She was too busy *chismiando* (gossiping) with her *tía* and other female relatives. I climbed onto his pick-up truck still harboring my intense erection, one of the perks of burgeoning adolescence. As I was about to put on my seatbelt, my *tío* said, "Sit closer to me, *mi'jo*. We're just going around the corner." I said nothing and slid toward the middle of the truck.

It was a warm summer night in the Lower Valley in El Paso, and I was about to seduce a thirty-year-old man at the age of twelve. He put his muscled arm around my shoulder squeezing me tightly. My hand had "accidentally" fallen on his leg. I turned to look at him and noticed that he had undone three of the silver clasps on his sweat soaked Western-style shirt. I had seen him bare-chested before but never had been this close to him when he was shirtless. I almost gasped. The fur on his chest was a thick mat of coarse dark manliness. He saw me staring at his chest and asked me playfully, "You like all that *pelo* (hair), *mi'jo*?" I gulped and nodded. He smiled and turned up his stereo. He was playing low-rider oldies. He alternated this music with his beloved *conjunto* and country western music. The song playing was "Natural High" by Bloodstone. He started singing but his voice was so deep and hoarse that he clashed with the falsetto of the singer. I didn't care. Nothing could ruin this moment. This is the moment that would portend my destiny as a teenager and an adult as a hypersexual gay man. My hand on his leg fell toward the inside of his thigh and he kept squeezing my shoulder and upper arm. I wanted to shift my orientation in the truck so my hand could reach his crotch, but I was frozen. I sang the words of the song softly along with his drunken rendition, "Take to the sky on a natural high/Loving you more 'til the day I die." He pulled over in an empty lot saying, "I have to take a piss, *mi'jo*." I said, "Me too, *tío*." There wasn't much traffic on Alameda that night and Coyolxauhqui (moon) was nowhere to be seen.

The conditions were perfect for what I had envisioned. He unzipped his pants, and so did I. It was difficult for me because I still had an erection. My *tío* was half hard and he opened his button fly all the way to the bottom. I have to look, I thought. Oh God, I *have* to look. I could hear his violent stream of piss hit the ground several feet away. I was standing there with my erection in my hand forcing myself to produce some urine. I was dry. He kept pissing all that Lone Star beer. He didn't say a word, just sighed at the relief of urinating. I decided to look. I shifted my head down and tried to shift only my eyes but I cocked my head ever so slightly toward him, and he caught me. "Are you trying to look at your *tío's verga* (prick), *mi'jo*?" I shook my head quickly wanting to run away until he said, "It's okay, *mi'jo*. Go ahead and look." I took his invitation and shifted my body forty-five degrees to my right and witnessed a magnificent sight: my *tío's* huge (at the time I considered it huge) uncut penis, his hairy crotch, and his dangling testicles. He looked down and noticed my appendage still in my hand. He had ceased urinating and shook the remaining drops from his beautiful uncircumcised penis. He turned toward me with his shirt completely open and his penis and testicles plainly exposed for all to see. Actually, they were for me that night. He pulled me closer. I started breathing harder and harder and more rapidly. My heart was racing. "Are you okay, *mi'jo*?" I could only gulp and nod. I took his manhood in my hand and started to stroke it lightly. He moaned. I grabbed his hairy testicles and rubbed them slowly with my fingers. Without saying a word, he pushed my head down to the ground. I knelt on the patchy grass and opened my mouth wide. I started to pleasure him and he responded, "That's the way, *mi'jo*. Oh yeah, *chupame* (suck me) …" After several minutes, I heard a long inhaling sound. I had no idea what that was and became alarmed. I took my *tío's* penis out of my mouth and looked up at his hairy crotch and chest. He was making the inhaling sounds, but why? He inhaled a second time. I asked, "What's wrong, *tío*?" He responded, "Here, *mi'jo*. Put this under your nose and inhale deeply. It was a small dark vial of liquid. It smelled like spray paint or the liquid paper my friends and I sniffed, just much stronger. I did what he said and inhaled. I was transported to another realm of pleasure and consciousness. I heard him say, "Now with the other side." I took an even deeper inhalation this time. It was pure ecstasy. I couldn't believe what was happening next. My *tío* knelt down before me and started to pleasure me. I could feel his whiskers on my testicles, and I heard him stroking his penis while devouring my sex organ. He took another inhalation of what I would later learn are called "poppers." He handed the bottle to me, and I took two deep inhalations. The pleasure was unbelievable. Before I knew it, I was about to climax. I started to convulse, and my *tío* only proceeded to deep throat me even further. My husky, masculine, hairy, womanizing *tío* was about to swallow my ejaculatory fluid. He grabbed my ass and pulled me closer into him as if he wanted us to fuse into one being. I came like I had never come before. He swallowed every drop. "Did you like that, *mi'jo*?" I could only nod. My body wasn't capable of speech. I was still on my own natural high. We were still both hard, but he took me into his truck. He laid me down on my back and slid my shorts off. He took off his boots and jeans, which was difficult for him since he was drunk. He even fell on his bare ass once. We both laughed shortly, not wanting to break the sexual tension. He was completely naked except for his unbuttoned shirt. "Take off your shirt," I commanded. I was surprised at my assertiveness. He smiled and acquiesced. My husky, masculine, hairy, womanizing *tío* stood naked in front of me. He laid me back and put his weight on top of me. He threw a half empty bag of sunflower seeds on the floor along with some empty beer cans. He looked down at me smiling. His weight was both uncomfortable and welcome. His hairy chest contrasted with my smooth torso. He leaned down with his mouth toward me and kissed me. I had French kissed other *boys* but not a man. His moustache and stubble sent me into a delirium. I was still dazed by the poppers, but now I was making out with my husky, masculine, hairy, womanizing *tío*! He started kissing and nibbling my chin, my neck, my earlobe. I felt myself ready to ejaculate again. He must have read my mind because he placed his hairy nipple in my mouth. He moaned. I started sucking on it. He gave me his other one. He tasted just like I thought he would—pure manliness. I inhaled his hairy, sweaty armpit and winced at the remnants of his Speed Stick deodorant. I ejaculated again—the semen pressed between my penis and his hairy abdomen. He laughed, "*¡Chinga'o, mi'jo* (Fuck, son), you cum a lot!" We started to make out again for a few minutes until he pulled out something from his glove compartment. It was a small bottle of Vaseline. Before I could offer any protestation, he placed the vial of poppers under my nose again. I took the biggest inhalation I could in both nostrils. My husky, masculine, hairy, womanizing *tío* was performing oral sex on me again and inched his tongue lower and lower until he reached my not-quite-so-virgin hole. He proceeded to lube my asshole, and we connected as one organism for the next half hour. I forgot the excuse my *tío* gave when we returned, but we had more secret encounters from that day on. The desert kept our secret.

Several years later, after I got my driver's license, I explored the seedy underbelly of El Chuco in search of paternal love. My *tío* had told of certain areas in El Paso where I could find the warmth I continuously craved. One such spot was curiously named an "adult bookstore." A bookstore? Real books? Like those sold at Waldenbooks or B. Dalton's? Maybe I could get the latest Stephen King! I had been wanting to pick up his latest, the apocalyptic thriller, *The Stand*. I had never heard of an "adult bookstore." Does this mean that there is no child section or teen section? The sign said the store was open twenty-four hours. A twenty-four-hour bookstore! Awesome! Just like Whataburger. That might be nice … no little brats running around the store. But why would a bookstore be located in such a sleazy strip mall—in between a pool hall and a dive bar?

As I tread lightly toward the threshold, my curiosity piqued, a middle-aged moustached burly Chicano comes out of the bookstore and stares at me. He asks me what I was doing there. I said to look for some books. He chuckled, put his hands on my shoulders, and squeezed. He pushed me against the wall. He carried an intense look on his face and pressed his lips against mine. I felt the same delirium as I did with my *tío* and inhaled his masculine scent.

After he released me, he patted me on the head and told me to have a good time. I opened the door and entered into a new world. As I entered,

I quickly realized that I would not be finding the latest Stephen King novel but would encounter something much more exciting. A clerk, an older Chicano male, asked me for my ID. I showed him the fake ID I used to frequent bars in Juárez. He barely looked at the ID but stared at me intensely. I asked him what was in the back of the store. "That's the arcade." I tried to look like I understood.

Later, I searched for my father in other locales. I remember entering a bathhouse for the first time. I was twenty-one. A close friend and I were visiting Houston, and we had just left one of the many gay clubs in the city. He lived in San Francisco and was a frequent patron of gay bathhouses and sex clubs. I had never visited one. The surrounding area was industrial; nothing else was open. After paying the fee, we entered and he proceeded to "show me the ropes." We separated in order to begin our individual sex hunts. When I saw men of all ages, races, and body types walk and cruise each other in such an environment, I felt extremely liberated. I stood there in awe of the men, wearing only towels, some completely nude, cruising me, and offering their bodies to me. Motionless for a few minutes, my eyes adjusted to focus on an older stocky Chicano male reminiscent of my beloved *tío* who looked to be about in his late forties, tall, hairy with a salt and pepper goatee. He gave me the "look" to follow him to his room. I surrendered myself to him and subsequently became addicted to gay bathhouses and sex clubs.

In those encounters, I found my father briefly for moments, sometimes minutes, especially if they called me *mi'jo.*

CHAPTER 19

How to Compromise Yourself

Daniel Vidal Soto

Abstract Residents of a racist southern town, a father warns his son that life is unfair and unjust and that he'll "need to kiss the white man's ass" to succeed, and it won't be pleasant. Ironically, this comes to fruition in a more literal sense when the son has his first sexual encounter, with a white man, that turns out to be an alienating, disagreeable experience.

I

My father told me life is simply unfair, and to get anywhere I'll need to kiss the white man's ass. It won't be fun, it won't be easy, but it just needs to be done. He worked with rural Texans who still believe in the Almighty and the baby Jesus, Manifest Destiny, and the American Dream.

D. V. Soto (✉)
Brooklyn, NY, USA

A. R. Del Castillo, G. Güido (eds.), *Fathers, Fathering, and
Fatherhood*, Palgrave Studies in Literary Anthropology,
https://doi.org/10.1007/978-3-030-60877-4_19

165

II

My first queer experience was with a white man. For weeks I had wanted to sleep with him, building up glances and light winks. The night I decided to go through with it, I knew exactly what to wear. After showering, I grabbed my beater and boxers. I wanted oral only, I thought, I established, no penetration.

III

When I was young, mother got into a car accident, which broke her spine. There were days we wouldn't eat; dad worked overtime. I missed him, them. He worked in the garage, bringing car engines back home. He worked on commission, and though he was technically at home, the only memories I have are the sounds of clanking metal.

IV

I knocked on his door, and he let me in. Boiled me some tea, laid the cubes of sugar next to the bags. I told him I thought I was curious. But it was scary, my parents would disown me. I want to go forward, I said. I wanted to experiment, and he said, like I thought he'd say, we can do something about it.

V

At this time, my sister was a baby and mom had to fill the bottle with half water, half milk; memory's guilt wouldn't let me drink milk until I was old enough to legally purchase cigarettes. They found a lawyer to defend mother's case. She was bedridden for days, and even her smile changed afterward. When I was young I'd tell her, I can always tell which photo of you is before and after your wreck cuz your smile is different. She must have just noticed; she looked at the picture as if looking at a reflection she would never get back.

VI

I asked him when we would be able. Tonight, I've got some time, he said, if you could. Or wanted. He wanted to lean in, and I felt myself move forward. The ass, I always go straight for it, he doesn't move my hand.

VII

It's not even about compromise, my father says. Even justice doesn't work for you. The lawyer they hired took all the earnings after he found my parents were new to the system. Mom stayed in the bed much longer than we anticipated, and my sister, three years older than me became a mother figure. I don't remember much of my mother from my childhood; there are flashes of reading books, playing with puzzles. But mostly, I remember being alone in the living room, pretending to need a toy from the next room, just so I could hear her breathe; it was the most we ever shared.

VIII

He's a bad kisser, the kind of lips that don't move, but are just there passively voyeuristic. A taker. And I should've known from that massage that left me tense. He begins to feel my stomach and chest, rubbing his fingers over my ribs. Said, you're *caliente* (hot). He grins, puckering his lips, apologizes for not pronouncing it correctly. I cared, and I didn't.

IX

From my earliest memories, I was surrounded by white people. It was a small town, the only thing my parents could afford before moving to the city. It was disgusting, a red town with one main road, one building with all three: library, city hall, and fire station. There were two laundry mats, and one Chinese one Mexican restaurant. The school was a small shithole, and there were only four other students like me, and we knew we weren't white before we knew we were human.

X

The second night, there's still the tea, the sugar cubes. There's even that music with no real beat, but a muffling and vague togetherness; horrible for the event, and I can't get into the mindset. Outside looking in, going along with the movements. I wanted to push away but let him move his arm around my thigh to the back. I wanted to move back, but he ran right after. He asked, and I said no in my mind, but my mouth moved forward, a kiss to evade the question.

XI

Dad used to tease me that I'd marry a white girl, but now he says I'm going to marry a white girl who claims to be Mexican. He was concerned that growing up in River Oaks would mean the end of his generation, and he'd still speak to me about carrying our name. Many of my cousins who have grown in the US did not marry Mexicans, mostly white men, or a light-skinned *mestizo*. Soto, Vidal, then Daniel. That is who you are, and this is how your children should learn.

XII

He lay me down like a heavy doll, my arms moving only when he fidgets with their hinges. I wanted to be drunk, inebriated somehow. He had posters of Tokyo, pictures of koi fish. He had a clear plastic container with various tea leaves, origami. From the floor, I could see the rows of manga DVDs and comics lining his shelf. He had paper lanterns, and on the top of the shelf I could see chopsticks and anime toys. At the end of it, he said, you fuck good, best out of anything, my Latino. He leans in to kiss me on the forehead, and I leave without saying a thing.

CHAPTER 20

A Performance Recovery: Cruising Fathered Memories Through Dependency Circuits

Joe Earvin Martinez

Abstract This performative writing attempts to repair the distance between a queer brown son and Mexican father. Martinez recovers memories from his childhood and young adulthood and invites his father to cruise through circuits of chemical dependency, depression, and queer sex. Martinez associates drug-induced psychosis, a shared experience he and his father know firsthand, with Munoz's theory of "Feeling Brown." For Martinez, Muñoz is a queer theoretical daddy who teaches him to think through his memories in hopes of repairing—through critical difference—the possibilities of mature affection and recovery between queer brown son and Mexican father.

I don't recall ever once discussing my father or my relationship with him. I suppose after finally reaching a point in recovery from my depression-sex-drug dependency I was exhausted and tired of suffering; I was and still am looking for new directions, alternative paths to take that empower me in the most mindful ways.

J. E. Martinez (✉)
Palmdale, CA, USA
e-mail: joe.martinez.645@my.csun.edu

A. R. Del Castillo, G. Güido (eds.), *Fathers, Fathering, and Fatherhood*, Palgrave Studies in Literary Anthropology, https://doi.org/10.1007/978-3-030-60877-4_20

This ongoing distance between my father and me has become a bit of a tired subject—both experientially and textually. Many of the flashes of memory this text circuits through have been pulled from old writings and are my deepest feelings of loss, resentment, and yearnings for love during my depression-sex-drug-dependency—a year-and-a-half's worth of introspection (ages 22–24). Writing has always aided me in questioning and rethinking the relationship between my dad and me. This writing, I believe, is a failed, but critical attempt at rethinking and reframing this father-son relationship. Failed perhaps because it re-enacts the abandonment and madness that chemical dependency sows in tangled emotionality for those involved. (Whose story is this to speak?) Critical perhaps because it does just that, leaving the writer (me) and his father (mine) vulnerable to judgment. Yet, in this failed attempt, the reader (you) may be reminded of what's at stake when sharing stories of trauma. Thus, I regret to inform you that recovery is a long and durational performance and the time it takes to turn one's pain into beauty does not happen through trial and error alone—it invites vulnerability.

Am I fortunate to have had my father in my home and in my life despite his own chemical dependency? What has witnessing, since the age of twelve, drug-induced hallucinations taught me about these affect realities, affective performances? What has experiencing my own hallucinations taught me? When our drug-induced bubbles burst, do we (our egos) burst with them? Does this affective saturation become and point to the possibility for othered fantasies of affection, love, and intimacy? Such questions do not simply ask that my father and I think through this relationship, but that we act through it. I hope this piece encourages this commitment to action between me and him, queer brown son and Mexican dad.

Queer in Aztlan[1] affirms the experiences of queer Chicanos, José Esteban Muñoz's *Cruising Utopia: The Then and There of Queer Futurity*[2] affirms my experience as a queer brown male. Through my depression, this text invited me to love again, to understand my experience and to treasure it. More importantly it invited me to confront my shame and to write it out, to look for hope in all my brooding, my failure. It literally

---

[1] See Adelaida R. Del Castillo and Gibrán Güido, *Queer in Aztlan: Chicano Male Recollections of Consciousness and Coming Out* (San Diego: Cognella, 2014).

[2] See José Esteban Muñoz, *Cruising Utopia: The Then and There of Queer Futurity* (New York: New York University Press, 2009).

sparked a flame in me, affirming my experience as a queer brown male—a queer prince of color: cruising, drugs, HIV, failure, "Narcissism," depression, and drug-induced and muscle twitching gestures—histories retold that will forever invite retelling and reframing.

Muñoz's articles "Feeling Brown, Feeling Down: Latina Affect, the Performativity of Race, and the Depressive Position"[3] (2006) and "Feeling Brown: Ethnicity and Affect in Ricardo Bracho's *The Sweetest Hangover (and Other STDs)*"[4] (2000) have inspired the framework of this performative piece. He writes, "This, as I will contend, is negotiated through a particular affective circuit. The version of depression ... a project that imagines a position or narrative of being and becoming that can resist the pull of identitarian models of relationality" (2006, 676–677).

You will find in this writing my own experience in knowing the schizoid and paranoid affect through the rounds of a spark wheel turned by the calloused thumbs of kin-related addicts. My intent is to mend—through memory—what feels like opposition between my father and me and perhaps feelings of opposition between fathers and sons within and outside the nation-state, across borders. Muñoz calls this "national affect" (2000) if "... what unites and consolidates oppositional groups is not simply the fact of identity but the way in which they perform affect" (68).

THIS PERFORMANCE OPENS

With a snap!

Between two male bodies, a father and son. A dividing line. A split.

He sits beside his father on the couch, shifting his weight as his bottom is seated. "Please. Please. Please. Can we move into my Nina's house?" Mother and sister walk the space, listening, feeling for a yes. Lights from the T.V. project onto this larger darker face and it nods, "Alright." The small body jumps up to hug his father, the cushion underneath is now pressed by the tips of curled toes and boney knees, abdomen stretched—joy, excitement, a high pitched "yay!" Little arms wrap around the body that sits and pulls away in discomfort, "Alright, alright! None of that." Voice low. Lips

[3] See José Esteban Muñoz, "Feeling Brown, Feeling Down: Latina Affect, the Performativity of Race, and the Depressive Position," *Signs* 31:3 (2006): 675–688.

[4] See José Esteban Muñoz, "Feeling Brown: Ethnicity and Affect in Ricardo Bracho's *The Sweetest Hangover (and Other STDs)*," *Theatre Journal* 52:1 (2000): 67–79.

curved upward straighten, the boy moves away, aware of the growing distance, the feeling of difference. Feeling brown. Pulling. Pulling. Pulled.

This performance pulls at a sense of touch and sound.

He sits by the toilet, knees bent, toes curled in, voice unsure, straining, wet tears spilling. They draw out words from my mother's mouth, "Joey, what's wrong?" Pulling words out of my own mouth, "I don't have any friends."—"Well, what about Danny, isn't he your friend?"—"No, he makes fun of me."—"Okay, but stop crying, your dad's in the other room listening."—Was he?—silence—absence—silence—shock—small hands brushing tears off his cheek.

Round and Round: Splits of Mind, Winding Roads

If one has ever experienced or witnessed a crystal-meth-induced hallucination, the user feels and searches for an external threat that feels like a shadowy figure. And after the high and hallucination comes the downer—regret, shame, fear, and depression itself. For Muñoz, the reparative position enables us to "resist a disrepair within the social that would lead to a breakdown in one's ability to see and know the other" (2006, 682).

For me, it is after the high and hallucination—the paranoia and schizophrenia—that the crack and crystal meth user begins to experience belonging, much after euphoria and paranoia, when the mind is perhaps more at ease and in a mature state. After my father comes down from his high, he lays in bed or on the couch watching T.V. silently. I do wonder if it is here that he is regretting and feeling shame for his drug use and addiction. I do wonder if it is here that he thinks most about his past actions and the consequences that come with it, fearing the loss of his family. In the search to find affective fathers and self, I find at the round and round of a spark wheel, where calloused thumbs rub hard, a split takes place....

8811 Woodman Avenue

Three stories high. We knew. The reverberating roll of the black gate and vibrations of the windowpane, he was home. A white Yukon XL pulling into its reserved parking in the complex below. Three stories below. Heads poke out, four of them in a shared room, four siblings, three stories above.

He rummages through our belongings, intentionally finding things to be sold: radios, surround sounds, Nintendo gaming consoles, a Playstation 2, money in our wallets, time spent working, education, our hearts, our homes. There is a price to be made of us all.

The round and round of a spark wheel, his thumb strikes at it, friction, release. A white, cloudy smoke. A smoky white hit. Numbness. Blank stares. It is the contact zone of heart and mind and body and spirit and love. Desire, he buys it with our hearts.

Fatherless nights: His desire morphs into estrangement, departing.

Fathered mornings: A daughter exclaims, "I won't respect you until you respect yourself!"

Father's mourning: with his baseball pitching arm, he shoots a remote control at our mom's mirror. "I don't give a fuck if you guys hate me!" An impenetrable mirror, it remains still, nailed to the wall. His reflection zooms, darts from the mirror's sheen, down into the hall, and our reflections remain still.

The four of us thought, "we don't hate you." Confusion grows, and so do we.

Wood Man Avenue

He stays locked up in the bathroom every night. Sounds of that spark wheel. He remains still. A wood man. Sounds, movements, sights. "Martha, who's there? Martha, who's there?!!" An external threat.

"Daddy, no one is here." She says softly.

He is disillusioned by movements in his paranoia. Disillusioned. Petrified.

It's too early for me, so I listen, drifting into a dream.

Awakened. "Joey, let's go get some food." I walk past my father and my uncle in the bathroom. He chugs down the beer, I chug down an orange juice from the Jack-in-the-Box nearby. Three stories below. Three lights away.

743 Avenue H-7

Their thumbs roll, friction, release. A white cloudy smoke. Numbness. Blank stares. It is the contact zone of heart and mind. Desire, they stole it from our hearts.

They rummage through our belongings, intentionally finding things to be sold: radios, surround sounds, Nintendo gaming consoles, a Playstation 2, money in our wallets, time spent working, education, our hearts, our homes. There is a price to be made of us all.

His thumb ... cloudy smoke ... white ... Numbness ... Blank ... heart and mind ... he buys...

We have always dreamed of a house: four bedrooms, two living spaces, a kitchen, a garage, a yard, a dog, two dogs, puppies.

Puppies running through our home, pooping on the carpets. They run in after burglars pry open our back door, a glass door.

Balanced on the windowsill sits my mom's luminous fish tank with golden-shiny fish. Its fluorescent lights illuminate the living room at night. The light draws them in, so the tank was stolen, too.

In debt, he owes what belongs to them. So, they react.

Robbing us of our safety, we migrate back down the 14 South. Winding roads. Past mountains, like hurdles, reaching the 5 North—off Osborne. Make a left. Make a right. Make a left. Brandford Street and Laurel Canyon.

12571 Brandford Street

… belongings … radios … a Playstation 2 … time spent working … homes … us all.

… thumb rolls, friction … A white … smoke … smoky white hit … contact zone … our hearts.

He's robbing us of family, too. Tension rotates every morning: my mom—my aunt—my cousin—my sisters—my brother—and me. Tension so tight, we cut it—Snap! We move once more. He moves with us, too. His released body—mind at ease—numb and calloused thumbs.

Robbing her of safety, we are forced to migrate back up the 14 North. Winding roads, past mountains, like hurdles. Exiting Pearblossom. Down Sierra highway. Make a left. Make a right. Make a left. Rockie Lane and Avenue S.

40739 Rockie Lane

He … belonging … finding … surround sounds, Nintendo … money … education … price…

… roll, friction, release. A white cloudy smoke. Numbness … Desire, they buy it…

He's robbing my aunt of her home. Really *our* home. We did what we could to fill the space, empty space: two floors, five bedrooms, three-car garage, two living spaces, three bathrooms, a kitchen, a dining room, a yard, front and back.

Three couches, a bed frame, four mattresses, a crib, multiple plastic drawers, a prize-won 60-inch television set.

A white smoky hit. A white smoky hit. Awhitesmokyhit. Asmokywhitehit...
Awhitesmokyhitawhitesmokyhitawhitesmokyhitsmokywhiteahitsmoky
whitehit

But we feel close in this space. Up and down the 14 and 5 North. Seven bodies fill a 1997 Saturn sedan. To work. To school. Past mountains like hurdles. Exiting Pearblossom. Lefts. Rights. Lefts. Rights. We feel each other. Shoulders touching. Knees. We hear each other. The baby cries.

But no matter our traveling, our efforts, our routines, the large empty space rejects us. We move back again. Robbing us of our safety, we migrate back down the 14 South. Winding roads, past mountains, like hurdles. The 5 North. Exiting off Lankershim. Make a left. Make a left. Make a Right. Neenach Street.

11777 Neenach Street

... her belongings ... sold: radios ... gaming consoles...

Their thumbs roll ... smoky hit... Numbness. Blank stares. It is the contact zone of heart...

He begins hallucinating. "Martha, who's there?" Hands and face pressed against the limo tint of my aunt's pearl white Escalade.

"Jose, you better not touch my fucking car." Bat in hand.

"Jose, get away!"

A seventeen-year-old boy begins crying and shouting, "I fucking hate you!"

We hear shattering glass. But it was the neighbor's truck. He was in search of an illusory man that my mom was having an affair with. A shadow-man. An external threat.

They both took those smoky white hits. Robbing us of security and trust. Some more tension. Some more lies. Some more efforts.

... release ... mind ... body ... spirit ... love. Desire, she fights it for our hearts.

Tension rotates: my aunt—my mom—my sister—my brother—my cousins—my dad—and me.

Snap!

She exclaims, "You're acting like a fucking bitch!"

"Well, then get the fuck out! Everyone! Get the fuck out!"

I walk in to see my aunt throw a water bottle onto the kitchen floor. It spins and spins, spinning some more...

"Alexandra, shut your fucking mouth!" My mom screams.

"No, if she wants us out then I'm leaving!"

I walk back to the room and start packing, too. Again. We all do.

Robbing us of family and home, we move back up the 14 North. Winding roads, past mountains, like hurdles. Exiting Pearblossom. Down Sierra highway. Make a left. Make a right. Make a left. Make a right. Make a left. Make a right. Monaco Drive.

5743 Monaco Drive

Familiar feelings. Tension rotates: my aunt—my mom—my sisters—my brother—my cousins—and me. Trying not to pull, we cleaned. We cleaned. We cleaned. We worked. We don't want mouths speaking behind our backs. It was home, my aunt's home. My aunt's television. My aunt's couches. But it was our food, utilities, our space, but we felt out of place.

She walks in with a smug look, so we clean some more.

It feels like we burden her. It feels like Brandford Street all over again. But more intense because we are all adults. It feels like she wants my mom out or, at least, my dad. She wants them out of her living room, where they sleep. And the baby, she's now five. I suppose she wants her out, too.

She wants us all out, says so behind our back. The other sister said it to our faces.

His thumb rolls, friction, release. A cloudy smoke. A white smoky hit. Numbness. Blank stares. It is the contact zone of heart and mind. Desire, he buys it with our hearts because there is not much else.

We move again. No warning. We move in a hurry. My brother and I, young men, filling the truck. We move in a hurry, hoping the tension does not snap.

Two lights away. We move down the street. Our own home. Not my aunt's.

6323 Katrina Place

His thumb rolls, friction, release… Desire, he buys it with our hearts.

My thumb rolls … green cloudy smoke. Blank stares. Blank pages … I buy … lose heart.

His thumb … My thumb rolls, friction, release. A white smoky hit. A green smoky hit.

A crash and shattering. This time a mirror breaks. Crack. The splitting comes from my parent's bathroom.

My brother and I look to each other, get up and run. He runs to the bathroom. I run to my room. Bat in hand ... praying that I don't have to use it.

I walk to the bathroom with a heavy lowered arm, memories flashback. This fear feels familiar.

8811 Woodman Avenue

A hit to my mom's face, I run and grab his heavy arm. A nine-year-old boy tries his best to lower it.

"What happened?" Bat in hand.

"Nothing. He got mad and threw the mirror." Mirrors—glass, reflections—seem to be his enemy.

"Oh, you mean he just wants attention?" Mad at both of them, I walk out. Past him. Past her.

"What? W ... was that bat for me?"

I ignore him. The anger, the door threshold, keep us divided, keep us split. Cracked. My heart shatters.

At age twenty-two I moved out.

11326 Reseda Boulevard

My thumb rolls, friction, release. A cloudy smoke. Numbness. Blank stares. Blank pages. It is the contact zone of heart and mind. Desire is consuming my heart and mind.

Note to you

The last time you hallucinated you were arrested because you thought that my uncle had a gun and you told the neighbor to call the police.

You kept asking "Martha, who's there?"

I told you, as my hand reached your shoulder, "Leave my mom alone, go to sleep."

"Don't touch me. Don't fucking touch me." You are enraged. What did you feel when my hand touched your shoulder?

I lifted my hands and closed my eyes, "Leave my mom alone. Just go to bed." I grew angrier; I thought I had moved past our difference, my resentment, my own feelings of self-destruction. I thought that in my own recovery, I was mature enough to forgive you for your feelings of not belonging.

THE MIRROR

What is narcissism? I ask myself.

After moving to Reseda, my depression worsened. On my own, in a rented room. I smoked weed almost daily. And like other queer sons, I used Grindr for a touch (maybe two or three) and a night of excitement of male bodies touching other male bodies. I cruise late nights to feel my own hands, to touch my own.

I give myself away. I am older now, mature and ready. Shame isn't the only thing I carry. Every seeing eye becomes an advance for a connection between bodies. I yearn for muscles like mine that lay heavily defined on the bones of my arms. I want legs like mine, powerful and dangerous. I want legs that can kick down doors of burning houses. I search for solid teeth that bite down on me hard, leaving red bruises and scars.

Sex-Addicted Weekends
  (Green dot)
  Bio: Latino, 5'7," 7 in. UC, Verse, 420 Friendly, PNP
  "Any pix?" Unapologetic and abrupt.
  Mirrors: The same impenetrable one, my grandmother's.
  A selfie here: Back arched, spine turned, stomach in, chest out, briefs tight around the waist, thighs, cock and balls.
  A selfie there: Knees locked, feet planted wide, my phallus hangs low, swinging.
  A selfie here: In the bathroom. In the shower. In the private room of a bathroom spa, Melrose. In the beds of strangers. With strangers.
  A selfie there: Grindr, Adam4Adam, Photobooth, iPhone, e-mail, Craigslist
  Father. Do you remember when I left home at 2am? You're on the couch. Coming down from your high. You don't know who I left with, but I walk out the door—heart racing—to PnP with 2 looking for a 3rd.
  Whoosh. Whoosh. Whoosh. Blood Rushing. What am I going to tell you?
  "I'm leaving with some friends, I'll be back." Door closes. 2 strangers waiting for me.
  We drive off.

Drug-Addicted Weekends
  A hit here. A line there. A booty bump here. A needle piercing there.

Rounds of a spark wheel ignite flames that flicker like desire.

Father. Do you remember when I left home at 2 am?

They are good-looking medical assistants, carrying a bag of syringes. The night my skin is pierced; I accept their offer in a hotel. I have crystal dick, a limp dick. The less attractive one becomes jealous and mean whenever my crystal dick becomes hard, and when his "boyfriend" lays on his back. I want to leave because of his nasty, insecure comments.

Infected Weekends

STIs: discharge and pain and itch and pain and pain and itch.

HIV: swollen lymph nodes and fever and intuition and intuition and intuition.

Curious. Unprotected. Risky. Careless. Raw.

Depressed Days and Longing Nights

Lowered shoulders. Slouched. Craned neck. Tilted, looking down at the flesh that drives me—it smells like ass, sweat and balls, piss, and cum. I am quiet in the halls. Reserved and urging. I am tired. Exhaustion is explicit.

Two days later I sent a text to my brother. "Can you come pick me up?" Hours later my brother, my cousin, and our family friend arrive to pick me up. I leave immediately without telling the two.

In the back seat. Green sweater. I reek of sex and drugs. What did I put my body through? No food. A fist and me. Piercing after piercing. Underneath the green sleeves my arms twitch subtly.

Twitch. Twitch.

They pass the blunt to me. I take a hit to release me of the pain, risk, and pleasure my body has just endured.

To My Best Friend, Elizabeth

"My body feels tired—I woke up and it was shaking lightly. My body wants someone to hold it, to let its heart, stomach, shoulders and mind know that everything's gonna be okay. My body wants someone to keep it from worry and fear. My body wants another body to help it transform, to help it hold itself, to keep itself from shaking, to keep itself from worry, from fear, from shame. My body wants another body to transform with—a lover's body loving another body. A listening body. A tender body. A careful body. An embracing body. A speaking body. A silent body."

Rounds of a spark wheel ignite flames that flicker like desire. Drugs and sex had me gazing—brown-eyes-to-brown eyes—at myself in mirrors. "Who am I?" Hallucinating in my bedroom, a voice responds angrily, "Who are you?!" Hands move away from my face; my eyelids open wide. I now know better than to ask this question again.

Is the depressed and addicted reflection a superficiality of egotism and uncertainty? Perhaps not. Depression and sex addiction are most certainly laborious to the body, my body. Fifteen hours of sleep a day is not healthy. Eight to sixteen hours of drug-induced sex at the Melrose spa isn't either.

So, is it appropriate to consider these narcissistic projections as constitutive of depth and sincerity, of reparation? What about vain reflections of visual artifacts such as naked bathroom selfies? Or do well-endowed men constitute depth (8 inches and more)? What about the pin pricking needle that pierces my veins, carrying blood and meth just beneath my skin?

As a queer brown son, I live the variations of knowing depth. I do believe, despite the splits between me and my mirrored self, that my depression and addiction are/were like any other, an access point to/of self-reflexivity, self-knowing, and self-feeling. These drugs, these deep reflections may not be "narcissism," perhaps because I happen to be a queer *brown* son who shares a cultural, performative, and historical discourse with a straight father.

(My) Mourning (My) Father

You are quiet and tired. You are quiet in the halls. Exhaustion is explicit. Does your body shiver at night? Do your bones feel brittle? Does your blood feel clean?

Drugs, I believe, have you questioning, too. So, why do you remain still? Stagnant. Why do you remain quiet? Almost numb? And more, why do you shatter mirrors? Do you not feel your value? Do you not see it?

My father, you are silent in your crack addiction. You stand in dark hallways of the house, quiet. Contemplating mistakes and reckless acts from the past and future, but never the present. No, never present.

And we see you, me and my siblings and my mother too. A shadow as rigid as the wall that your coarse hands hold onto.

Are you balanced? Is your world falling? Spinning?

Speak. Please.

We hear
your voice. It's hoarse and numb, those toxins leave your cords dry and damaged. That terrible cough. Is it because of the morning's shower steam?

Your speech sounds husky, almost dead, and shaky when you say, "Let me get the keys." To the car late in the night.

We know
that eventually you will drive off, white headlights hitting my window glass, window shades, white lines cast on the walls of my room. We know, we hope, you'll come back each night.

We see
your pupils dilated, black. Your weight loss, hair loss.

You stay silent in the halls. Confused about your pain. Is it silent shame? Regrets?

Months ago, father, I was caught up in rage, loneliness, shame, and myself. Like you, father, I was stuck in my reflection. Lost almost. Narcissus Narcosis. Drugs. Mirrors—glass and reflections and technologies—my enemies as well.

Father, I cannot fight your demons. I will not try and ward them off any longer—those hissing sounds, snake-like, shy and hushed. I want. I won't. To be closer to you? That is your work and your pleasure—to be closer to me. I have my own shadows to tame, my own monsters to dance with.

But you do not understand, father. I don't blame you. Blame is not my concern. That is childish. At the age of twenty-four, my flesh is coming to terms with all of it. Perhaps you know nothing about these terms; what are the desires of a queer prince of color? Perhaps they are your biggest fears and they drive you to silence, to addiction, and a deep, mystic reflection where you stay stuck.

Maybe you didn't know of my late-night journeys to the edge of the world, ready to jump, looking for an escape. Maybe you didn't know and maybe you can't know. We don't share words. But maybe we share the same dreams and fantasies.

But did you know?

There were moments while hallucinating from having taken too much meth that like you I suspected I was being followed ... my fingers at the window blinds—eyes peeking out. Like you, my eyes would follow cars on the rearview mirror. Like you, my pores oozed toxins. Like you, I asked, "Who's there?" Like you, paranoid and schizoid. Did you know?

Do you remember the night I came home exhausted and high? I felt scared and wanted my paranoia to subside. A book in hand of a queer brown father—orange and purple koi on the cover—he shows me the map for another place and another time. I tell you and my mom that this queer brown father gives me hope. You tell me to go to sleep and dream....

The Night Before

Driving on the 14 North to Palmdale. I can feel the crack cocaine on the steering wheel. It's sticky and gross. My dad and uncle drive the car too often, I don't think they feel the residue themselves—calloused thumbs. The stickiness reminds me of when I was smoking meth, injecting meth, snorting lines, and booty bumping. I should have wiped down the steering wheel with alcohol wipes. I hate this feeling.

I start feeling the drive again. Did the residue seep into my bloodstream? I want to fuck. I want to get fucked. This night drive back home feels like those lonely nights a semester, two semesters ago. Cruising. Grindr. Bathhouses. Gang Bangs. Slings and swings. I want to download Grindr. I want to find a man with a big dick. To touch me. To hold me down. To fuck me. And to fuck me again. I don't care much to top. I just want to bottom.

I tell myself, "No." My body starts to shake. My chest begins to contract and expand like it did when I would spend hours having sex with some older white man, while on G, crystal meth, and poppers. With my left knee now steering the wheel, I wrap my arms around my shoulders. I squeeze my biceps. They're so small-scrawny now. I squeeze harder. "It's okay." I breathe deeper. I squeeze harder. My fingers reach for my shoulder blades, I try to give myself a big hug. Like those hugs good friends give. I give myself a hug, I want to be a good friend to me. So I hug myself, so that I can love myself. These urges upset me. I hate myself.

DRAWING BLOOD

Father, into tubes pulled from steel syringes, I see red. At times, multiple tubes. When it pierces my skin—bronze, thick—I feel our closeness. I used to believe we were so distant. Some may believe that after the moment of diagnosis that HIV and AIDS create a larger divide between those of positive and negative statuses and identities. Even in our chemical dependencies, the risk of contracting the virus was disparate for us both.

Perhaps those who are positive feel distant when conversations on health arise in the classroom, between family and friends. Or maybe those who contract the virus through sexual acts feel guilty for their irresponsibility to protect themselves and others. Are those who contracted the virus through intravenous drug use reminded of the cool rush that surges through their left arm each time they have their blood drawn at hospital visits? It's possible we may withdraw altogether into the night left cruising solo in the cities not-so playful parks. Maybe those who are negative will let slip an HIV/AIDS phobic statement, which jeopardizes trust, friendship, and safety.

Blood can forge differences.

Blood can forge alliances.

And when we consider the history of the blood of mixed people—including mestizos—perhaps this viral mutation of blood, of genetics—HIV/AIDS—this mixedness—deepens us. Its volume deepens our histories, tangles up our relatedness, and saturates our purities. Where instead of HIV-negative statuses uphold the negation of generations (past/present/future) of queer men of color, HIV/AIDS-positivity must positively bring forth life to the queerly mixed worlds we find ourselves in the making of. Thus, if Muñoz's work is also in the spirit of challenging binaries—POZ/NEG—Me/You—and if feeling brown is at once a queer and decolonial labored sense, then the question/mutation of HIV/AIDS must be one that is felt together—deeply—and found in-between our histories, memories, and statuses.

Father, my HIV-positivity doesn't make our lives more distant—it—pulls—us—in.

CHAPTER 21

"Make Me Your Toxic Son, Daddy": The Bio-Familial Bonds Created by Gay Men Through "Bug Chasing" and "Gift Giving"

Omar O. González

Abstract A lasting outcome of the HIV epidemic, according to the author, is the stigmatization of HIV-positive men who may respond by self-segregating, closeting their seropositive status. However, through blog monitoring of tumblr.com and bbrt.com topics on "bareback" condom-less sex and a first-person encounter, the author explores gay identification through the fetishization of desire as *those wanting to be infected* by the HIV virus ("bug chasers") and *those wanting to infect* ("gifters"). Gonzalez finds the practice of familial bonding expressed through father/son roleplay suggestive of the heteronormative procreational project whereby "bug chasers" are seeded or impregnated by the HIV toxic seminal loads of "gifters" whose DNA is carried to fruition by the former. This subculture subverts serosorting discrimination against HIV-positive men and privileges them as desirable.

O. O. González (✉)
California State University, Northridge, CA, USA
e-mail: xicano73@ucla.edu

© The Author(s), under exclusive license to Springer Nature
Switzerland AG 2021
A. R. Del Castillo, G. Güido (eds.), *Fathers, Fathering, and Fatherhood*, Palgrave Studies in Literary Anthropology,
https://doi.org/10.1007/978-3-030-60877-4_21

185

Although not as seemingly impactful as the Stonewall Rebellion in 1969 or the assassination of San Francisco city supervisor Harvey Milk in 1978, the publication of Lawrence K. Altman's article, "Rare Cancer Seen in 41 Homosexuals," in *The New York Times* on July 3, 1981, represents another Anzaldúan rupture, or *arrebato*, for the LGBTQ community and continues a legacy of stigma, genocide, and activism. Randy Shilts documents the early years of the epidemic in his journalistic tome, *And the Band Played On: Politics, People, and the AIDS Epidemic* (1987). He uncovers a combination of dismissive apathy by white supremacist heteronormative institutions (the disease is relegated to the 4 H's—homosexuals, Haitians, hemophiliacs, and heroin users) and incredulous fear by gay men (the disease represented a Reagan ploy to force them back into the closet) that made for a constellation of cacophonous voices and flaccid action by the federal government against a vanguard of virile activism of such well-known groups as the AIDS Coalition to Unleash Power (ACT UP) and regional ones like ALLGO (Austin Latina/o Lesbian and Gay Organization).[1] Unfortunately, the most lasting outcomes of the epidemic are the stigma and fear of the illness perpetuated by HIV-negative gay men against those living with the virus forcing them into another closet, lest they be branded with the scarlet letter of "A(IDS)." For a growing segment of gay men, however, the stigma itself has gone from an irrational fear to an alluring fetish. This fetish has come to be known as "bug chasing," the overt act of an HIV-negative man seeking to be "gifted" by an unmedicated[2] "poz"[3] man. Once the "chaser" seroconverts, he carries his "gifter's" DNA forever, marking the latter as a sort of v(amp)iral patriarch, creating a familial bond out of the ruins of an epidemic. Attempting to form some semblance of community, "chasers" and "gifters" co-opt the heterosexual procreative process to construct their own families, as the "chasers" deliver their "gifters'" babies upon their deaths.

Contrasting this relatively new subculture, the father/son roleplay fetish among gay men is not a new phenomenon. The online publication, *Handjobs* (a hardcopy publication from 1991 to 2014) publishes illustrated stories of the differing manifestation of the incest taboo between

---

[1] ALLGO was founded in 1985 and is the longest surviving Latinx LGBTQ organization in the United States.

[2] The term "unmedicated" in the context of "bug chasing" refers to an HIV-positive man who knowingly eschews HIV medications, effectively allowing his viral load to increase making him toxic.

[3] Poz is slang for HIV positive.

men—father/son, uncle/nephew, grandfather/grandson, stepfather/stepson, co-workers, friend's father, and so on. These stories almost always include an underage boy, technically classifying the sex acts as statutory rape. The October 1998 issue titled "Damp Daddy" features a ruggedly masculine white man, nude except for a towel and a strategically placed title. The contents of the issue include a variety of stories with such titles as, "Just Next Door," "Daddy's Fantasy," "Dinner with the Coach," and the feature story, "Damp Daddy." Each story highlights the fetish of inter-generational same-sex desire. Never is identity discussed, only desire and pleasure. The subject of morality is absent; the characters never ponder upon their actions with any arbitrary value system. The publication contains a variety of erotic drawings, some influenced by the *Tom of Finland* aesthetic. Moreover, published in 1998—two years after the advent of the HIV medications known as the "cocktail" which reduced the mortality rate from AIDS complications drastically—only one small advertisement for a (900) number mentions the topic of safer sex. One of the stories, "Dinner with the Coach," does incorporate the usage of a condom into the plot, but the other stories all highlight unprotected oral and anal sex and higher risk acts, such as "felching"[4] and "ATM."[5] Although the stories in *Handjobs* broach acts that would be deemed as "unsafe" by HIV service providers and medical professionals, the publication does not include any mention of the epidemic, thus serving as escapist fantasy. Although *Handjobs* is now an online-only publication, its perseverance represents the enduring appeal of incestuous fantasies.

The rise of "bug chasing" and "gift giving," though at first unbeliev-able given the horrors of the first fifteen years of the epidemic, is, I argue, an inevitable backlash to the dogmatic discourse of safer sex practices and the discriminatory stigma under which people living with HIV negotiate. Even before the Centers for Disease Control concluded that people spread the virus sexually (as well as intravenously and via childbirth), the medical establishment socialized gay men to distrust their bodies, their fluids, their desires. For twenty-two years, from 1983 to 2015, blood banks enforced a homophobic ban on gay men from donating blood. In 2015, the Federal and Drug Administration replaced the lifetime ban with a one-year

---

[4] Felching is the act of performing oral sex on an anus after a man has ejaculated in the orifice.

[5] ATM is an acronym for "ass to mouth" which signifies the act of a man inserting his penis into a mouth for fellatio directly after egress from an anus.

deferral, meaning that a gay man must wait twelve months from his most recent sexual contact to donate blood. The stigmatization of gay sexual acts and the resulting fluids continues through the act of "serosorting"[6] on the gay dating apps and rejection of HIV-positive men by those who believe they are negative. For nearly four decades, gay men have negotiated the fear of the dreaded HIV-positive diagnosis, a modern scarlet letter of shameful depravity. Some men, however, are coming to terms with the closet of hiding a poz status.

From an outsider's perspective, the gay "community" is a confederacy of sexual nation-states, akin to Athens or Tenochtitlan. Each faction is divided according to one's sexual tastes, perhaps based on body size—bears or twinks—or by race, where Asian and Black men are sometimes excluded—or by sexual practice, BDSM or vanilla? Another faction arising in the last fifteen years is that of the "bug chaser" and the "gift giver," a realm where HIV-positivity is coveted; it is what the "Gift" chasers are seeking entrance into, the so-called POZ-BROTHERHOOD, as it is referred to in online forums. The HIV virus represents the Holy Grail for "bug chasers," as some have eschewed the prescribed actions of insisting their partners wear condoms or take PrEP, as the pillars of homonormativity dictate. Common among these disparate groups is a complicated legacy of the effects stemming from the effects of the HIV epidemic. Stigma against HIV-positive men, despite the current campaign of "U=U",[7] persists, which, I argue, has led to the self-segregation of HIV-positive men into a secret society of sorts, one that some HIV-negative men are seeking entrance to, a last refuge from an irrational fear of seropositive status. The "POZ BROTHERHOOD" represents yet another fracture of the gay community, one that fetishizes the virus instead of fearing it.

[6] Serosorting is the act of discriminating against serodiscordant sexual partners. In this context, an HIV-negative man who seeks only other HIV-negative sexual partners, thus discounting HIV-positive men who hold an undetectable status.

[7] The U=U (Undetectable=Untransmittable) campaign according to the website, www.preventionaccess.org, "was launched in early 2016 by a group of people living with HIV who created a groundbreaking Consensus Statement with global experts to clear up confusion about the science of U=U. The Statement was the genesis of the U=U movement that is changing the definition of what it means to live with HIV. The movement is sharing the message to dismantle HIV stigma, improve the lives of people living with HIV, and bring us closer to ending the epidemic." Although the U=U campaign is nearing four years, stigma resulting from the fear of the virus still exists because of its pervasive associations with wasting, disease, and death.

Based on blog analysis from personal blogs on the websites Tumblr. com and BBRT.com, a site dedicated to men who are seeking to "bareback" (condom-less sex), some "bug chasers" are seeking a deeper bond with their "Gift givers," desiring to be owned and claimed through a material, biological bond. They become their "gifter's" son, as they carry their strain in perpetuity. On Tumblr.com, the user "Latino Bug Chaser" posts on his profile: "Starting this blog to journal my thoughts and experiences as I embrace The Gift. Latino guy here. Not crazy, not insane. Just taking a less traditional approach. While many try to fight the odds, I have come to terms with the inevitable conclusion and instead chase the Virus. Through the chase I lose the fear and only by embracing it can I be free." Latino Bug Chaser is a young man living in East Los Angeles and at last count had over 70,000 followers. He routinely posts about his love of bareback sex and claims he is a "passive chaser," as he is taking PrEP yet still desires the virus.

One follower, "neveragaindickhole," mentions the bonds gay men create by barebacking: "First I'd like to say on behalf of [a]ll the tops out there, we applaud your decision be[h]ind this blog and welcome you to receive all our gifts, charged or not, so willingly inside of your body, where they can grow and flourish inside you and make you achieve your fullest potential....." Latino Bug Chaser in turn responds "Hello there. ... Thanks for the kudos. I've always been a romantic so for me, even it it's a one-night stand, sharing that special moment of intimacy when a Top is breeding me with his cum is a gift to me. You're right. It doesn't have to be a charged load to make it special. Your cum contains your DNA so the fact that my body will absorb it means that a little bit of your very essence will live in me." This type of exchange is common on Latino Bug Chaser's blog. The men who post such comments express their appreciation for his candor and bravery regarding such a taboo—*desiring* to be HIV positive. Latino Bug Chaser's blog is an outlet and may even serve as a prophylaxis; some men have written they use the blog posts and videos posted as masturbatory material. Latino Bug Chaser's blog elicits its own share of hate correspondence, but he takes each piece of correspondence with pleasant aplomb. He realizes the taboo terrain upon which he is venturing. Although he never uses the vernacular of "Daddy" and "son" in relation to "bug chasing," he frames the sharing of DNA between men—HIV+ or not—as a bonding ritual between partners. The bottom carries the top's essence forever, more so if the bottom seroconverts, thus carrying the top's unique HIV strain.

On the website, www.bbrt.com, the "bug chasing" community seeks men with profiles containing the terms, "toxic," "Gifter," or "poz." I created a profile with the name "ToxicPozCock" and described myself as a man in his late thirties who chose to go off his HIV regimen. I describe my HIV status as "Do Not Care," one that I chose from a drop-down list. One such exchange I had with a user, "aaandreww," provides further insight to the "bug chaser's" mind:

TPC: Definitely want to seed your ass
AAA: down to convert me?
TPC: You wanna be poz?
AAA: yes I do
TPC: I'm so ready to fill you with poz cum
AAA: come poz me.
TPC: You wanna be my poz boy?
AAA: yes can you make me your poz boy
TPC: Yes you'll be my poz son forever.
AAA: please be my poz daddy

This type of exchange is not uncommon. Another user with the profile name "UrGoodBoy" discloses his desire to seroconvert and that he has stopped taking PrEP. Even though this user has a boyfriend, he says he is very "vanilla" and is wanting to explore a darker, kinkier side to his sexual desire. On bbrt.com, the father-son sexual fetish becomes more layered due to the direct bio-bonds created through the taboo action of unprotected anal sex with a top who *willingly* "impregnates" a bottom who desires the status of HIV toxicity. Based on the blogs I have analyzed and the profiles with which I have interacted, "bug chasers" have an almost maniacal need to be "inseminated" or "impregnated" by a "Gifter" as a means to form kinship ties and to belong to a tribe. Others have responded that a poz status, especially a toxic status, would represent the ultimate action as self-described "pigs." In fact, on the bbrt.com website, men "Oink" at each to show interest in another's profile.

As I researched this community further, I found myself being drawn into the taboo fetish of "Gift-giving" and "bug chasing." My fake profile, "ToxicPozCock," continues to receive interest from men around the world, all desperate and eager to be "gifted." Some want me to inseminate them anonymously without ever seeing my face, and some want a deeper connection, craving a father-son type arrangement in which when I convert him to a poz status, he would become my son—effectively owning him.

I began a conversation with a man desiring a cross between the two. He wanted me to be his "poz Dad" and receive regular "poz breedings," but he wanted to keep things anonymous. Curious to explore this further, I arranged to meet him at a hotel one night. I would tell him the room number and I would wait outside until he was ready for me to walk in on him in a sexual position—on all fours on the bed. As agreed during our chat, he would be clothed only in a ski mask and a blindfold underneath, a jockstrap, and sneakers.

It was a typical southern California evening by the coast in mid-December. I chose a hotel by the ocean in a swanky beach community. I entered the room after receiving the text he was ready. As per our agreement, I did not say a word and grabbed his nearly full bottle of Truvada, an HIV-med now known as PrEP, Pre-Exposure Prophylaxis. I grabbed the bottle of life-saving medication and went to the bathroom and flushed the blue pills down the toilet, save one. I returned to the bed, and solely using the language of kinesthetics, I dominate him sexually over the next few hours. I broke our agreed-upon code of silence only to reaffirm his desire "to be pozzed," to which he would reply how badly he wanted "to carry my AIDS baby," "to make him pregnant with my strain," "to knock him up with my toxic load," "to give him the 'fuck flu,'"[8] and "to make him toxic." During the session of taboo manlust, my mind entered altered states of consciousness from ones of critical consciousness to others of visceral, primal desire. I *knew* I could not "poz" him, yet part of me *wanted* him to carry my specific mutation of the virus. I wanted the pride of knowing *I* created my own spawn in my own queer way. In that revelatory moment, I became Lestat the Vampire, reborn from the Anzaldúan Coatlicue State[9] from the conclusion of Anne Rice's epic, *Memnoch, the Devil* (1995), a novel in which the protagonist is guided through the

---

[8] The "fuck flu" is slang for the initial flu-like symptoms a person often experiences when he/she/they seroconvert with the HIV virus.

[9] In Gloria Anzaldúa's landmark text, *Borderlands/La Frontera: The New Mestiza*, the Coatlicue State represents a person's psychic, emotional, physical, and spiritual response to severe trauma as a means of survival. Having to process the experiential is also represented by the case of Vampire Lestat. After his time with Memnoch (the Devil) and visiting Heaven and Hell, Lestat is left incapable of integrating the significance of these moments ontologically and retreats into a frozen state of being—neither (un)dead or alive—until he regains the ability to process his experiences.

totality of human history, Heaven, and Hell and dares to bite the neck of Christ. In her earlier chronicle of the vampires, *The Vampire Lestat* (1985), Rice calls the seroconversion of a human mortal into a vampire as the "Dark Gift." In his mind (and in some dark recess of my own subconscious), I bestowed my own "Dark Gift" unto this unknown young man, or he believes so; therefore, he is now *my* creation, *nuestra creatura* (our creature), constructed out of the chaos of decades of disease and death. "My son," or "*mi'jo*," is reborn through the power of transubstantiation running through my veins. He and any other son I create represent my posterity, my legacy, my progeny. Those of us living with HIV, once shunned to the shameful closet, now assert our agency and realize the virus and the disease that defines it is as organic to our identities as any other part of our phenotype. Entering the fifth decade of this epidemic, many of us in the poz community use this attribute as any other defining feature, as other gay men would use a large penis, a "bubble butt," or chiseled pecs. Going further, some have used the virus to build genetic bonds with each other in a procreative process that, for a lack of better terminology, is a "Father/son" relationship. Thus, through the act of "Gift giving," gay poz men are creating new bio-bonds that, I argue, are stronger than our birth ones as the former are not some random heteronormative accident but a connection based on agency, desire, and survival.

PART V

Situating Spent and Shifting Fatherhoods

INTRODUCTION TO SECTION

Queer sons do the work of reuniting with homophobic, gone, and emotionally distant fathers as if on sacred treks to lands with different measures of time and units of meaning for being and knowing.

Comfort

CHAPTER 22

Our Shimmering and Ephemeral DNA

Gibrán Güido

Abstract Following an itá life-reading, the author reaches out to a father he hasn't seen for years. Still Güido appreciates that his father has given him his name, that of the beloved author of *The Prophet*, Kahlil Gibran. The author also conceptualizes the sharing of DNA with his father as more than just a chemical trait, but rather as spiritually telling of "microscopic life patterns." When they reunite, they begin a mixed but gentle process of catching up on years of lost time. Güido's brother takes part in this reconciliation having defended him against the father long ago. But the brothers have different reasons for appeasement with the father, one is linked to religious calling, the other is open to the spiritual healing of acceptance.

There is power in a name, which parents give us to make known our presence in the world. Our name reminds us of our origins, our kin relations, and binds us no matter the trials we encounter in our lives. Families become broken, bonds between children and fathers grow fragile, shatter, and linger over the course of our lives. And no matter our need to reject or disavow pain, our fathers remain with us. We carry them microscopically in the life patterns of our DNA and see their features in our own.

G. Güido (✉)
University of California San Diego, La Jolla, CA, USA

A. R. Del Castillo, G. Güido (eds.), *Fathers, Fathering, and Fatherhood*, Palgrave Studies in Literary Anthropology, https://doi.org/10.1007/978-3-030-60877-4_22

Because of my name, I take my father wherever I go, recall him whenever someone speaks my name, or acknowledges my presence. My name is really one of the few things my father has given me. Having read *The Prophet* in his younger days with only a grade-school education, my father gave me the name of his favorite author, Khalil Gibran, and as such forged a link between all three of us. Khalil, an author of vast spiritual depth, writes so often of love, love-loss, and pain as I find myself doing. Perhaps there is something prophetic about my father's gift to me as there is in the remnants of fatherhood in my own writing. Impressions of him lurk in my written work as I attempt to move forward with my own ambitions of putting pen to paper.

Spirituality, too, has guided and protected my decision to grow empathetically. Had it not been for my spiritual leanings and my initiation into Santería (Afro-Cuban religion) I would not have been able to write this piece. Santería priesthood is a long and arduous process, one of sacrifice, self-reflection, and humility—nourishing the body/mind/spirit to shed a former life in preparation for a new one as if a child in embryonic stasis until the birth of a new sense of self. As part of my yearlong initiation I take part in an "Itá" or life reading. A "blueprint" to a life, an aid to help balance oneself in order to provide spiritual healing and guidance to others. Through the Itá reading the Santero elder offers me *consejos* (advice) regarding my relationship with Changó (an orisha deity) and my father. He asks if I know if my father is alive suggesting he "sees" my relationship with him is troubled. I do not know if my father is alive, it has been eight or nine years since our last encounter. "If your father is dead," the Santero says, "he regrets having done any wrong to you and in order to make amends he will protect you in his afterlife. If he is alive, you must speak to him as soon as you can." I had not anticipated or prepared for this request.

The words of the Santero stay with me, but nearly a year passes before I comply with his request. I call and ask for the guidance of my *padrino* (my Santero godfather); I turn to a spiritual father figure for advice about my biological father. Should I contact my father, make amends with him, and begin the process of healing? Should I visit my father before my year is up or should I wait until after I become an ordained priest? Xuanito directs me to see him now. I had hoped he would encourage me to do otherwise.

How does one prepare for a visit with a stranger known as "father?" What would be my excuse for a visit to his home? Would he be as hostile as he had been when we last met? How would he receive an unexpected visit from his first-born son who he rejected years ago? I confide in my partner and ask him for advice. He is supportive of me even though he doesn't have any specific answers that appease my anxiety over the anticipated encounter. Finally, I decide to take my father a copy of a book I co-edited on queer Chicano sexuality as my reason for visiting him. Handing him a personal copy of this anthology would serve as a symbolic gesture. It would prove that despite his anger, disapproval, and abandonment I went forward. My essay in the book describes my father's homophobic reaction to my coming out to him. The anthology is proof that I have gone on to pursue a career that validated my experience and sought to provide others with a space to share their own queer identity and hardships.

I dedicate a copy of the book to my father and sign my name, but the book stays on the kitchen table for days. I need to emotionally and psychologically prepare for the encounter. Will I need to prepare physically in case I need to defend myself? The day arrives and my partner volunteers to come along with me in case anything goes wrong. That day I dress in white and wear my *collares* (necklaces) for spiritual protection. Invoking my *padrino* and the power of the words of the Santero priest, I knock on his door, took two steps back, and wait in anticipation.

My father answers the door by leaning forward through the doorframe. I will always remember his facial expression, his body language, and his shock at seeing me. We are both unsure of how to speak to each other so I make the first move. "Hello Dad, how are you?" Why I chose to use the word "Dad," I don't know, perhaps out of habit. "Hello, *mi'jo* (my son)," he replies. His choice for the affectionate diminutive "mi hijo" comes as a surprise to me. He invites me in, but I'm hesitant because I'm prepared for the worst, still I walk in and he apologizes several times for the mess in his home. He invites me to sit on the couch, the best seat in the house, but not before he moves stuff on it to the far left of the couch. He pulls up a chair from the kitchen table, it's wobbly but he tries to assure me that there's nothing wrong with his seat. The pleasantries begin. He asks how my brother and I are doing. Surprisingly, he asks about my mom, whether she's well; perhaps he wants to hear that she's not doing well and suffers without him.

As my father and I sit in the living room/kitchen space of his mobile home he asks more than once about my brother. I wonder if he still remembers my brother's assertiveness the last time they met and how my brother stood by me despite my father's homophobia. I do not give him the satisfaction of responding to his inquiries about my brother. Instead I change the subject and talk about how I'm doing. I tell him that I'm continuing my education and that I am now in a doctoral program and hope to become a university professor. The look on his face lets me know that perhaps he doesn't understand me. I tell him that I've brought him a book that I helped to organize and write and that it would mean a lot to me if he accepted it and read it. For me this represents a new opportunity for my father to give his eldest son one more chance. I want him to know there are others like me who want the love of their fathers but are denied it because of a lack of awareness and understanding. My gift to my father is another way of communicating that I want his love, concern, and approval. But I do not believe that my father understands the measure and importance of the gift I bring him.

My father and I collapse the years of silence between us by recounting to each other the most significant events in our lives. He tells me about his knees and how he had surgery on them. He details the procedure, the symptoms prior to the operation, and the prognosis. He feels the outcome daily and the years of aching pain prior. He thinks back to a time before he had bad knees and the many commercial spaces, homes, and public areas where he worked as a landscaper. A pause in his speech breaks his practice of dominating the conversation. I take the opportunity to physically make myself comfortable as I prepare an attempt to enter the conversation. I begin by telling my father about my experiences and the stress of graduate school. I tell him of the tasks and responsibilities I have taken on. Confidently and proudly, I tell him that after completing a master's thesis, co-editing an anthology, and chairing a conference for queer people of color I am pursuing a doctoral degree with the help of my family and my academic mentor. He responds with silence. I also tell him about my "breakdowns," and that I've been hospitalized twice. The first episode was so intense that I had no recollection of who I was, where I lived, or who family members were. I tell him that I wandered the streets of downtown San Diego and Balboa Park until the police picked me up; the second time my brother accompanied by our cousin and her child found me. I choose not to tell him about the psychological diagnosis because I haven't come to terms with it yet. He comments that the last time he saw me I was physically thinner and that I don't look the same. His comment pierces my protective emotional wall.

My father listens to me, but I believe he fails to realize the seriousness of the situation. He does not understand the urgency and harm I have undergone. I feel he retreats to old habits. He listens and assesses but does not register the gravity of what I have just told him about myself. Instead he shifts the topic of conversation back to himself. He discusses his relationship with his girlfriend. He tells me how she struggles with a work-related injury. How she must contend with her legal battles and how my father comes to her aid and confronts the attorney. In his story he is the protagonist who quells the lawyer with his bravado and makes the lawyer yield to his demands. His dominance inspires his girlfriend to expect a positive outcome to her legal case. After this exchange, my father sits back confidently. Silence follows and my discomfort increases. I decide to leave. I don't know how much time has passed. There are no clocks in his home to count the minutes, perhaps the hours that have gone by. I begin my departure and rise from the couch, he makes small talk, a way to stumble our way into a transition between my being there and my leaving. I reach the front door, push it open and stand on the broken, termite-ridden steps. I thank him for his time and for inviting me into his home. I tell him that I look forward to perhaps seeing him sometime in the future.

To my surprise, he offers to walk me to the car. My partner is waiting there for me, to hear about the outcome. We slowly walk to the car; he continues to make small talk. I get to the car first and signal to my partner that my father is not far behind. I am not certain how my father will respond to my partner. Perhaps he secretly hopes that over the years I've "changed" my sexual preference and that my partner is a woman. He reaches the driver's side and I move aside and my father introduces himself to my partner, Iván, who responds in kind. The darkness in the car has me question whether my father realizes my partner is a man. I wait to see how my father responds. But he acts naturally; he and Iván shake hands. My father doesn't hesitate to speak to him. He asks where my partner is from. Iván is uncomfortable but he rises to the occasion and politely interacts with the man I had told him so much about during all those moments of intimacy when I confided in him. After some small talk my father invites Iván and me to dinner at his home. Proudly, he promises to provide the best meal he is capable of making. He asks Iván if he likes *ceviche* (a seafood cocktail). But Iván is uncertain how to respond so my father gives him the option of fish or shrimp. Iván's prolonged lack of response encourages my father to offer both.

We drive home to join my mother and talk about my visit with my father. I make the decision to avoid this topic around my brother; I'm still wondering how to approach the subject with him. I don't know what to make of the wave of emotions I feel after reconnecting with my father. That night I lay in bed in the darkness reflecting on the events of the day while my partner lies next to me. Unable to understand what this encounter means for me, I slowly begin to drift, losing consciousness and in this liminal state I imagine the child in me saying to my father, "Goodnight, Daddy."

Afterward what seem like moments are days gone by and still I don't feel as though I can gather the courage to confide in my brother about my meeting with my father. My brother seems more of a parental figure to me now than ever before. I don't tell him about the visit to my father's home because I fear hurting him and betraying his trust in me or perhaps I fear he'll think I have trivialized the pain we've shared together for decades due to our estrangement from our father. Not willing to undermine our affection for and loyalty to each other, I decide to tell my brother of the visit while my mother is present. As I do his demeanor changes and his body rearranges itself as if preparing for unsavory news whenever the hint of my father is mentioned. I sit at the dinner table, the place where he, my mother, and I have had our most serious and intense discussions. The kitchen is the place where we have shared our deepest concerns and confided our worst fears to one another. By now my mother knows that I have reconnected with my father. After sharing with my brother the outcome of my first meeting with my father my brother decides, after considerable thought, that he is open to a possible reunion with him. Nonetheless, my brother and I discuss my father's invitation extensively as if generals in a war going over field strategies. I get back to my father on the phone several times; we've exchanged phone numbers and discussed a possible time and place for dinner, and, importantly, whether or not my brother will attend. I think to myself that perhaps the challenge at hand is not solely attributable to my father's behavior or my brother's defense of me and my sexuality but may have more to do with their similarities of character. At last, we both decide, dinner at six at my father's place and we'll be having shrimp *ceviche*.

The day comes and I arrive early, hoping that I can set the mood and make things comfortable so there's no conflict between my brother and father. The mess in my father's mobile home is basic to his way of living, a reflection of himself, and his economic instability. The small glass table in the kitchen will hold the banquet for the two estranged men he calls "*mi'jo*." My father again makes small talk, his inability to relax communicates his uneasiness in once again seeing my brother after all these years. He repeatedly looks out the window whenever the headlights of cars flash on entering the mobile home park. In the faint light of dusk I can see my brother approaching. I tell my father and he quickly looks out the window. I can see by his body language that he's preparing for the encounter, uncertain of its outcome. My father opens the door and invites my brother in before Omar has a chance to knock. Soon we sit at the table before the feast my father has prepared and I can tell that it pleases him to watch Omar and I enjoy his food; he asks us more than once if we're enjoying the *ceviche*, and repeatedly invites us to serve ourselves as much as we want.

My father and Omar dominate the conversation with little intervention from me. I feel I'm there to help facilitate the conversation as if a therapist or mediator. I remember how my brother ended what little contact my father and family had in order to protect me.

Finally, the evening ends with my brother having to leave early for his religious study group and I follow soon after, but offer to help my father clean up. My father assures me that there is no need to help. Perhaps the chore will offer my father time to reflect on our reunion. My father, brother, and I part ways; each to his own pursuits unsure of their future together.

Omar coordinates our next reunion; his assertive command of the matter is surprising. For some reason, I feel uneasy about our ensuing encounter, perhaps because I'm not sure of its outcome. Omar arranges for our next meal with our father to be in a public place. Perhaps I fear a public spectacle resulting from an unsure relationship with our father that would undo the mending achieved in our first meeting with him.

Finally, we all meet at the designated place and I pay for our meals in advance to smooth out any awkwardness over the bill. As we finish our dinner, still seated at the table, my brother begins to share glimpses of his life by showing cell phone photos to our father, snapshots of his most important moments. After the meal we all linger outside the restaurant and gather around my brother's car. We all knew of Omar's Air Force departure to Japan the next day, leaving my father and I to nurture the new relationship until his return. Before we all depart, Omar suggests, "Let's take a picture." My father's enthusiasm and my brother's suggestion make me uncomfortable, but we all gather together, close to one another. I can't remember the last time we were this close physically and emotionally. From the many photos he takes, my brother saves one on his phone, which he later shares on social media on Father's Day with a message for everyone to read: "It was 4 years ago right before I left for boot camp [that I saw] or spoke to my father. I'm not gonna lie, we had a real bad falling out, even though we literally live 5 min away from each other neither one of us made an effort. GOD really does work miracles, I can honestly say it wasn't until I turned my life over to Christ [that] I found the strength and courage to forgive him for all that he's done. This is our first picture together (father and sons) in, I want to say, over 10 yrs. The day before I leave to Okinawa. Just wanted to say Happy Father's day dad." My brother receives numerous comments of praise from friends and family with many "likes" on Facebook.

Since the time of this photo my father and I have had lunch once but several conversations over the phone. The topics vary but our bond continues to grow. He offers counsel, the kind I always wanted from him in my youth. He repeatedly advises me to face my challenges head on and not seek temporary refuge by consuming alcohol. These words of wisdom echo those I received from my Ita and Changó. And both my spiritual and biological fathers advise me to become a better individual to reach my fullest potential.

Recently, I was faced with a situation that could have impacted my future ambitions for an academic career and possibly require legal counsel, but the presence and comfort of my friend, Rosi, and my academic mentor's support made the matter bearable. While I was visiting Rosi, the vibration and ringtone in my pocket interrupts the sharing of a cigar and shots of Tequila I was having with her. I see that my father is calling and excuse myself. I prepare for the conversation by breathing in deeply and releasing tension from my body. To my surprise, he calls to tell me, *he loves me*. I have waited such a long time for this. His words are like a balm that allows a feeling of profound comfort during a moment in my life of intense apprehension. His words dissipate the fear I have been living with and ambition is possible once again.

CHAPTER 23

Querido Padre: Things I Want to Tell You and Other Thoughts

Adán Campos

Abstract Through the negotiation and narrativization of childhood memories that take place in the United States and Mexico, the author reveals a nuanced and complicated picture of the charismatically attractive, yet unpredictable individual who was his father. Raised by a single mother, the author revisits memories of his father contemplating who he and his father are, and their connection to one another. When the father returns to Mexico to reside in his home town, his unexpected, suspicious death puts an end to the possibility of the author—now a university student— ever knowing him in the present moment or of developing a meaningful father/son relationship where the son tells the father of his sexuality and same-sex desire and is able to experience his father's response.

In the summer of 2015, while packing for my move across the country to attend graduate school, I found a letter my father had sent me from prison when I was a child. He wrote:

A. Campos (✉)
Arizona State University, Tempe, AZ, USA

© The Author(s), under exclusive license to Springer Nature
Switzerland AG 2021
A. R. Del Castillo, G. Güido (eds.), *Fathers, Fathering, and Fatherhood*, Palgrave Studies in Literary Anthropology,
https://doi.org/10.1007/978-3-030-60877-4_23

Para mi hijo Adán:

Hi, Adán, ojalá que cuando recibas esta carta estés bien de salud. Yo quiero pedirle a mi niño que me haga un favor. Pero antes que nada quiero decirte que te quiero mucho y que te extraño y tengo muchas ganas de verte. Y el favor que te quiero pedir es que estudies mucho y que no hagas enojar a tus maestros ni a tu mamá porque, pobrecita de tu mami, trabaja mucho y llega bien cansada y le duele la cabeza cada que la hacen enojar. Pórtate bien y sé un niño bueno con tu mami y tus maestras en la escuela. Estudia mucho, mi niño, porque yo te quiero mucho, mucho y si te portas bien yo también me voy a portar bien contigo, te lo prometo. Te quiero mucho y por favor estudia, ¿ok? Contéstame, Adáncito. José Martinez[1]

This work represents my response to his letter, coming to terms with what my father means to me, and dealing with his untimely death in the spring of 2013.

*   *   *

Only you and mom call me Adancito, a loving nickname. As I re-read your letter I want to stop, but I see that you ask a favor of me. I continue reading and I'm surprised to find that you ask me to be a good kid and not upset mom or my teachers. That if I am good, you in turn will be good to me. Perhaps mom told you I was mischievous or maybe you knew, but how would you know, you weren't around. I'd like to think I didn't upset mom or my teachers that much, but you'd have to ask them. Like many Mexicans, you wished me good health, declared your love for me, and asked that I excel in school. You expressed concern for mom, a little surprising. *Sí, pobrecita de mi mamá* (Yes, poor mom), she's worked so hard her entire life and has practically nothing to show for it. You know, I really don't know the man who wrote this letter to

---

[1] "Hi Adán, I hope this letter finds you in good health. I want to ask a favor of my boy. But first I want to let you know that I love and miss you very much and want so much to see you. The favor I want to ask of you is for you to study hard and don't upset your teachers or your mom. Your poor mommy, she works so hard and gets home exhausted and her head hurts every time she gets upset. Behave yourself and be a good boy for your mommy and your teachers at school. Study hard, my boy, because I love you so much, so much. And if you behave I, too, will be good to you, I promise. I love you, please study, ok? Write to me, Adancito. José Martínez" (English translation by A.R. Del Castillo).

me. I know you fathered me, I know your name is José Martínez, and I know you're from Mexico.

*   *   *

I received the news while I was in class. It was my feminist theory class. The first message came via text from a cousin in Arizona, then an online message from a cousin in Mexico. I pretended I hadn't received them. I tried paying attention, but I couldn't hear the person at the front of the classroom even though I was only a few feet away. I could see her mouth move, her body walking back and forth. Then Pablo called, my older brother. I stepped out of class to speak with him. You had been murdered. Apparently, no one knew what happened, or didn't want to tell us. I left class. I didn't know if I should cry or continue with my day as usual. I went to the food court on campus. I hadn't eaten that morning. Ever since that day, once maybe twice, tears filled my eyes and ran down my face. I've asked myself again and again, how do I mourn the loss of a father who was not present? Of a man I do not know. How am I supposed to feel?

I had just seen you the year before in Mexico. I had not seen you for over two decades. I returned to the States hoping to see you again. Years after your death I realized part of me felt robbed. You were taken suddenly, without notice. I no longer had the opportunity to choose whether I wanted you to be part of my life or not.

*   *   *

You'd always arrive in your shiny car, music blasting throughout the entire trailer park. You'd step out, I'd see your boots touch the pavement before I saw your face. You'd walk toward us, your boys waiting diligently. Your shiny smooth shirt unbuttoned almost halfway exposing your gold chain, even more so when you'd wave at the hollers. You'd smile. *¡Hola, hola!* you'd greet the men strolling over to say hello. You'd chat some then come over to us. It was always the same. Now, like then, I see you, but can't touch you. You're abstract yet oh so real.

A man with pitch black hair and brown *indio* (Indian) skin. I wanted to grow up looking just like you. And I have. I wonder if you've also spent time rejecting the lie that our skin is too dark, too brown, our hair too thick, too black. Hairstylists always complaining that our hair is not easy to work with. I am told you were tall, towering over mom like a skyscraper. Before I saw you again as an adult I had imagined you taller than me. "He must have gotten shorter with time," mom said.

My father—drug and human smuggler. Abusive partner. This is what I know of you, my father. Because of who you were, I was able to dismiss you, not want you in my life. Why would I want a man in my life that beat my mother?

When I hear folks on your side of the family say they miss you and remember you as a good man, I get jealous—but just a little. You're my father, not theirs. They got to know you in ways I never will. You took that away from me for being the kind of man you were. But then I feel an invisible slap, why would I want to call you father, why would I get jealous? "Drugs, money, it all got the best of him. He had a good heart though," your family members say of you. I know they want to make sure they tell me the truth about you without crushing any hopes I may have of you.

You were the kind of man that breaks his promise. Mom told me that whenever you were in prison, you always promised to be a better man when you got out. That you found the Lord and now you knew how to live right by her, that you could live a different life. *Mi'ja perdóname* (Babe, forgive me), mom says that's how you always began. Mom believed you at first, "I was naïve and in love, what can I tell you," she says, "so I would go back." "Mmhmm," was mom's response when she realized it was all talk. Whenever you did get out, you changed for a bit. But then the old you came back. Maybe you would've changed had you lived, kind of looked like you could've when I saw you that day in Mexico, looking all tired, peppered hair, hunched shoulders, your skin dry and shiny because you've been working under the sun. Or maybe I fell for it like mom did all those years ago.

Your voice is recorded in my memory. I can even imitate you. It terrified me at times. Your voice could make any look down at the floor. I would watch you from a distance not wanting to hear you raise your voice. *¡Cabrón!* (You little shit)! Your words would hit me. It was as if you were grinding your teeth, yelling, but slightly opening your mouth so only I could hear.

Once when my brothers and I went to visit you in Arizona an uncle asked me what I wanted, I think it was for my birthday. "Rollerblades," I told him. Days later we were in someone's backyard gathered around a table, the kind that easily deposits splinters on wary children. A white box was at the center of the table. There were people there, some I recognized as family. "Open the box," you said enthusiastically. Everyone's eyes dropped on me. Surely, it was the rollerblades. I opened the box and there they were. White skates, two front wheels, two back wheels. They weren't the rollerblades I wanted with the wheels in a straight row, the ones shown on commercials. *¡Qué carbrón! ¿No te gustan?* (What, you little shit? You don't like them?) you yelled. You must have seen the disappointment on my face. No, I didn't like them, but I just stood there, silent. You grabbed the box from the table and stormed off. I just stood there, my arms to the side, looking at the empty table. Even now I haven't managed a poker face. I even laugh at the most inappropriate times. I just can't help it.

MOM AND YOU

Mom, always with three kids in tow, each pacing fast with stick legs, taught us the art of escape. We learned to flee before we learned to read or write. Pablo and I were responsible for getting ready while she dressed Diego, he was still a baby. We only had moments to get out, leaving with only the clothes on our backs. Always at night. These lessons proved vital as we embarked into the world and as we got older. Mom's three kids figured things out on their own, no one to ask, these first-generation US-born kids.

Then one day she crossed state lines with the hope that the distance was a border between you and us. Do you know what it's like to raise three kids as a single mother, a Mexican woman, speaking no English, not knowing how to read or write in Spanish, without papers, poor as hell, living in the United States? Mom did what she could. What she knew. That day, long ago, she ran. She ran and ran without looking back.

When we were kids mom took us to see you when you were caged in those concrete prison walls. *Adán, ven habla con tu papá* (Adán, come speak to your father), she tells me. I hesitate. I try not looking at you. I don't want to see you like this. But I listen to mom. I climb and sit on mom's lap. She hands me the phone. I have to hold it with both hands. It's heavy and looks like a public pay phone. My head is tilted down so I look up to see you. You smile. *¿Cómo estás, mi Adancito? ¿Qué? ¿No estás feliz que me estás visitando?* (How are you, my little Adán? What? You aren't happy you're visiting me?) you ask. I shake my head no. *¡Pinche cabrón, debes de estar agradecido…!* (You little shit, you should be grateful…). I look at mom, she grabs the phone as I struggle to hand it to her. I slip off her lap and my shirt rises slightly. I see you talking at me but can't hear a thing through the glass. *¡Bache, cálmate, son tus hijos!… no me andes hablando así* (Bache, calm down, they're your children … don't speak to me that way!), she scolds you. My mom, short Mexican single mother, she's always been my first line of defense in this world.

"He was your father, you three deserved to see him. But all those trips, they were hard. They were far. It was hard finding a ride out there. No one wanted to go. The lady we went with that time, her husband was locked up too, and she had a car, so we went with her," mom said when I asked her why she took us to see you.

I wonder how mom was able to survive all the blows. I wonder how she was able to survive this world, get from one place to the next. She was displaced, forced to migrate to the United States, violence accompanying her on the journey *pa'l norte* (up north). When she arrived in this alleged land of opportunity, she experienced hardships daily. And you had to come around, adding your violence. To speak of one's trauma can be like reliving it, it's hard on the body, the mind, and spirit. Maybe that's why many like mom hardly even speak of their lives before coming north, or their journey here. It's too painful.

For mom to tell us stories of you she has to be in the right mood. Ask her in the right way and she'll tell you. "He threw me on the floor, pinned me down with his knees on my shoulders. He started punching me in the face. I don't know how she knew but your tía (aunt), who lived in the trailer next-door, busted in and pushed him off me. She grabbed me and we ran out. We ran and ran until we saw a house with a high porch. We knew we could hide there from him. When we were on the porch I looked down at my nightgown and it was covered in blood, all the way down." How could you lay your hands on the woman who raised me, who sacrificed so much so that my brothers and I could have a better future? Asshole.

How Do I Make Sense of You and What You Left Behind?

What's the point in writing about a man who was hardly ever present? And now that he's gone, never will be? What's the point if he can't even read this? A man whose past I know more of from hushed whispers than of actual lived experience. Why would I want a man—a father—in my life that seems to only cause deep and lasting pain? Yet because of him I have learned not to repeat his mistakes.

I don't know how to communicate with you. I have written words on these pages only to return to them and have no clue as to their meaning. Even when my mouth opens to voice these words into existence, nothing comes out. I delete them, write them back in, and take them out once more. Then I write something else altogether.

Sometimes I don't trust my memories of you. They may give me a false sense of who you were. I recall each story of you told to me by those who knew you. Stories of you that have been filtered through family members you've hurt. All I have of you are fractions of memories and parts of stories. And this letter. Had I responded to your letter as a kid, maybe I'd have more of you.

I don't know whether to call you by your name or "father." The word slips from my lips like water slipping through my fingers. Father. I had not called you father before and meant it. The new f-word. Father. Saying the word feels like speaking English for the first time. Father. Father. Father.

You abandoned us, didn't try to stay in our lives. I tried convincing myself that your letters and calls from jail were enough. But they weren't. You just weren't there.

I knew I was fatherless, known it all my life. Even when you were in and out, having you around felt heavy, scary. Yeah, sometimes you made my brothers and I laugh, gave us money. But you didn't raise us. So I'm not sad I grew up without you. What I didn't know was whether to hate you, miss you, or celebrate your absence. I learned to live without you.

Your absence haunts me. I felt it when I knew you wouldn't surprise me on birthdays, graduation, or be there to send me off when I moved away for graduate studies. You've managed to stay in the cracks, creeping up at the most inconvenient times.

I wanted you here whenever the fridge was empty or when mom stressed over paying bills, or whenever I was bullied at school for wearing hand-me-downs. There were times I depended on the school lunches to keep my stomach from growling, letting others think *'amá* wasn't trying her best. It wasn't until high school that I stopped wondering, had you been around, if I would have been like my friends, showing off my new clothes or new gadgets. I dared not ask mom for anything, I feared it would become a burden for her, even if she smiled and said she'd try to get it for Christmas.

In middle school a counselor was informed of the economic hardships our family faced. One day I was pulled out of class, placed in a van, and taken away. I thought I was being kidnapped as part of some secret operation where I would be experimented on along with the rest of the kids in the van who looked poor like me. Pablo was in the van, too. We got to a building and once inside we were told to take clothing, toys, school supplies, and a backpack. I was excited but tried not showing it. I took my time picking out what I wanted.

On the school bus ride home I heard the kids making fun of us. I don't think I ever used the things we were given that day, they reminded me of the laughs, whispers, and finger pointing my brother and I were subjected to as we walked past the kids in the bus clutching onto our obnoxious white trash bags, great for displaying the poor kids' donations. "What's in the bag?" one of them asked me. "Nothing," I said and stared out the window the whole ride home. I did keep the Teddy bear I grabbed. I don't know what became of it though.

We have gotten by without you. We had to. In fact, we're thriving. Pablo, Diego, and I have said it before—we're better off without you. I still have a family without you. Your absence is not my burden to carry.

In many ways, I know your absence was liberating. Your absence freed me to be a different kind of man and to love differently. We didn't have to learn to communicate with fists and a loud voice, pushing our way through the world. Our mother's reminders of your fists and kicks, her endless sacrifices for us, helped us reject the demands of the world, outside the tiny apartments we lived in, to be men like you.

But I know I've failed at times. I was seduced by this world that deeply favors men. There were moments when my pain was so great that it took precedence over everything else. Had I learned to deal with my shit earlier maybe then mom wouldn't have had to deal with my occasional indifference to her pain. It took me a long time to learn to know how to deal with my emotions, understand myself in my complexity and depth. But in the process, I turned to the bottle far too many times, sometimes to remember and occasionally forget. I had to close myself off to the world in order to be open with my loved ones and myself. It's the only way I'd survive.

My Inheritance

You saved me from drowning once. I wanted to swim far and fast like the swimmers on television. I didn't have the outfit though—the cap or tight-fitting underwear. I had on some dark shorts and went into the water. "Don't go in too far," someone had warned. The next thing I know I'm trying to claw my way up to the surface but I keep going under, deeper and deeper. All I can see is a whirlpool sucking me in, and a figure above, then everything went dark.

When I recover I'm on the sand and you're yelling at me. I cough up water and I'm trying to breathe through my mouth but it's difficult. Someone, a woman I think, places a towel over me. I shake and shake. It's so cold. You stand to the side, wet, still yelling at me for almost drowning, for not listening. What can I say? I wanted to be like the swimmers on television. You almost lost me but you saved me. It was you who pulled me out of the water, wasn't it?

Because of you I like oysters. I often think of you whenever I eat them or the topic of oysters comes up. I think of the time we were at a restaurant and saw the platter of slimy food in front of you. I dared not eat from it, it appeared as if the slime would come alive in my stomach and find its way back out again. You insisted I try it, at least once, and that if I did you would leave me alone. I did, then another, and another. I've been eating oysters ever since. Eating oysters reminds me of sitting across the table from you, that having dinner with you is not just a thing of the past. You taught me to try new things, to be adventurous. When I eat oysters, I am eating with you.

Some of the letters and their envelopes you sent us from prison had drawings on them, Chicano prison artwork. That's how I began drawing: mimicking every line. "You're a good artist," friends would tell me in high school. I draw eyebrows and eyelashes like those of *cholas* (homegirls). I learned to draw with pen because all your drawings were in pen. Maybe that's why I don't like writing in pencil because I learned to be creative with a pen.

There are very few memories of us laughing together. Remember that day in Mexico when I was about eight years old and you grabbed my face, scratching it with your beard?

"Why do you have hair on your face?" I ask.

"Because that's what men get on their face. Wanna touch it?"

"Mmhmm," I reply. Your beard is not long. The hairs are so short and close to your face that when I try grabbing them they escape my small fingers. I notice the acne scars on your face and wonder if I will have them as an adult, turns out I do. My hand travels from one side of your face to your chin.

"It pricks," I say.

"Mira," (Look) you say then your hands grab my small face holding it still as your beard presses against my face, moving from side to side. I kick my feet; my stick arms fail to push you away from me.

"Ay," I yell repeatedly. You finally let go and laugh. I hold my cheek and smack you. We laugh. I didn't know your touch could be so gentle.

I did the same to my nephew, Ricardo, Pablo's youngest son, the day he asked me the same question I asked you. I thought of you when I did it.

"I don't want hair like yours on my face," Ricardo says. His words sting me. I couldn't help feeling he was rejecting a part of me. Then I remembered: Ricardo learned to be soft from his father; Diego and I, without knowing it, were accomplices in spreading softness. The hair on my face is too prickly for his softness.

"Come here," I teased him.

Maybe he'll remember this, too. He'll have something to remember me by as an adult. A reminder to stay soft and to push back against whatever tries to make him hard.

*   *   *

I unintentionally followed through on your favor but not because of or for you. I've done well academically, always had a job, and helped mom with the bills. I've even stayed away from men like you. I graduated high school because a teacher said high school graduates make more money than push outs. I decided to go to college because someone told me college graduates make more money than those with just a high school diploma. Mom never got to go to school. You didn't finish. Schooling for both of you meant a ticket out, that's why I went on. Those pieces of paper they give you after so many years meant leveraging them to get a better job even though there aren't any guarantees. It was the possibility of not having to worry about putting food on the table or a roof over my head, like mom has. I'm one of those sentimental firsts: the first to graduate high school, first to go to college (but not the first to graduate, Diego graduated with his bachelors before me), and now the first in a PhD program. Imagine that! It hasn't been easy, always having to figure things out on my own. There have been more obstacles than I can count. But I made it. What other option did I have?

School didn't help much though; we were learning what we really needed in real time. Mom taught me all the things I've needed to navigate these murky waters we call higher education. Translating government and bank documents, taxes and who knows what else for her, learning mom's pay cycles along with when bills were due, how much to pay which bill. I learned how to talk to these professionals when I translated for mom, talking to all those white folks when she used to clean houses.

My Daddy Issues and I

Even after your death you left your baggage. Here I am, writing about you. Here I am wondering why I want to know for myself whether or not I would have wanted you in my life had you lived. My hands shake a little; my breathing quickens and deepens; the room spins a little. Here I am, ashamed as I admit I may have daddy issues. I feel too soft, too open.

You know, when I applied to graduate school I didn't know the specific reason why I wanted to study masculinity. I recently realized that one of the main reasons I decided to study masculinity is because I wanted to explore the possibility of what life could have looked like had you been around. But don't give yourself too much credit; other things sparked my research interests.

As I speak these truths about you, I struggle being honest with you. Most importantly, I struggle being honest about you with myself. I try not holding back but I'm concerned that breaking these silences so openly lets others believe they have a license to demonize you. My family and I reserve the right to hold you accountable, others don't have that right.

MEETING YOU IN MEXICO

Mom and I had come to Mexico to visit and stay with your sister, my *tía* (aunt). I asked her if we could visit you and she agreed. As my aunt drove from Colima City to Cofraidi (the town you lived and grew up in) I wondered if you wanted to see me, hoping that I would return home as a changed individual, somehow becoming a better person after meeting you. This would be the first time I'd see you in my adult life. And there we were, sitting next to each other, two decades of absence suddenly filled. Sitting next to you felt like I had always been by your side. I didn't know then that this would be the last time I'd see you alive.

When we arrived in town, we parked at the home my brothers and I stayed in when we visited many, many years before. It was the house you lived in as a child. The town had changed, seemed smaller, not as busy. But now I saw it with adult eyes. The home looked unkempt. "Let's go find your father," *Tío* (uncle) Fernando said waving at me to follow after I asked for you, only minutes after we arrived. He drove me in that makeshift-looking truck of his that looked like it wouldn't start. I held onto the door handle throughout the ride. He drove rapidly on the cobbled streets, making for a bumpy ride. We turned left, drove, turned right, drove, stopped to ask questions, and drove again. We came to a stop. *¿Está el Bache?* (Is Bache around?) *Tío* Fernando asked a woman who glanced over at me suspiciously. She nodded her head no, "your father's girlfriend," he said, and with that we drove off. "He must be buying fish. He just got out of work so he must be there because it's lunch time and he's probably hungry," I listened hoping he was right. As he drove in the unfamiliar town I looked out for a fish store as if I knew what to look out for.

We drive down a street where all the stores have counters that open out onto the sidewalk. Then I spot a man standing at a counter. The man is short, his clothes noticeably worn and torn even from afar. He's hunched over the counter. My heart beats faster and faster. My hands sweat a little. I think I'm dreaming. I want to point you out, but wait. For a moment I want to tell *Tío* Fernando to stop the truck so I can jump out. I shouldn't be the one looking for you. But I stay. I don't want to regret that I didn't look for you. You kind of look like Diego from behind, the way you stand, or maybe it's because he inherited that dark brown skin of yours. I've thought of this moment many times throughout the years. What would I do if I were to see you once again? Would I be nice to you or *reclamarte*, hold you accountable for what your presence in my family's and my life has done? Then *Tío* Fernando says pointing in your direction "Look, he's right there."

Tío Fernando stops and parks on the opposite side of the street. You turn, immediately looking suspiciously at the truck. You walk over slowly, like a child greeting new people entering his home, toy in hand. You look directly at me as you approach. In the flesh, you have wrinkles and peppered hair. But where it's black, it's pitch black, and thick, like mine, Pablo's and Diego's hair. Your smirk, the glow in your eyes is gone, seems like life's picked you up in a whirlwind and dropped you haphazardly. *Tío* Fernando begins to speak, asking you questions, but you just nod at him, looking directly at me. Occasionally, you answer him with "hmmms" and nods. Then *Tío* Fernando goes silent. Our eyes lock, we study each other, and the silence grows. Your eyes go from looking at me like the boy who was playing with his truck, got it taken away, was offered it again once his sadness was visible, but rejects the toy, to looking at me with the same eyes as the man in the pictures and in my memories. Slowly, I watch emotion creep into you, saw it in your eyes, the kind men long for until their hearts go numb. I think you wanted to hide your watery eyes but couldn't look away. I wait for you to make the first move. You nod toward me and with a low voice, as if you wanted to cry, ask *Tío* Fernando ¿*Y este?* (Who's this?) But I shot back "What, you don't recognize me?" At that moment I saw your chest cave in, as if your body suddenly deflated. You stood frozen, your lips parting and eyes slightly widening. "Adán," you declare softly, without question. *¡Claro!* (Of course!) I respond. Immediately you begin making your way around the front of the truck toward me. I step out, and we hug awkwardly, but a hug *de cariño* (of affection) nonetheless.

"How are you?"

"I'm good, and you?"

"Good, good. Who you here with?"

"Mom."

"Where is she?"

"Your mother's home."

And with that you left, speeding off on your bicycle. I fear you'll fall and injure yourself as you wobble away on the stone road. You raced off to see a woman you had not seen in years.

We arrived seconds after you. You didn't come to a complete stop when you jumped off your bike. You looked frantic until you saw mom. You didn't know what to say, you greeted her like a socially awkward person greets someone in a packed room. The entire time we were together you hardly looked at me, you stared at mom most of the time, occasionally conversing with me. "I speak some French," I say to you. "That's good, you," you respond. I wonder if you care about me as I sit next to you. I wonder what kind of father you could be. I wonder what the rest of my life could be like if you were in it.

I couldn't bring myself to say it. "Don't say anything," I told myself tightly grabbing onto the armrests of the white plastic chair I'm sitting in, the kind that is always present at backyard fiestas. *'Apá, soy gay* (Dad, I'm gay), I imagined myself saying out loud. Would our meeting be cut short if you disapproved? Would you know what to say? Would you have cared either way? The feeling of wanting to tell you felt new, but it was secretly buried deep inside. I didn't want to ruin the moment. So I squeezed it real tight inside of me so my mouth wouldn't betray me. The feeling of telling you lingered for years. Now you're gone. If you had lived I would have told you.

The sky was turning grey and my aunt suggests we drive back before we get caught in the storm. The winds were erratic and the waters at the shore roiled tall waves. I looked over at you and didn't know what to say. After so many years I knew I wanted to speak with you. I was secretly embarrassed for being so excited to speak with you so I tried not to say too much, left it up to you to fill in the awkward silence. I saw you hold your tongue too, frustrated. Maybe you didn't know how to speak to a son you didn't know, or with a woman you hadn't seen in years, or where to even begin. Maybe it's because there wasn't much to say about yourself, except to tell us how tragically your life had gone. When we were leaving, you told mom how much you hated picking coconuts for a living and that you wanted to open up a *bodega* (store). That's when I saw the ambitious father many talked about. I briefly saw that spark in your eyes again. Mom handed you American bills. *No, no,* you managed to say as your eyes got watery. *¿Como crees? Ten* (Don't be silly, take it) mom said to you, grabbing your hands, placing the bills inside them, closing your hands. She said something to you, kissed you on the cheek, and with that, we left. We visited for what felt like just half an hour. For a while after returning to the States all I could do was wish our reunion had lasted a lifetime.

Shortly after returning to Colima City I went on an errand with a cousin. In the car, she told me you defended a gay cousin. She said you went drunk to the bully's home. Slurring your words, you yelled from outside the bully's home to leave the queer alone, "So what if he's gay!" you yelled. You defended him. I'm sure you would have defended me were I in a similar situation. But could you have been sober? Did you have to yell? Still, it made me smile inside.

How can I forget reuniting with my father after so many years? I often recall how the air left your body when I asked if you knew who I was. You knew it was me the moment you saw me yet your eyes begged the question, how was it possible? I know, I was asking myself the same thing. Yet there we were, facing each other, both grown older.

I only have you in memories and fear they'll fade over time. I cannot show proof that you are my father, claim you. A short time ago I said out loud to myself that I wanted my father back. That maybe, just maybe, you could change.

*   *   *

As kids my brothers and I visited you in Mexico during school's spring break, I was in the third grade. We stayed so long in Mexico kids at school thought I wasn't returning, but it seemed like such a short stay.

While in Mexico you took us to the beach. Once there the clouds darken, and I fear water will pour from above sweeping us into the vast ocean, swallowing us. You sit on the sand blowing air into a water tube, your cheeks fully round. Then you rise, smiling, your ass covered in sand. *¡Vente, ándale, vas a divertirte!* (Come on, hurry, you're going to enjoy this!), you finally say grabbing a hold of the air-filled plastic tube. As you run into the water I know not to trust you, you wanted me in there with you. You paddle away from shore with your feet; my heart beats faster and faster. I fear the waters will drift you farther into the sea where I can no longer see you.

¡Vente, cabrón, no tengas miedo! (Come on, dude, don't be afraid!) you call out to me as I stand at the shore staring at you and all that surrounds you.

Cálmate, Bache (Calm down, Bache), your girlfriend of the time tells you.

You keep yelling at me from a distance in the water. I run to you to shut you up. Immediately water splashes onto my face, finding its way into my mouth. I spit it back out. It's salty. I hadn't tasted seawater before. I spit and spit but can't get the taste out of my mouth.

"It's just water, *cabrón!*" you yell.

I rush back to shore but you yell to get back in. I get back in because we've come a long way and by the look in your eyes, you wanted to have fun with us, your boys. I would have been perfectly fine just standing there at the edge, the ocean barely touching my toes, fully clothed, pants rolled up to my knees.

I end up on the water tube with you. I look into the vastness that is the ocean then look at the shore, look back at the ocean then the shore again.

"There's nothing wrong, *cabrón*, relax," you say.

You hold me in your wet and freezing arms.

"Ooh!" you say as you grab and hold me at the edge of this swaying plastic tube as if I'm falling overboard. I scramble, clawing at your neck and hair, trying to hold on to something so as not to drift away to some far unknown place. You laugh. I stay quiet in the comfort of your arms until we get back to shore. I fear the water tube isn't sturdy enough to keep us safe; the waves are stronger than I expected and seem like they'll flip the tube over. Or worse yet, carry us off into the abyss. Maybe we'll fall over and a shark will snatch us up before we get a chance to paddle our way back. Once we return, I'm sure you won't always be the nice guy I want you to be. But in this moment, as you hold me in your arms, I know the ocean won't take us away.

CHAPTER 24

No Last Name

Yosimar Reyes

Abstract The author was twelve when he met his father who had driven from Texas with his American wife to bond with his boys. As if time had stood still, the father failed to mention the more than ten years of lost time and abandonment. But the author wanted to believe in the father, find answers to his mother's silences, take his father's name, and develop a meaningful father/son relationship. Dad treated the boys to a brief stay in Carmel, good restaurants, and the promise of a possible trip out of state. When he left, the boys called him daily until the phone calls became less and less accessible then the line was disconnected. Through it all the mother's love stayed strong and weathered the attraction.

My father picked up Pelón and me in a white Toyota minivan. Our dark faces reflected on its shiny, white paint. In the passenger seat, next to him, sat a white woman he introduced as his wife. "This is Celeste," he said. My father's green eyes glimmered as if this were one of his most significant accomplishments—to have married an "Americana"—or, as my family would say, *Una mujer con papeles* (a female American citizen).

Y. Reyes (✉)
San Francisco State University, San Francisco, CA, USA

© The Author(s), under exclusive license to Springer Nature
Switzerland AG 2021
A. R. Del Castillo, G. Güido (eds.), *Fathers, Fathering, and Fatherhood*, Palgrave Studies in Literary Anthropology,
https://doi.org/10.1007/978-3-030-60877-4_24

They had traveled from as far as McAllen, Texas, to meet us in East Side San Jose. Celeste stepped out of the van to greet us. "Nice to meet y'all," she said in her Texas accent.

She stretched her long, white arms and hugged both of us at the same time. Pelón and I, confused by Celeste's affection, stood blank-faced with our arms by our side, as we did the many times we were introduced to relatives from Mexico we didn't know. Once in our neighborhood, they were hesitant to leave the van parked where it was for fear someone might break into it. After all, their new white minivan stood out amid the beat-up cars and worn-down apartment buildings on our street. We assured them that the neighborhood was pretty safe as we walked up a flight of stairs to our small, two-bedroom apartment.

"We live in number 35," I said, pointing to our door. The "35" was missing the number 5 that was never replaced, so it looked like we lived in number 3.

Our neighbors peeked through their windows as we walked up the stairs. It was rare to see a white woman on our street, much less a white woman entering an apartment complex full of Mexicans. Knowing our neighbors were staring, my brother and I walked proudly up the stairs. We raised our heads and smirked, knowing they were watching us. We knew that once Papi left, the neighborhood kids would run up and ask us who they were. Nonchalantly, we'd reply, "Oh, that's just my dad and step-mom."

Once upstairs, Abuela (Grandmother) opened the door into our small living room. She greeted Papi, and in no time, they began talking about Mexico. Memories swirled in our living room, bringing up Guerrero, my mother, my parents' young love, but never bringing up where he had been all this time, the heartbreak or our abandonment. I stared into Papi's face, listened to the way he spoke, and watched his green eyes. Mami told us that back in Mexico, Papi was known as *Gato* because he had eyes like a cat. Unlike him, I was ordinary, my skin was dark, and my hair stuck up like a broom. I wanted his eyes, so when people would ask me who I got them from, I could reply, "my dad has green eyes, too." Noticing my staring at him, Papi turned toward me and nervously said, "Gordo, show us your room." I turned to my Abuela, unsure of what he meant. Abuela, not uncomfortable, responded, *Este es el cuarto. Dormimos en el suelo y los cuartos los rentamos para alcanzar la renta. Sin papeles tenemos que ajustar con lo poco que tenemos.* (This is his room. We all sleep on the floor and rent out the rooms to pay the rent. Without legal papers, we have to make do as best we can.) Embarrassed by Abuelita's response, Pelón sat on the couch tearing at a hole in it.

My brother was the only one with memories of my father. By the time I was born, he was no longer in the picture, and by the time I turned three, my mother had already crossed us into the United States. I never grew up missing him, but my brother had vivid memories of our lives in Mexico and could still recall the day Papi first left.

Taken aback by the news that we shared a living room with my Abuelos, Papi and Celeste stared at each other in silence. Celeste, in her awkward Texan Spanish, said, *Está muy bonito su casa. Me gusta mucho los fotos.* (Your home is beautiful. I like the photos.) Pelón ran into the closet and brought out a book where he sketched portraits of our family. He placed the book on Papi's lap, breaking through the awkwardness in the room. Papi paged through the book. He traced his fingers against my brother's pencil marks; the lead smeared on his fingertips.

"Mi'jo (my son), these are good. You have an eye for art like one of my bothers. You know, one of your *tíos* (uncles) is a painter in Mexico," Papi said. My brother's face glowed at our father's acknowledgment.

To get to know us, Papi began to ask us questions. "What grade are you in now? What do you want to be when you grow up? When is your birthday?" We talked about our favorite music, some books we read, and how we were doing in school. Never did he apologize for leaving us; never did he apologize for taking twelve years to meet me. He simply went about the conversation as if our separation had no impact on us.

*   *   *

Celeste had researched beautiful places to visit in California, and she came across the City of Carmel, so that's where they had planned to take us. Abuela packed our clothes in plastic grocery bags. In our family, vacations were not a concept we understood, so having luggage just in case of a trip was not something we owned. The farthest we had gone was to a lake in Pleasanton, and even then, we didn't pack a change of clothes. Abuela had packed lunches, *tortas de frijol* (bean sandwiches) wrapped in aluminum foil, though Celeste said we wouldn't need them because she was going to take care of us. As we jumped into the minivan and buckled our seat belts, excited for us, and yet still concerned, Abuela leaned close to us and whispered, *Si se quieren regresar nada más llámenme y yo los voy a encontrar* (If you want to get back just call me and I'll go for you).

On our way to Carmel, Celeste and Papi talked about how different California was compared to Texas; they spoke of all the hills and the beautiful weather. My brother and I simply sat in the back of the van alert to our surroundings since we did not know where we were going.

When we arrived in Carmel, Celeste helped us carry our clothes inside the grocery bags into the hotel. "Don't y'all love it? It's right by the beach, so I figured it would be perfect for a family getaway," she said, sounding more eager than any of us.

The streets in Carmel were clean. The only noise we heard was the ocean tides crashing against the rocks. The people walking on the street smiled and waved at us. We stood out like gardeners working on people's front lawns, except for Celeste, who blended in with the rest of the people on the street.

We stayed in a nice hotel and ate seafood for dinner. Papi even bought a $12 chocolate bar, which according to the person selling them was "artfully crafted." We spent two days in Carmel wandering through art boutiques, walking on the beach, and taking family pictures in front of beautiful houses. We were a family: me, Papi, Pelón, and Celeste, a portrait that Pelón had never drawn.

The night before we were to return home to the East Side, I gave Papi a letter I wrote to him when I heard he would come from Texas to visit us. I used my seventh-grade cursive to sign the end of the message: Yosimar Reyes. Papi took the time to read the letter. His eyes moved back and forth, trying to decipher my *pocho* (Mexican American) Spanish. Once done with the letter, he neatly folded it, placing it inside the envelope. He turned toward me and said, "*Pero, mi'jo,* (But son), your last name is not Reyes. *Tú eres Jiménez.* Your last name is Jiménez." Confused, I told him that in school Mami signs all my paperwork with her last name. I told him I had never written Jiménez next to my name. Dumbfounded, he said, "Well, from now on, you should get used to writing Jiménez next to your name. There is no reason why you shouldn't feel proud to be a Jiménez."

Papi dropped us off back home. We jumped out of the car, our skin darker than before, after spending days in the sun. I held Papi's hand as we walked up the two flights of stairs to our apartment. Celeste and Pelón followed carrying gifts we brought for our grandparents. Our neighbors peeked through their window; we walked with our crooked smiles stretched across our faces because we had a story to tell.

"Gordo, you have to listen to your Abuela. If you do good in school, next summer I am going to buy you a plane ticket and you can stay with me in Texas. Things are going to be different now. I'm going to call and make sure that you are always ok." I had never been on a plane before, and the idea that hundreds of miles away, someone cared for me, made me feel important. For once, I mattered.

At school the next day, I told all my classmates that from now on, my last name was Jiménez. I even told my teacher, Ms. Gutiérrez, that she needed to change my name on the roster.

In the weeks that followed, every time I had to write my name on an assignment for school, I wrote: Yosimar Jiménez. It felt like I was a different person, as if slowly all the missing pieces in my life, the ones my mother kept hidden from me, were finally coming into place.

Ms. Gutiérrez, unsure of what had come over me, decided to call my mother. Unaware of this, one afternoon, I arrived home and found my mother sitting on my Abuela's couch. I could already tell she was upset by the way her leg shook, which happened every time she was angry. *Me llamó tu maestra ... ¿puedes explicar cómo te apellidas Jiménez?* (Your teacher called ... can you explain how it is your last name is Jiménez?)

I have always been scared of my mother's anger, so I stayed quiet.

A ver, dime. ¿Cómo, chingados, que ahora te apellidas Jiménez cuando ese hombre nunca te ha dado nada? ¿Cómo que te apellidas Jiménez cuando tu abuela y yo nos estamos matando por ti? (Well, tell me. How the fuck is it that your last name is now Jiménez when that man has never given you anything? How is it that you are now a Jiménez when your grandmother and I are killing ourselves for you?)

I could see how my mother's anger took over her body. Whenever Mami became upset, she would go into a rage and become a wild woman whose words would hit at the most tender places. But this was different than the time she got mad at me because I was acting up in school; this was a different kind of anger; it was anger at knowing she could potentially lose me. I didn't want to believe her. I wanted to believe everything Papi had said. I tried to think that Mami was only mad because I finally had a relationship with the man she seldom mentioned.

¡Como quisiera que ése desgraciado viniera ahorita para que te largues con el! (How I wish that wretch would come now so that you would get the hell out of here along with him!)

For a moment, I felt she hated me. She hated Papi and the idea that I could grow up to be like him—it was something she could not live with.

!Desde este momento ya eres Jiménez, igual a tu pinche padre! (From this moment on you're a Jiménez just like your lousy father!) Mami stopped speaking to me. When she would come over to visit Abuelita, she would not look at me. To her I was just another body occupying our crowded apartment. *No le hagas caso, mi'jo. Luego se le pasa* (Don't mind her, son. She'll get over it), Abuela would say. I found comfort in Papi's voice on the telephone. I was finally getting to know that side of me I never knew existed. I learned about Texas and how different his life was from ours.

Night after night, I dialed the 956 number. At first, Papi always answered. Eventually, it became Celeste, who always answered. We went from two-hour conversations to 10-minute talks. Sometimes he answered. Sometimes he didn't until one day we heard on the other end of the line: *We're sorry, the number you have dialed has been disconnected or is no longer in service*. At first, we thought it was Celeste playing a joke on us. "Dial again, stupid," Pelón said.

We took turns dialing and every time we received the same message. We whispered "Papi" into the telephone, hoping that in some way, our voices would go through the line, and we would hear, "Hola, mi'jo." (Hi, son), but we only heard: *We're sorry, the number you have dialed has been disconnected or is no longer in service*. "Maybe we should call back tomorrow," I said to Pelón. We called the next day and the day after that. We called until we just gave up.

*   *   *

Mami sat on her front porch. She no longer lived with us because she had remarried; she had a new life. She promised that once she saved up enough money, she would come back for Pelón and me, and we would both stay with her. The sun beat against her skin, she saw me coming from up the street, but instead of going inside her house and avoiding me, she waited until I approached her. Her face was cold and hard like the last time I spoke to her. I walked up to her, scared. She sensed my fear but did not give in and stared straight into my eyes. My throat slowly unraveled. In a cracked voice, I managed to utter "Mami," I paused and waited until the heaviness in my stomach settled. *Quiero que me perdones. Mami, de hoy en adelante ya no quiero ser Jiménez. Nada más voy a ser Reyes, Mami* (Forgive me. Mami, from now on I no longer want to be a Jiménez. I'm only going to be a Reyes, Mami). She sat silent. Her cold stare reminded me of the many times I came home crying because someone had hit me or teased me, but instead of coming to my aid, she would say, *No llores. Tienes que aprender a defenderte.* (Don't cry. You must learn to defend yourself.) "I'm not always going to be around to protect you, Gordo." She had a strange way of teaching us life's lessons.

She saw me crushed. Her cold, hard face broke, and Mami became Mami again, the same Mami who rushed me to the hospital every time I was sick, who every new school year took me shopping for new clothes, who every time she filled out paperwork wrote: Yosimar Reyes.

She got up from her seat. Her body became a vast shadow engulfing me. *Papi, yo te voy a querer como seas. Jiménez o Reyes. Yo siempre te voy a querer.* (Sweetheart, I will always love you whoever you are, Jiménez or Reyes. I will always love you.)

In our living room there once was a portrait of Pelón, Celeste, Papi, and me. We're standing on a boulder with an immense blue sea beneath us and Papi's arms are stretched out hugging the three of us. We're all smiling. When the neighborhood kids would ask us, "Hey, what happened to your dad and step-mom?" We would simply answer, "He's busy working in Texas, but one day he's coming back for us. He's going to come back."

After many years my father reached out to us again trying to pick up the pieces from his last exit. But we are men now, Pelón and I have demons of our own. We made men of ourselves without a blueprint. Often I wonder if this queerness I embody is the universe asking in its own way for my mother's forgiveness.

CHAPTER 25

Communion

Jesus D. Mendez Carbajal

Abstract An openhearted but conditional acceptance of blemished fathers and ancestral patriarchs that calls for new ways of being masculine and the willingness of all involved to change, heal, and move forward without blaming or getting even for the intergenerational harm that resulted. The non-binary child and adult (son) specifically ask what the consequences are of not forgiving the father and how precisely do they/them (he) go about forgiving their (his) own.

If we forgive our fathers, we forgive ourselves,
If we forgive ourselves, we don't drown or dwell in pain and sorrow,
We grow.
We learn that it's okay to stumble in life, to even keep falling
          because one day we'll learn.

If we forgive our fathers, mothers, caregivers,
We open our hearts to feel love and to heal.
If we forgive our fathers, we humanize them, put them back together
Piece by piece, limb by limb, help them become whole again...
We help them re-member their wholeness.

J. D. Mendez Carbajal (✉)
San Diego State University, San Diego, CA, USA

© The Author(s), under exclusive license to Springer Nature
Switzerland AG 2021
A. R. Del Castillo, G. Güido (eds.), *Fathers, Fathering, and Fatherhood*, Palgrave Studies in Literary Anthropology,
https://doi.org/10.1007/978-3-030-60877-4_25

227

If we forgive our fathers, we may begin to forgive our grandfathers, great grandfathers and all the men of our lineage.
By doing the hard work of forgiveness, we heal intergenerational trauma.
We cry out our father's tears, release their pain by our own right, through our bodies.
If we forgive our fathers, we acknowledge, heal, and care for the masculine essence
in all of us

What if we *don't* forgive our fathers?
Should we let them drown in their pain and sorrow?
Should we let them fend for themselves, leave them unprotected as they did us?
What if we don't forgive our fathers and continue living our lives as if nothing's the matter?
What then?
Will we compromise our mental health because we keep lying to ourselves, pretending everything is ok?
Buying into the bullshit that everything is always fine.

What if we don't forgive our fathers?
Do we turn into hypocrites who don't follow their own advice?
Who don't listen with open hearts?
Or should we hurt them as they hurt us?
Do we pass on this pain?

What if we don't forgive our fathers?
Do we close our hearts to love?
Do we continue walking down the yellow brick road hoping this will fix itself?
If we don't forgive our fathers, are we the ones to be criticized for having kept silent,
when we should have spoken up?
Do we move out, distance ourselves, and disown our families?

What happens if *I* don't forgive my father?
Do I let the pain grow and deaden me from inside?
Do I let myself rot in despair and sadness?
Am I really going to have to be the one to call his shit out?
Maybe.
So then, how do we forgive ... how do I forgive my father?

CHAPTER 26

Chrysalis

Jesus D. Mendez Carbajal

Abstract Frustrated by the wasted time and lack of communication, understanding, and empathy, a non-binary adult (son) reaches out to the father by forgiving them (him) and asking to be forgiven themselves (himself). The non-binary adult (son) also thanks the father for making them (him) a better person through all the good and all the flawed practices of fathering and fatherhood.

I'm now 21 years old and I'm through with staying silent.
I'm here to ask your forgiveness and to forgive you, too.
All my life we've had a rocky relationship.
I don't want that anymore.
I'm here to cash in my overdue father-son time, father-son love,
      cash in my endless coupons and redeem lost time, most of which has
      expired.

I forgive you for not giving me the best example of what a queer brown
boy needs.
I forgive you for not opening up sooner and I hope you forgive me for not
asking sooner.

J. D. Mendez Carbajal (✉)
San Diego State University, San Diego, CA, USA

A. R. Del Castillo, G. Güido (eds.), *Fathers, Fathering, and
Fatherhood*, Palgrave Studies in Literary Anthropology,
https://doi.org/10.1007/978-3-030-60877-4_26

I forgive you for not being there for mom and me.
I can't hold a grudge against you because you've done your best.
When you know better, you do better.

So, I forgive you
        for not knowing better when I needed it the most.
I forgive you
            for resorting to what you knew, using the tools, methods and
            knowledge
            your alcoholic father taught you.
I thank you
            for all the bad and all the good you've done,
            you've helped me know better what kind of person,
            parent, partner, sibling, cousin, elder I want to be.
'*Apá, te perdono* (father, I forgive you).

PART VI

Fatherhood Patterns and Passionate Fathering

INTRODUCTION TO SECTION

A critical analysis of Chicanx/Latinx father and queer son relationships in literature and film brings one author to assess his relationship and identity with his own father. Father figures as godfathers, grandfathers, and others nurture a poet's love and hope for queer men as part of a people, class, and humanity.

Un Sueño about the Future (A Dream of the Future)

CHAPTER 27

Like Father, Like Queer Son?: Gay Chicanx and Latinx Males and Their Fathers

Daniel Enrique Pérez

Abstract This study finds Chicanx and Latinx father-son relationships depicted in literature and film tend to stereotype father figures as absent or uninvolved in the lives of children. Fathers are represented as domineering men who uphold traditional family values, humble hardworking men who have some authority at home, but none in the workplace, or failed men who have no authority at home or workplace. Despite such drawbacks, these fathers exert heteronormative beliefs and behavior on the family, which is particularly disruptive for queer sons. The essay finds father-queer son relationships require sustained negotiation and the reconfiguration of masculinity revealing that queer sons may have more in common with their fathers than expected. The essay ends with the author's reflections on his relationship and similarities with his own father.

D. E. Pérez (✉)
University of Nevada at Reno, Reno, NV, USA
e-mail: dperez@unr.edu

© The Author(s), under exclusive license to Springer Nature
Switzerland AG 2021
A. R. Del Castillo, G. Güido (eds.), *Fathers, Fathering, and
Fatherhood*, Palgrave Studies in Literary Anthropology,
https://doi.org/10.1007/978-3-030-60877-4_27

233

INTRODUCTION

Like most queer Chicano males, I rarely talk about my relationship with my father. While gay men often form intimate bonds with their mothers, several of us have more vexed or distant relationships with our fathers. I contend that this is a topic that many gay men in general have difficulty discussing. This essay explores the realm of fatherhood as it relates to relationships between queer Chicano, Mexican, and Latino males and their fathers. Here, I will focus on the depiction of these relationships in different cultural texts—fiction and non-fiction, written narratives, and films. Instead of seeing the rendition of father-son relationships in Chicanx and Latinx cultural production as authentic representations, I explore these as actually generative of several themes I argue are common to much of this body of work. Although the depiction of these relationships is scant in literature and film; there are a few that merit consideration because they reveal common themes that can lead to a better understanding of how these relationships may develop and are represented in varying cultural texts. This essay will demonstrate that although relationships between fathers and their queer sons, as depicted in Chicanx and Latinx cultural texts, often portray them as vexed and mired with conflict, they also highlight the similarities between queer Latinx males and their fathers.

FATHERHOOD AND LATINO MASCULINITY

Notions of gender may frequently be reconfigured and expanded with respect to fathers and Latino masculinity, but even so there remain certain characteristics that shape the way Latino fathers are portrayed, especially in popular culture. Latino fathers are often portrayed as men who are absent in the lives of their children either because they work long hours and spend much time away from the domestic space or because they are not physically present for a number of reasons—immigration, divorce, abandonment, and other circumstances. Father figures as depicted in literary and filmic texts are often absent. They typically do not play a prominent role in the day-to-day rearing of young children. The father may be away at work for long hours, he may have left the family to pursue economic opportunities, he may have abandoned the family for other reasons, or he may be emotionally absent. In his personal essay, "My Literary Fathers," Ray González describes his father in the following way: "my father is guilty of adultery and of abandoning his family to go live another life. He didn't want anything to do with us after the divorce" (1996, p. 172–173). This is one example of the type of chasm that might develop between a father and son due to circumstances over which the son has no control. What is important here is the dearth of representations of intimate Latinx father-son relationships in cultural production. While one may find the presence of fathers and sons in narratives and visual culture, it is uncommon to find examples of the two developing close bonds with one another, spending quality time together, or in other ways one might typically conceptualize a healthy or successful father-son relationship. As Charles Ramírez Berg, *Latino Images in Film: Stereotypes, Subversion, Resistance*, explains in his analysis of the "absent father" figure in film and television, while Anglo families are often depicted as "complete and ideal," ethnic families are portrayed as "fragmented and dysfunctional" (2002, p. 121). Ramírez Berg claims that this portrayal of the missing Latino father "is indicative of abnormal Oedipal development" and that Chicano male children are not "able to identify fully with the father ... nor can [they] take his productive, 'masculine' place in society" (p. 121).

When they are present, fathers do play an instrumental role in family dynamics. As Alfredo Mirandé demonstrates in his sociological study of father-son relationships *Hombres y Machos: Masculinity and Latino Culture*, with respect to caring for the family, Latino fathers feel responsible for providing financial resources as the main breadwinner, protecting the family, and instilling values in their children. When these fathers were asked what their "most important responsibility or duty" was to their children, their answers ranged from "financial or physical responsibilities (e.g., taking care of their basic needs) to moral, emotional, or spiritual development (e.g., giving them moral guidance)" (1998, p. 108). Evidently, as patriarchal figures, Latino fathers hold a range of responsibilities integral to the development of children.

Latino fathers often feel responsible for upholding family traditions and serving as a moral compass. I've argued elsewhere that one of the primary goals attributed to fathers portrayed in Chicanx and Latinx cultural texts often has to do with the reproduction and replication of the family by not only having children themselves, but by facilitating these processes among their offspring (Pérez 2009). When father figures play a prominent role in their families, they are often invested in assisting their children in following some of the traditions and sacraments associated with creating their own families. One of the best examples of this dynamic is found in the film *Mi familia* (1995). In the film, the patriarch and matriarch of the family do their best to rear their offspring in a way that facilitates their children's development into what they perceive to be successful parenthood. However, a salient aspect of the film is the inability of their offspring to successfully have children and/or replicate a nuclear family of their own.

The film centers largely on the narratives of three siblings who are unable to successfully reproduce the nuclear family, which I consider comparable to *queer subjectivity* in as much as the children implicitly reject heteronormative gender and sexual norms (Pérez 2009).

Latino fathers are also portrayed as either domineering men who are stern and strive to uphold traditional family values; as humble men who work hard and may have some authority in the domestic sphere, but not in their work environment; or as failed men—those who have no authority in the domestic or work space and who are what Ramírez Berg refers to as "psychologically flawed" and "cannot succeed no matter how hard they try" (2002, p. 121). The father figure in *Mi familia*, José (played by Eduardo López Rojas), would most likely fall into the first two categories whereas the father figure in the film *Real Women Have Curves* (2002) Raúl García (played by Jorge Cervera Jr.) might fall into the middle one. While José is a humble, hard worker who attempts to instill traditional family values in his children, Raúl is a humble, hard worker who is not adamant about his daughter following traditional family customs. In *Real Women*, the mother, Carmen García (played by Lupe Ontiveros), functions as the female patriarch (Pérez 2009) who attempts to impose traditional family values on the children. It is important to note that the fathers in these films have to contend with the way their subjectivities are circumscribed by their relationship to the dominant culture. Their roles as fathers are often shaped by extenuating circumstances—the need to work long hours, or separation due to economic or immigration issues. A good example of the latter is Reyna Grande's father in *The Distance Between Us*. In the memoir, Grande refers to her father as "the man behind the glass" (2012, p. 10) because she must rely on the memory of her father to keep him close because his extended absence has left her without other ways of remembering him. He remains fixed in a certain place and time. Eventually, "the man behind the glass" becomes a fantasy figure that is always inaccessible—a lesson Grande learns when she is finally reunited with her father after several years. In fact, the title of the memoir and "the man behind the glass" remain markers of the impossible relationship between the two that ensues even when they live under the same roof.

Conflicts between a Latinx father and his children are commonly depicted when the relationship between the two is portrayed in cultural production. This tension is often rooted in the father's unsuccessful attempts to uphold family traditions, which would typically involve ensuring his children get married to a member of the opposite sex and begin establishing a family and a home of their own so the family lineage may continue. I argue this is also one of the main conflicts between queer Chicanx, Mexican, and Latinx males and their fathers. Since queer males do not typically uphold the expectations of their culture—namely, to reproduce the family—they are often ostracized, ridiculed, or marked as failed men.

Queer Chicanx and Latinx Males and Their Fathers

In Rigoberto González's memoir, *Butterfly Boy*, the distance between the author as a young adult and his father is rather stark even when they are in close physical proximity. In the book, González and his father are placed in an uncomfortable scenario: after years of living apart and going their separate ways, the two decide to take a long bus ride to visit the family in Mexico. However, they quickly discover that despite being related by blood, the two are markedly different, especially now that González has obtained a college degree. The two consistently argue and fail to see eye to eye throughout their trip. González clearly does not identify with his father. Instead, his father is portrayed as the Other. In one passage, González confesses: "I wish he could read my mind to spare me the energy of having to put it into words, everything from my resentment for his having left me to the fact that I'm gay and that he has nothing do with that" (2006, p. 107). González obviously resents his father and is unable to forgive him for not being a successful father. The author and his father are marked by a series of traits that differentiate the two. At the time in which the present-day narrative takes place, González has a college education and has access to economic resources whereas his father remains trapped in a working-class social location.

There are several father figures in the works of gay Chicano and Latino authors who can help shed some light on the complexities of the relationship between the two. In the works of John Rechy, the father figure is often absent or plays a minor or secondary role. When present, he fits the image of the domineering father who rules with an iron fist. A good example of which is the father of the unnamed protagonist in *City of Night*, who we now know is largely based on Rechy's own father. The unnamed protagonist describes this relationship in the following way: "Once, yes, there had been a warmth toward that strange red-faced man—and there were still the sudden flashes of tenderness…" (1963, p. 14). He then adds that there was also a "terror" between the two that his mother never understood. Later, he describes the violence the family had to endure: "My father's violence erupted unpredictably over anything. In an instant he overturns the table— food and plates thrust to the floor. He would smash bottles, menacing us with the sharpfanged edges" (p. 15). Violent imagery of this nature is repeated in *We the Animals* (2011), by Justin Torres; Pap, the father figure, is domineering and violent. Violent fathers are also present in the works of Michael Nava, especially those in his Henry Rios Mystery Series. Fathers in the short stories that comprise *Everything Begins and Ends at the Kentucky Club* by Benjamín Alire Sáenz are similarly portrayed. In the collection, one will find several examples of either absent or domineering fathers who rule with an iron fist. A good example is the father in the short story "Sometimes the Rain." Ernesto, the young male protagonist in this story, explains how he became the brunt of his father's violence: "My youngest brother died of meningitis. My father's grief and disappointment turned to rage. The rage was pointed in my direction" (2012b, p. 128). Although the above include some works of fiction, as I pointed out earlier, there are some parallels between authors' lives and those of fathers described in the texts. These narratives are useful for an examination of the relationships between queer Chicanx and Latinx males and their fathers. They can be seen as testimonios of complex and vexed relations in flux, with tensions brewing and erupting often. These sons search for ways of being in a society where they confront racism, homophobia, xenophobia, and patriarchy on a daily basis.

What remains a constant theme in these texts despite the gender or sexual identity of the children is the attempt by Chicano, Latino, and Mexican fathers to establish and transmit gender norms to their children. There are several examples of these processes in Chicanx and Latinx literary texts as well. For example, in Rudolfo Anaya's *Bless Me, Ultima* (1972), the father is invested in raising his son as a Mares—the father's side of the family, which is associated with several masculine characteristics—whereas Antonio's mother attempts to raise him as a Luna—marked by feminine traits. In *Rethinking Chicana/o and Latina/o Popular Culture* (2009), I argue that Antonio is neither a Mares nor a Luna, but something in between, akin to queer subjectivity. A similar phenomenon happens between the young male protagonist in both José Antonio Villarreal's *Pocho* (1959) and Tomás Rivera's *…y no se lo tragó la tierra* (1971). These portrayals closely resemble the dynamics between father and son highlighted in Mirandé's work. In the latter, men were asked to identify the males they most admired and it was found the most educated men were more likely to select nonfamily members—friends, historical figures, college professors—instead of their own fathers (Mirandé 1998). This dynamic is evident in all of the texts mentioned thus far. In *Bless Me, Ultima*, Antonio identifies with Ultima, a curandera, instead of his mother or his father—a social location that lies in between the two diametrically opposing gender tropes that run throughout the narrative. Similarly, in *Pocho*, Richard Rubio identifies with writers and other individuals who are versed in art and culture and engage in nonheteronormative social and sexual acts—a professor who is also a poet, gay male creative writing class-mates, Joe Pete, and others—but he rejects his father as a role model. These young men disassociate from their fathers and search for father fig-ures and role models in other people.

Because the relationship between father and son is often mired not only by generational differences, but multiple cultural differences, it is rare to find examples of successful mappings of normative gender and sexual norms onto younger males. In other words, although fathers in literature and film may attempt to instill cultural, gender, and sexual norms in their sons, it is rare to find examples of a successful transmission of such norms. I suspect this has something to do with cultural differences (Mexican vs. American, for example), differences in the educational achievements of the two, socioeconomic tensions (working class vs. middle to upper class, for example), and sexual identity. Any one or any combination of these factors may facilitate the type of gender and sexual transgressions we wit-ness between young Chicano, Mexican, and Latino males and their fathers in cultural texts. Moreover, as Alexander Doty suggests, in popular culture queer narratives and cultural texts are economically viable in ways that heteronormative ones often are not (Doty **2000**). This might help explain why narratives like *City of Night*, *We the Animals*, and *Pocho* have also been commercially successful. The narratives and memoirs described above reveal that Chicano, Mexican, and Latino males who surpassed the educa-tional levels of their fathers tend to veer from the heteronormative cus-toms prevalent in their respective families.

In the short story "Sometimes the Rain," the protagonist, Neto, finds his friend and erotic interest, Brian, beaten in the face and discovers that Brian's father was the culprit. They then have an exchange about how their violent dads hate them and Neto suggests, "Maybe our dads went to the same father school" (Alire Sáenz 2012a, p. 142). Neto's comment underscores that many males learn how to be fathers from their own fathers or other father figures—uncles and grandfathers, for example. This is the "father school" to which these individuals typically have access. Like gender, fathering is a learned behavior and something that is not normally taught in a formal institutional setting. In his cross-cultural analysis, "Fathering: Paradoxes, Contradictions, and Dilemmas," Scott Coltrane explains the difference between *fathering* and *fatherhood*: "*Fathering* (in contrast to *fatherhood*) refers more directly to what men do with and for children. Although folk beliefs suggest that fathering entails behaviors fixed by reproductive biology, humans must learn how to parent" (2006, p. 449). Latino fathers typically learn how to be fathers from other men, not from any type of formal education or training. And if their fathers aren't present in the household, these men often learn from other family members or from cultural cues they receive in the media and popular culture. What makes the latter somewhat precarious is that the identities of brown and black men in the media are often circumscribed by narrow and negative stereotypes. Latino masculinity in US popular culture and the media in general is often associated with negative characteristics. Despite Mirandé's study, which highlights the cultural differences between perceptions of what it means to be "macho" in the United States, *machismo* is now imbued with a number of negative characteristics, like exaggerated masculinity, authoritarianism, and violence (Mirandé 1998). As Rudolfo Anaya contends in his essay, "I'm the King: The Macho Image," the macho image has both positive and negative traits associated with it: "Being macho is essentially a learned behavior; as such it is a conditioned behavior. We males learn to act 'manly' from other males around us; the 'macho' that preceded us was learned from the cultures from which it evolved. Many forces impinge on the Hispanic/Latino cultures, so throughout history, machismo—or the conditioning of male behavior— has attracted all sorts of positive and negative elements" (1996, p. 59). Indeed, Mirandé points out that being "macho" in Mexican culture has positive traits associated with it—honor, respect, and courage, for example (1998, p. 78).

In addition to the varying notions of "macho," Mirandé points out that there are multiple ways in which Latino men express their gender: "Latino men do not constitute a homogenous, monolithic, unvarying mass, as was depicted in the traditional model. This suggests that there is not one masculine mode but a variety of modalities and masculinities that are not only different, but often contradictory" (1998, p. 15). For Mirandé, masculinity is context specific and continually shifting. Similarly, in "The Latin Phallus," Ilán Stavans highlights the way Latino men learn to be shape shifters. He describes his own experience growing up in Mexican culture and witnessing how males demonstrated acts of affection between one another. However, such acts became taboo after a certain age: "My father had taught me to show affection in public. When departing, he would kiss me without inhibition. But as I became an adolescent, I heard my friends whisper. Was I secretly a deviant?" (1996, p. 153). Evidently, fathers and their male offspring are taught to feel shame about showing affection in public after the child reaches a certain age, a phenomenon that typically is less taboo between fathers and their daughters as the latter get older.

Like the examples from literature and film that I highlight above, the distance between the father and his offspring is a salient aspect of these cultural texts. Chicano, Mexican, and Latino fathers, whether physically present or not, often do not form close emotional bonds with their sons, for a number of reasons, which research suggests does have implications on gender identity and expression. Scott Coltrane's research builds on the work of anthropologists Barry Hewlett (2000) and Nancy Chodorow (1974), which suggests that when fathers are involved in the care of male infants the children develop an intimate knowledge of masculinity. However, when fathers are not present, the boys lack a clearer sense of masculinity (Coltrane 2006). It is this phenomenon that presents an interesting lens from which to examine the relationship between queer Chicano, Mexican, and Latino males and their fathers. Young males are often expected to learn gender norms from their fathers, but what happens when a young man does not have a father who is truly present in his life?

Disidentification and Distancing: Reconfiguring Gender Norms

As mentioned above, a common theme in narratives that describe the relationship between queer Chicano, Mexican, and Latino males and their fathers is the distance between them. This distance may be emotional, physical, or both. The distance may be by choice or due to inevitable circumstances that do not permit the formation of close bonds between the two. Regardless of sexual identity or gender identification, the depiction of young men and their fathers is typically one that is rooted in the son distancing himself from the father, and not wanting to be like him. Disidentification is a common theme and practice. José Esteban Muñoz defines the process as one that "scrambles and reconstructs the encoded message of a cultural text in a fashion that both exposes the encoded message's universalizing and exclusionary machinations and recircuits its workings to account for, include, and empower minority identities and identifications" (1999, p. 31). Therefore, disidentification permits young males to redefine gender roles and expression for themselves. Moreover, as Mirandé's study indicates, it is not the case that young males merely abandon the idea of searching for a father figure; they often look to other father figures as models—nonfamily members and historical figures, for example (Mirandé 1998). Sometimes women fill this gap, especially working, single mothers who assume the role of primary provider and protector of the family. These processes facilitate a reconfiguration of gender norms as sons search for and embody alternate forms of gender expression and sexual identification.

In essence, the narratives examined above provide alternative ways of seeing gender and masculinity that move beyond the stereotypes found in popular culture. Queer Chicanx and Latinx men reconfigure masculinity in many ways. These narratives underscore the ways in which men sometimes appropriate other forms of masculinity or ways of expressing their gender. Whereas their fathers are sometimes emasculated by the dominant culture, their children, despite their sexual identities, are often able to replicate some valued masculine norms, like financial security and taking care of the family. They are able to appropriate some norms that allow for the articulation of new forms of masculinity. Evident in these narratives is that as these men achieve higher education goals and move up the socio-economic ladder, they replicate some of the roles that a father or husband would typically play in a family. In John Rechy's memoir, *About My Life and the Kept Woman*, the author describes some of the things he did to improve the life of his mother and his siblings. In one passage, he contends, "I had to protect my mother" (2008, p. 42). Rechy, like many other queer Chicanx and Latinx males, becomes a surrogate husband or father for his family, providing physical protection and financial assistance when possible. This is just one way in which one might witness queer Chicanx, Mexican, and Latinx males assuming roles and developing characteristics associated with fathering.

There are several examples in literary texts of the way the social standing of sons, including gay sons, exceeds the social standing of their fathers. One might expect this in Chicanx and Latinx literature because the writers themselves are often already defying normative gender codes by engaging in a task that is largely deemed unmanly. As I have argued elsewhere, writers or the act of or preoccupation with reading and writing are largely associated with femininity in Chicanx and Latinx literary texts, regardless of one's sexual identity. In John Rechy's *City of Night*, for example, the unnamed protagonist goes out of his way to hide his intellect, his interest in reading, and the fact that he wrote some of the books that appear on the bookshelves of some of his clients in order to reproduce a form of masculinity that is more widely accepted and desirable in the given social context.

LIKE FATHER, LIKE QUEER SON: A CLOSER LOOK
IN THE MIRROR

While queer Chicanx and Latinx males may engage in disidentificatory processes when it comes to their fathers, there are often biological and behavioral factors the two have in common that should not be overlooked. Try as they may, biologically related sons and fathers cannot discount their resemblances and genetic links. As underscored above, in cultural production there are few examples of queer Chicanx and Latinx males who identify their fathers as their role models. However, I contend queer Chicanx and Latinx males are not so different from their fathers although it is difficult to find examples in cultural production of queer Chicanx and Latinx males who *recognize* they are like their fathers. I suspect this has more to do with their *desire* not to be like their fathers. In reality, these men may not be all that different from one another, despite the nonheteronormative gender and sexual behavior in which the son may engage.

In the documentary film *El canto del colibrí* (2015), directed by Marco Castro-Bojórquez, one will find testimonies of fathers who come to terms with the realities of their queer children's lives. Whereas more traditional narratives between fathers and their queer children center primarily on disidentificatory practices, what I find most compelling about this documentary is the way it represents a progressive response by fathers to their children's coming out stories and their nonheteronormative gender and sexual identities. These narratives highlight the degree to which a father might have a more nuanced view of his child's gender and sexual identity. In a couple of scenes, the fathers comment on the hope and desire they have for their gay sons to be active agents when engaging in erotic acts. They reiterate the common belief in Latinx cultures that while men who are penetrated are considered stereotypically gay, those who penetrate are less likely to be. The sons do not reveal the sexual positions they assume or prefer, adding an element of mystery and providing the fathers with the freedom to create their own narratives about the roles their sons assume in erotic exchanges. Nevertheless, I see discourses like these as attempts to negotiate and create an identity that recognizes unique *and* common traits between the two figures. The two appear to be redefining and negotiating a form of masculinity that allows the sons to engage in same-sex acts while remaining their father's son, recognizing physical and behavioral characteristics that the two share. One will find other progressive responses and interactions between Chicanx and Latinx fathers and their queer sons in texts like Alire Sáenz's *Aristotle and Dante Discover the Secrets of the Universe* and the short film directed by Adelina Anthony and written by Ernesto Javier Martínez, *La Serenata* (2019). However, I contend that in Chicanx and Latinx cultural production fathers are overwhelmingly depicted using the negative stereotypes I outline above, which underscores the need to present more nuanced and positive portrayals of them.

My initial title for this essay was "Masculinities in Flux." However, after delving further into this topic, the theme of children discovering that they are more like their fathers than they expected continued to arise, regardless of the child's gender or sexual identity. I reworked this essay and chose "Like Father, Like Queer Son?" because I believe that despite the common narrative of Chicanx and Latinx children disidentifying with their parents, children will often find visages of their parents when they look in the mirror and examine themselves more closely. Beyond biological inheritances, sons often emulate the behaviors of fathers, even if they weren't raised by them.

In *Madre and I: A Memoir of Our Immigrant Lives* Guillermo Reyes describes the first and only time he met his father. As an illegitimate child, Reyes was not raised by his father, and Reyes' mother rarely shared information with him about his father. Even though his biological parents never married or lived together (his father was married to another woman and had his own family), Reyes' mother, María Graciela Cáceres, insisted her only child take his father's first and last name. María Graciela Cáceres, like her mother, was an illegitimate child herself who never bore her father's surname. María insisted Reyes' birth was planned and that her child was *un hijo natural*. In Chile, *hijos naturales* are children conceived by women who are recognized by their fathers; the use of the father's surname is the litmus test used to verify recognition. Although his mother and father never married or lived under the same roof, Reyes' mother insisted on controlling the narrative in order to protect their social standing. As Reyes recounts, "The illegitimate child became *el hijo natural*, a linguistic improvement, a child born of nature" (2010, p. 36). Reyes' mother employed these tactics to ensure the father recognized Reyes and to prevent her son from being marked as an illegitimate child. She also wanted her son to be educated, like his father—an erudite literature instructor who was teaching night school when the two met; she was his student. Reyes' mother never earned a higher education degree and stemmed from a long line of illegitimate children. Her actions were designed to prevent her son from the fate she inherited from her own mother.

Reyes and his mother left Chile when he was ten years old; he was raised in the United States and developed a strong interest in film, literature, and theatre; he only met his father once, when he was fourteen years old. Reyes returned to Chile at that age for a visit and finally had the opportunity to meet his father. When he did, he was surprised by his father's swarthiness and height: "He was a short, pudgy man, much darker than I expected, with a brown tinge on his skin that appeared Polynesian. I could live with illegitimacy, but at the time it seemed a greater shock to me that my father had turned out to be nonwhite ... I had not counted on this particular discomfort. It bothered me, and it silenced me" (p. 44). Reyes' discomfort stems from the misrecognition of this stranger as his father. As he explains, he had never seen a picture of his father and his mother never described him to Reyes (p. 44). This was the only encounter Reyes ever had with his father; when he returned to Chile at the age of nineteen, he learned his father had died the previous year of "a rare form of leukemia after a long struggle" (p. 47).

Despite never really knowing his father and living in separate countries, Reyes and his father had several things in common including the same name, political beliefs, and passion for theatre and literature as well as having become educators after acquiring higher education degrees. Once in the United States, Reyes eventually obtained a BA in Italian and an MFA in theatre and became an accomplished playwright and university professor. In 2011 he met his older half-brother, Gonzalo Reyes, for the first time and was surprised to learn that Gonzalo and his immediate family recognized physical *and* behavioral characteristics that Reyes shared with his father. For example, having learned Reyes was an accomplished playwright and theatre professor, they told him his father had taught high school theater classes and directed school plays, which Reyes does to this day, "You inherited the artistic side because none of the other children of our father wrote plays or directed them like he did" Gonzalo told his brother (Reyes 2019). Reyes learned that like himself, his father was a writer and often tried to isolate himself from others to write plays and short stories. He also learned that some members of his father's family were exiled in Italy, which led Reyes to question why at a young age he had developed an interest in learning Italian and studying Italian culture. Reyes insisted he was unaware of his similarities with his father and his father's family until after 2011. While these resemblances between father and son may seem coincidental, I believe they invite us to explore ways in which sons might share qualities with their fathers, even when fathers are uninvolved in their upbringing. I contend that if we took a closer look at our fathers and their lives, shared traits between fathers and sons might reveal themselves in a similar fashion.

These narratives suggest that despite gender variances, queer Chicanx, Mexican, and Latinx males may emulate their fathers in more ways than they think they do. There remains a dearth of studies or depictions in cultural production of queer Chicanx and Latinx males and the way in which they resemble their fathers. Nevertheless, the examples cited above are intended to open the door and invite others to explore this realm, in the same way that this essay and this collection open the door for exploring topics that we often avoid.

Personal Reflections

Up until this point, I have avoided talking about my own relationship with my father. However, this essay would not feel complete without a few reflections and revelations on this matter. Like many other queer Chicano males, I grew up without my father. I was the middle child in a family of three boys. My parents divorced when I was nine years old, and my mother never remarried. My father was a terrific father to my two brothers and me when my parents were married. However, he was not the best husband to my mother. Besides being a heavy drinker on the weekends, he was a *mujeriego* (womanizer), and my mother eventually stopped letting him get away with it. My father lost his home, his wife, and custody of his boys. We were able to see him on weekends, but no longer living with his sons made it difficult for even a good father to have an intimate relationship with his sons. I was fortunate to have two parents who, even though they couldn't remain married or communicate civilly with one another, demonstrated unconditional love for my brothers and me. Both of my parents always expressed immense love and interest in caring for my brothers and me. They never abused or neglected us.

I often saw my parents as being very different from me. My father was especially not like me because he didn't really raise me, despite his willingness to do so. The vexed relationship my parents had did not permit my father to be the type of father I believe he wished he could be. Nevertheless, as he and I age, I find resemblances between us, not just the life he lived, but his voice, his character, our mannerisms. For some of these I am eternally grateful. My father is and has always been a great man in spite of his flaws. He is very well respected in the family and in his community, and he is genuinely a good human being. He is generous, compassionate, and loving.

As a single mom, my mother worked long, hard hours in the fields or as a seamstress and often could not be home for us, but we never questioned whether or not she loved us. My mother had no choice but to assume the role of father figure for my brothers and me. She became the primary provider and protector of the family. She adopted a form of masculinity that shaped me during my formative years, one that reconfigured gender norms beyond strict masculine-feminine binaries. In my conversations with other queer Chicano and Latino men, I've noticed that anytime we try to talk about our fathers, the conversation inevitably shifts to a conversation about our mothers. For me, this is natural to do because my mother was a father figure. Nevertheless, to avoid a divergence, I will do my best not to discuss my mother any more than I already have. This essay is about queer Chicanx and Latinx males and their fathers. We must be willing to go there.

I feel fortunate to have a father who did his best to try to see his sons on weekends and who attempted to play the fatherly roles expected of men when he could. My father is smart and remains a good man whom I admire unconditionally. He never had a chance to get a formal education. He obtained his General Education Diploma (GED) when he was in his thirties while he was working full time, raising a family, and literally building our home. He was a landscaper for the City of Phoenix, and later, a maintenance man for the community college I attended when I was eighteen. He always worked outside doing manual labor, but he also always did his job proudly. One of the earliest memories I have of my father in the workplace was a school trip my class took to the Phoenix Art Museum when I was in grade school. When we went to the museum, my father was working with his crew on the museum grounds. He wore a green city uniform, and by this time, he had worked his way up to being the foreman of the crew. I remember being proud of him. My father was quite handsome in his uniform, and my classmates recognized this. My father acknowledged me as I acknowledged him. I was never ashamed of my father or the work he did. Whether my dad was mowing a lawn or sweeping the basketball court during halftime at a basketball game at my community college, he did his job with great pride. He also treated everyone with the utmost respect and kindness. As a result, everybody admired and respected him, which made it easy for me to be proud of him. Nevertheless, I knew that I didn't want to follow in my father's footsteps; he had obviously instilled in me that if I went to school, I could have better working conditions and a better life.

When I was a teenager, I often wondered what my life would have been like had my parents not divorced. I know we would not have been thrown into abject poverty, and my father would have played a much more instrumental role in my upbringing. To this day, I wonder if I would still be as queer as I am. I know it's an unpopular stance, but I vividly remember being erotically attracted to girls when I was a child. I remember ogling adult magazines and finding myself erotically charged by women. But I also recall ogling magazines, like *Hustler*, which I found under my father's bed when he lived as a bachelor. I soon began recognizing the beauty of the male body and found myself erotically attracted to men. It may just be a coincidence that I recognized this same-sex attraction after my parents divorced, but somewhere in the back of my mind I've associated the two incidents with one another. Whereas some queer Chicanx, Mexican, and Latinx males might remember same-sex thoughts and attraction at a very early age, I was a relatively late bloomer. For the most part, I naturally exhibited traits that would be deemed normal for a young heterosexual male. My voracious appetite for learning was the one thing that set me apart from most males in my family and community, not my gender expression or my sexuality.

In the short amount of time that my father lived with us, he showed us boys how to camp, fish, hunt, change a tire, change the oil in the car, play sports, build things, and do all the "normal" things that boys were supposed to do in the cultural context in which I was raised. He was also the one who encouraged me to keep studying; he dubbed me the smart one at an early age. He facilitated the spelling bees, recognized my aptitude for learning, and fostered my educational advancement in the limited ways he could. He recognized that I was *different* from my brothers, a label that went part and parcel with not following in his footsteps, or those of my brothers.

Like my father, uncles, and male cousins, my brothers began having children with their girlfriends and eventually dropped out of high school when they were teenagers. It was the norm. There were no males or females in my family who even had a high school diploma. Thus, ensconcing myself in school, rejecting the gang members who attempted to induct me into their group, rejecting the girls who tried to get me to seduce them, and choosing books over booze and drugs marked me as *queer as fuck* even though I did not really engage in same-sex relations until I was twenty-one. In all other regards—my appearance, mannerisms, and demeanor—I was a cisgender male. Nevertheless, my actions defied the gender codes that were used as a litmus test for assessing acceptable forms of masculinity and male behavior in my family and culture. I learned to play all the ball games: baseball, basketball, kickball, and football. I learned to fish, change the oil in the car, lay bricks, hunt, drive a 1957 Chevy pickup truck with a standard transmission, and work in various manual labor jobs throughout my childhood. But I also learned to read novels, studied French, fell in love with math, and befriended geeks who held similar interests.

One of the most important lessons I learned from my father was that I must learn things quickly; he also showed me that the best way to learn was hands-on. As early as seven years old, I remember being underneath the car, tools in hand, trying to change the oil. I recall working with my father and brothers on the weekends mowing lawns in nice neighborhoods and toiling away in the fields. These experiences instilled a work ethic in me that to this day I admire in myself; it was one of my father's defining characteristics. Since I was a child, there has not been a time in my life when I have not worked. And I have never been afraid of hard work. When I was a child, if ever I believed I couldn't do something my father asked of me, I would yelp, "But Pa, I don't know how to change the oil in the car." Or, "Pa, I can't start the lawn mower." My dad's response was always the same: *Pues, vale más que aprendas devolín* (Well, you better learn fast). He would allow me to struggle with fixing and learning things on my own, but he would also provide the guidance I needed when necessary. This approach was also the way he encouraged me to study when I was a kid. He staged the spelling bees and bought us an expensive set of Encyclopedia Britannica that we obviously couldn't afford. He bought us clothes we needed to go to school even though we had to put them on layaway and pay for them in small installments. He was side-by-side with us underneath the car, making sure we could identify parts and fix them. However, these lessons only lasted until I was nine years old, until the divorce happened. After that, we were thrown into abject poverty: no more spelling bees, no more new clothes for school, no more stability, and no more father in our home.

When my parents lived together, they loved and fought ferociously. I remember one Saturday night my parents went to a wedding reception together. We stayed home under the care of a young uncle. Both of my parents had been drinking heavily at the party; they had driven in separate cars because they took other relatives with them to the wedding. They left the party around the same time, but my mother got pulled over by the police; she was taken to the police station for driving under the influence. However, this was the 1970s, and cops were much easier on women than men during this era. The police didn't arrest my mother or charge her with anything. While at the police station, she called my father and asked him to pick her up. My father had arrived at home by this time; my brothers and I were fast asleep and knew nothing about what was transpiring. My father got upset because my mother had been pulled over for drinking and driving. He decided to jump in his 1957 Chevy pickup and drive to Casa Grande, where his parents lived, approximately fifty miles south of Phoenix. Low and behold, he got pulled over for drinking and driving on his way to Casa Grande, and he was not as lucky as my mother. He was arrested and charged. Both my parents spent that night at the jailhouse, and our lives were never the same. My father lost his driver's license, wife, home, and the boys.

As my father grew older, he settled down and eventually "found God." When we were young, we observed the typical Catholic traditions: catechism, first holy communion, mass on Sundays, and so on. But as my father grew older and more religious, he began spending much more time with the Church and doing things for God. I was also religious as a teenager, and there was a point in my life when I considered joining the priesthood; I even researched seminaries. Besides my affinity for the pageantry of the Church, becoming a priest seemed like the best way to be able to continue my education since I was from such a poor family. I opted for an alternative way to pay for school: I joined the US Navy. Besides the financial motivations, I realize now that I was running away from home and ensconcing myself in homosocial spaces in order to avoid following in the footsteps that were expected of males in my family—to get married and have children. I also needed to explore the sexual urges that I had for men and I had begun to question the existence of God altogether. Being away from my family made it possible for me to explore these other realms.

I eventually came to terms with my sexuality and my atheism. I first tried coming out to my father as an atheist when I was approximately twenty-three years old, but it didn't go over so well; to this date, we have never even had the "Pa, I'm gay" talk. Nevertheless, I know he knows, and both my sexuality and my atheism remain topics we don't discuss.

Although these silences create a gulf between my father and me, it is not much different from the chasm that existed between us when I was a boy and he lived elsewhere—a gulf that never existed between my mother and me. Nevertheless, I never question whether or not my father loves me. He doesn't have to accept me as his gay, atheist son. For him, having a son who has been successful in life in ways he had never imagined is more than enough.

Like most Chicanx and Latinx males, I had no desire to follow in my father's footsteps. However, as I grow older, I recognize traits from my mother *and* father in me—some I cherish; others worry me. It is inevitable. I've learned to accept that whether I like it or not, I *am* like my father—my habits, my physicality, and my general way of being often resemble his. Like my father, I have been promiscuous and harmed those I love through inappropriate actions. I am imperfect in many of the same ways that he was. However, I also recognize that my father did his best to raise my brothers and me under very difficult circumstances. He could have abandoned us. Instead, he took the bus across the city of Phoenix to "pick us up" when it was his turn to see us. With money so scarce, our outings sometimes involved taking the bus to Phoenix Sky Harbor Airport and watching the planes land and take off; I had no idea where the planes came from or where they were going; I didn't know anyone who had ever flown on an actual plane somewhere. But the planes came and went from this city we called home—we were stuck there; they were not. Planes would eventually serve as a vehicle for my own escape, my own transgressions, but as a child, they were merely a fantasy—dragons with large metal wings that landed and took off.

I don't believe children are truly unlike their biological parents, no matter how hard they may wish or try not to be like them, no matter what their gender or sexual identity may be, and no matter who primarily raised them. Certainly, genetics play an important role in shaping physical characteristics; we cannot discount biological inheritances. However, this study suggests that we may also emulate our parents in other ways—their behavior and other ways of being. I must admit, the things I like most about myself now are also the things I admire most about my father. He is smart and remains among the kindest of human beings I've ever known. He is selfless, hardworking, well-rounded, intelligent, and a beautiful human being overall. People love my father because he exudes love and kindness wherever he goes. He is down-to-earth, friendly, and warm-hearted. I now do my best to be like my father. Instead of running away from him, I find myself striving to be like him. A part of me recognizes that I am like my father in many ways, and I feel quite lucky that, above all, my father knew how to continually demonstrate unconditional love for his children and others. I hope I am able to do the same in my thoughts and deeds.

When I look in the mirror, I recognize my father. He is there…with me, in the same way he was there with me underneath the car, showing me how to repair things I believed I couldn't. He's in the imperfections I perceive among my own physical and personal traits—the blotches on my skin, my crooked teeth, my tenacity, my stubbornness, my kindness, and others. He's present in my life even when he is not physically in it. Perhaps the search for a father figure beyond our own fathers is a search in vain. Certainly, we will find mentors and father figures who are very much unlike our fathers. However, no matter how much we try to escape the specters of our fathers, they are present and their influence is unprecedented, whether they were present in our lives or not. Perhaps we can learn to recognize and embrace the qualities in our fathers that are actually good for us, even if our fathers are imperfect, like us.

Conclusion

As I have shown, although the depiction of father-son relationships found in cultural texts may be shaped by negative stereotypes, the relationship between queer Chicanx and Latinx males and their fathers is much more complex and multifaceted. Although there is no universal experience, this analysis demonstrates that there are commonalities in the way these relationships are depicted in Chicanx and Latinx cultural production. The narratives that describe these relationships reveal common and important processes in the way young males disidentify from their fathers and identify with alternate father figures. These processes often result in a reconfiguration of gender norms. While queer Chicano, Mexicano, and Latino males may attempt to reconstitute gender norms that align with a new identity, if they look closely enough in the mirror, they will often find their fathers reflected in the mirror. And whether we like it or not, we *are* our fathers in more ways than we are typically willing to accept. The old adage, "Like father, like son," is not dependent upon one's gender or sexuality. Instead, the relationship between the two should be seen as a complex matrix with inevitable links between two people who share several traits in common.

REFERENCES

Alire Saénz, B. (2012a). *Aristotle and Dante Discover the Secrets of the Universe.* Simon and Schuster.

Alire Saénz, B. (2012b). *Everything Begins and Ends at the Kentucky Club.* Cinco Puntos Press.

Anaya, R. (1972). *Bless Me, Ultima.* Tonatiuh International.

Anaya, R. (1996). I'm the King: The Macho Image. In R. González (Ed.), *Muy Macho: Latino Men Confront Their Manhood* (pp. 57–73). Doubleday.

Coltrane, S. (2006). Fathering: Paradoxes, Contradictions, and Dilemmas. In M. S. Kimmel & M. A. Messner (Eds.), *Men's Lives* (7th ed., pp. 448–465). Pearson.

Doty, A. (2000). *Flaming Classics: Queering the Film Canon.* Routledge.

González, R. (1996). My Literary Fathers. In R. González (Ed.), *Muy Macho: Latino Men Confront Their Manhood* (pp. 165–185). Anchor.

González, R. (2006). *Butterfly Boy: Memories of a Chicano Mariposa.* University of Wisconsin Press.

Grande, R. (2012). *The Distance Between Us: A Memoir.* Washington Square Press.

Mirandé, A. (1998). *Hombres y Machos: Masculinity and Latino Culture.* Westview Press.

Muñoz, J. E. (1999). *Disidentifications: Queers of Color and the Performance of Politics.* University of Minnesota Press.

Pérez, D. E. (2009). *Rethinking Chicana/o and Latina/o Popular Culture.* Palgrave Macmillan.

Ramírez Berg, C. (2002). *Latino Images in Film: Stereotypes, Subversion, Resistance.* University of Texas Press.

Rechy, J. (1963). *City of Night.* Grove Press.

Rechy, J. (2008). *About My Life and the Kept Woman: A Memoir.* Grove Press.

Reyes, G. A. (2010). *Madre and I: A Memoir of Our Immigrant Lives.* University of Wisconsin Press.

Reyes, G. A. (2019). Interview by the Author. Phoenix, Arizona, 28 June.

Rivera, T. (1971). *...y no se lo tragó la tierra / ...And the Earth Did Not Devour Him* (Evangelina Vigil-Piñón, Trans.). Arte Público Press.

Stavans, I. (1996). The Latin Phallus. In R. González (Ed.), *Muy Macho: Latino Men Confront Their Manhood* (pp. 143–164). Anchor.

Torres, J. (2011). *We the Animals.* Mariner Books.

Villarreal, J. A. (1959). *Pocho: A Novel.* New York: Doubleday.

FILMOGRAPHY

El canto del colbrí. Written and Directed by Marco Castro-Bojórquez. Produced by José Alfaro, Katie Cruz and Liz Salinas, 2015. Film.

La Serenata. Written by Ernesto Martínez and Directed by Adelina Anthony. Produced by Aderisa Productions and Rebozo Boy Productions, 2019. Film.

My Family/Mi familia. Written and Directed by Gregory Nava. Produced by Francis Ford Coppola, Anna Thomas, and New Line Cinema, 1995. Film.

Real Women Have Curves. Written and Directed by Patricia Cardoso in Collaboration with Josefina López. Produced by George LaVoo, HBO Films and New Market Films, 2002. Film.

CHAPTER 28

My Padrino

Xuan Carlos Espinoza-Cuellar

Abstract A cherished Santero father figure, the author's *padrino* (godfather), brings hope and healing into his life.

My godfather is an organic intellectual
With endless remedies for heartache
His best remedy so far is his embrace
And when he says to me "my son, everything will be alright"

My godfather is an organic intellectual
He knows hundreds and hundreds of sacred plants
He sings to them, summons their energies
He says to me "*la primera alabanza es el canto*" (the first form of worship is song)

My godfather is an organic intellectual
His mind is filled with eternal sacred chants
I bow down, forehead to the floor
I salute him, "*dide*" (rise up) he says, and lifts my soul

X. C. Espinoza-Cuellar (✉)
University of Nevada Las Vegas, Las Vegas, NV, USA

© The Author(s), under exclusive license to Springer Nature Switzerland AG 2021
A. R. Del Castillo, G. Güido (eds.), *Fathers, Fathering, and Fatherhood*, Palgrave Studies in Literary Anthropology,
https://doi.org/10.1007/978-3-030-60877-4_28

CHAPTER 29

God Is Never Ashamed of Us

Xuan Carlos Espinoza-Cuellar

Abstract A youth is curious about why his grandfather, who helped raise him, attends church in a particular way.

My *abuelo* (grandfather) is a kind man
Olive skin
Curly hair
My grandpa said "ask me anything"
So I asked
My *abuelo* taught me how to walk
How to feed squirrels
One day we went to church
He was wearing *huaraches* (leather sandals)
And I asked him
"Why don't you wear shoes instead?"
"Because I'm going to the house of god, and he sees us as we are—poor, brown, Indian, fat—God is never ashamed of us."

X. C. Espinoza-Cuellar (✉)
University of Nevada Las Vegas, Las Vegas, NV, USA

A. R. Del Castillo, G. Güido (eds.), *Fathers, Fathering, and Fatherhood*, Palgrave Studies in Literary Anthropology, https://doi.org/10.1007/978-3-030-60877-4_29

257

CHAPTER 30

You Will Love

Xuan Carlos Espinoza-Cuellar

Abstract In an act of faith and fatherhood, the narrator in this poem conveys to a queer young man, whom he refers to as *mijo* (my son), daily-life commonsense as well as truths, observations, and advice regarding same-sex relationships with men. The narrator tells the young man never to forget the importance of family, mother, grandmother, class, and Mexican culture, language, and people as vital parts of one's identity. Throughout the poem, as though a heartbeat, the narrator declares the presence of love in the young man's life and future.

You will love
And it will hurt sometimes
Your frijoles will burn sometimes
And sometimes you'll put too much salt or not enough
An insult or two
But *mijo* don't ever let him hit you
And leave before you hit him back

X. C. Espinoza-Cuellar (✉)
University of Nevada Las Vegas, Las Vegas, NV, USA

© The Author(s), under exclusive license to Springer Nature
Switzerland AG 2021
A. R. Del Castillo, G. Güido (eds.), *Fathers, Fathering, and Fatherhood*, Palgrave Studies in Literary Anthropology,
https://doi.org/10.1007/978-3-030-60877-4_30

You will love
And it will suck sometimes
Cocine en olla de barro (Cook in an earthenware pot)
Persígnese en la mañana (Cross yourself in the morning)
Use condones y lubricante (Use condoms and lubricants)
Y guarde un cuchillo debajo de la cama (And keep a knife underneath the bed)

You will love
And it will feel good sometimes
No le eche tanta sal a la carne (Don't put too much salt on meat)
Póngale un vaso de agua a sus muertos (Give your dead (on the altar) their glass of water)
Take lots of pictures
And in times of trial, don't forget about the good memories
Invoke them, *que esas lo van a sacar de dudas* (for they will stop you from doubting)

You will love
And it will get intense sometimes
Límpiese con un ramo de flores blancas (Cleanse yourself with a bouquet of white flowers)
Hágase un baño de agua florida con cascarilla (Make a spiritual bath with Florida Water and
cascarilla)
Get tested at least twice a year,
Y coma bien, no se malpase (And eat well, don't go without)

You will love
And it will be sad sometimes
Use grape seed oil instead of Mazola
Chia seeds in your water, *pa' la diabetis* (for the diabetes)
Honey instead of refined sugars
Masturbate once a day *o las veces que quiera* (or as need be)
And never let your sexual desire depend on a man
For all men despite their beauty can be damaged

You will love
And you will be on top of the world sometimes
Don't eat so many tortillas,
Soda is not good for your kidneys, drink water or brew your own iced tea *o hágase su juguito natural* (or make yourself a natural juice)
Sea humilde y buena gente (Be a humble and kind person)
No need to be mean and *creido* (conceited)
Créase de su identidad y su lenguaje (Believe in your identity and language)

Ya lo material va y viene (Material things come and go)
Pero eso sí, que no se lo hagan pendejo que por ahí hay mucho cabrón abusivo
(But don't let anyone take you for a fool because there are many abusive
assholes out there)

You will love
And you will break up sometimes
Don't overdo it with the drinking
Write a lot of poetry
Listen to a lot of Jenni Rivera
Go out and enjoy your singlehood
Que es bien bonito no rendirle cuentas a nadie (Because it's really great not
having to be accountable to anyone).

You will love
Pero no se olvide de uste' mismo (But don't overlook your needs)
Love yourself
Quiérase musho (Love yourself)
Pa' que ningún cabrón le vea la cara de pendejo (So no asshole takes you
for a fool)
Pero antes de que llore por cualquier wey (So before you cry over just any guy)
Acuérdese de su 'amá   (Remember your ma)
De su 'guelita (Your grandma)
Y de su familia (And your family)
Y piense que un hombre por más rico que coja no es todo en la vida (And know
that a man is not everything in life, no matter how good he fucks)
Acuérdese que venimos de una raza de gente fuerte y hermosa (Remember that
we come from a beautiful and spirited people)
Pero que eso no nos quita lo hijos de la chingada (But that doesn't mean we're
not bad asses)
Y de eso también hay que estar orgullosos (Of that we should also be proud of)
Porque ser hijos de la chingada es lo que nos ayuda a sobrevivir (Because being
bad ass is what helps us survive)
*Nomás no hay que ser hijos de la chingada con la gente que como nosotros sufre
y lucha* (But never be abusive to those who suffer and struggle like us)
Sea hijo de la chingada con la gente que nos quiere chingar (Be fierce with
those who want to fuck us over)

You will love,
And love is the only thing that will bring you happiness
Beauty and health
Love *pues y cuando le digan que no puede amar a otro hombre* (whenever they
tell you that you can't love another man)
Mándelos a la chingada y dígales con palabras de profeta (Send them to hell
and tell them with the words of a prophet): YOU WILL LOVE

SELECT BIBLIOGRAPHY[1]

Acereda, A. (2012). Nuestro más profundo y humilde secreto: Los amores transgresores entre Rubén Darío y Amado Nervo. *Bulletin of Spanish Studies: Hispanic Studies and Researches on Spain, Portugal and Latin America,* *89*(6), 895–924.

Acero, R. M. (2003). *Novo ante Novo: Un novísimo personaje homosexual.* Madrid: Pliegos.

Aguilar-Ramírez, A. (2014). Maybe Ever Changing. In A. R. Del Castillo & G. Güido (Eds.), *Queer Aztlán: Chicano Male Recollections of Consciousness and Coming Out* (pp. 71–77). San Diego, CA: Cognella.

Alarcon, N. (1995). Tropology of Hunger: The 'Miseducation' of Richard Rodriguez. In D. Palumbo-Liu (Ed.), *The Ethnic Canon: Histories, Institutions, and Interventions* (pp. 140–152). Minneapolis, MN: University of Minnesota Press.

Aldama, A. J., & Aldama, F. L. (Eds.). (2020). *Decolonizing Latinx Masculinities.* University of Arizona Press.

Aldama, F. L. (Ed.). (2003). *Arturo Islas: The Uncollected Works.* Houston: Arte Público.

---

[1] A multidisciplinary selection of print sources on queer Chicano/Mexicano and Latino male sexuality and identification on but not limited to the family, cultural norms, performance, and performativity. These sources cite from the visual arts, theatre, social science, history, theoretical discourse, literary criticism, fiction, poetry, biography, and autobiography.

© The Author(s), under exclusive license to Springer Nature Switzerland AG 2021
A. R. Del Castillo, G. Güido (eds.), *Fathers, Fathering, and Fatherhood*, Palgrave Studies in Literary Anthropology,
https://doi.org/10.1007/978-3-030-60877-4

Aldama, F. L. (Ed.). (2005). *Dancing with Ghosts: A Critical Biography of Arturo Islas*. Berkeley, CA: University of California Press.

Alire Saénz, B. (2012a). *Aristotle and Dante Discover the Secrets of the Universe*. New York: Simon and Schuster.

Alire Saénz, B. (2012b). *Everything Begins and Ends at the Kentucky Club*. El Paso, TX: Cinco Puntos Press.

Allatson, P. (1999). 'Siempre feliz en mi falda': Luis Alfaro's Simulative Challenge. *GLQ: A Journal of Lesbian and Gay Studies, 5*(2), 199–230.

Allatson, P. (2007). 'My Bones Shine in the Dark': AIDS and the De-scription of Chicano Queer in the Work of Gil Cuadros. *Aztlán: A Journal of Chicano Studies, 32*(1), 23–52.

Almaguer, T. (1991). Chicano Men: A Cartography of Homosexual Identity and Behavior. *Differences: A Journal of Feminist Cultural Studies, 3*(2), 75–100.

Alvarez, P. (2014). Gil Cuadros' AZT-Land: Documenting a Queer Chicano Literary Heritage. In A. R. Del Castillo & G. Güido (Eds.), *Queer Aztlán: Chicano Male Recollections of Consciousness and Coming Out* (pp. 293–302). San Diego, CA: Cognella.

Álvarez, E. F., Jr. (2014). Crevices y cicatrices: Finding Liberation Through My Body. In A. R. Del Castillo & G. Güido (Eds.), *Queer Aztlán: Chicano Male Recollections of Consciousness and Coming Out* (pp. 83–90). San Diego, CA: Cognella.

Amuchástegui, A., & Szasz, I. Coordinadoras. (2007). *Sucede que me canso de ser hombre: Relatos y reflexiones sobre hombres y masculinidades en México*. México, DF: El Colegio de México.

Anthony, A., Dino, F., & Herrera y Lozano, L. (2011). *Tragic Bitches: An Experiment in Queer Xicana & Xicano Performance Poetry*. San Francisco, CA: Kórima.

Anzaldúa, G. (1987). *Borderlands/la frontera: The New Mestiza*. San Francisco, CA: Aunt Lute.

Arreola, S. G. (2010). Latina/o Childhood Sexuality. In M. Asencio (Ed.), *Latina/o Sexualities: Probing Powers, Passions, Practices, and Policies* (pp. 48–61). New Brunswick, NJ: Rutgers University Press.

Baca Zinn, M. (1991). Chicano Men and Masculinity. In L. Kramer (Ed.), *The Sociology of Gender: A Text-Reader* (pp. 221–232). Basingstoke: Palgrave Macmillan.

Balderston, D. (1998). Poetry, Revolution, Homophobia: Polemics from the Mexican Revolution. In S. Molloy & R. McKee Irwin (Eds.), *Hispanisms and Homosexualities* (pp. 57–75). Durham, NC: Duke University Press.

Balderston, D., & Guy, D. (Eds.). (1997). *Sex and Sexuality in Latin America*. New York: New York University Press.

Barbachano Ponce, M. (1964). *El diario de José Toledo*. México, DF: Era.

Barrera, R. (1999). *Salvador Novo. Navaja de la inteligencia*. México, DF: Plaza y Valdés.

Benavidez, M. (2007). *Gronk.* Minneapolis, MN: University of Minnesota Press.

Blanco, J. J., & Zapata, L. (1983, octubre 8). Cuál literatura gay? Sábado: Suplemento de *Unomásuno*, p. 11.

Bonfil, C., & Florescano, E. Coordinador. (1995). Los 41. In *Mitos Mexicanos* (pp. 219–224). México, DF: Aguilar.

Bracho, R. A. (1999). Daddy. In J. Cortez (Ed.), *Virgins, Guerrillas, and Locas: Gay Latinos Writing About Love* (pp. 157–163). Jersey City, NJ: Cleis.

Bracho, R. A. (2005a). *A to B.* Alexandria, VA: Alexander Street.

Bracho, R. A. (2005b). *The Sweetest Hangover (and Other STDs).* Alexandria, VA: Alexander Street.

Bracho, R. A. (2006). Huevos de oro: On Passion and Privilege. In R. Bernstein (Ed.), *Cast Out: Queer Lives in Theater* (pp. 191–194). Ann Arbor, MI: University of Michigan Press.

Brandes, S. (2003). Drink, Abstinence, and Male Identity in Mexico City. In M. Gutmann (Ed.), *Changing Men and Masculinities in Latin America* (pp. 153–178). Durham, NC: Duke University Press.

Buffington, R. (2003). Homophobia and the Mexican Working Class, 1900–1910. In R. McKee Irwin, E. J. McCaughan, & M. R. Nasser (Eds.), *The Famous 41: Sexuality and Social Control in Mexico, 1901* (pp. 193–225). Basingstoke: Palgrave Macmillan.

Cantú, L. (2000). Entre Hombres/Between Men: Latino Masculinities and Homosexualities. In P. M. Nardi (Ed.), *Gay Masculinities* (pp. 224–246). Thousand Oaks, CA: Sage Publications.

Cantú, L., Jr. (2001). A Place Called Home: A Queer Political Economy of Mexican Immigrant Men's Family Experiences. In M. Bernstein & R. Reimann (Eds.), *Queer Families, Queer Politics: Challenging Culture and the State* (pp. 112–136). New York: Columbia University Press.

Cantú, L., Jr. (2002). *De ambiente:* Queer Tourism and the Shifting Boundaries of Mexican Male Sexualities. *GLQ: A Journal of Lesbian and Gay Studies, 8*(1–2), 139–166.

Cantú, L., Jr. (2009). N. A. Naples & S. Vidal-Ortiz (Eds.), *The Sexuality of Migration: Border Crossings and Mexican Immigrant Men.* New York University Press.

Carlos-Manuel. (2014a). Immigrant, Maricón, and Mexican, any Questions? In A. R. Del Castillo & G. Güido (Eds.), *Queer Aztlán: Chicano Male Recollections of Consciousness and Coming Out* (pp. 35–44). San Diego, CA: Cognella.

Carlos-Manuel. (2014b). La vida loca: An Apolitical in-Your-Face Odyssey of a Mexican Immigrant. In A. R. Del Castillo & G. Güido (Eds.), *Queer Aztlán: Chicano Male Recollections of Consciousness and Coming Out* (pp. 235–268). San Diego, CA: Cognella.

Carrier, J. (1976). Family Attitudes and Mexican Male Homosexuality. *Urban Life: A Journal of Ethnographic Research, 5*(3), 359–376.

Carrier, J. (1985). Mexican Male Bisexuality. *Journal of Homosexuality, 11*(1–2), 75–86.

Carrier, J. (1999). Reflections on Ethical Problems Encountered in Field Research on Mexican Male Homosexuality: 1968 to Present. *Culture, Health and Sexuality, 1*(3), 207–221.

Carrillo, H. G. (1993). Another Crack in the Mirror: The Politics of AIDS Prevention in Mexico. *International Quarterly of Community Health Education, 14*(2), 129–152.

Carrillo, H. G. (1999). Cultural Change, Hybridity and Male Homosexuality in Mexico. *Culture, Health and Sexuality, 1*(3), 223–238.

Carrillo, H. G. (2002). *The Night is Young: Sexuality in Mexico in the Time of AIDS.* Chicago, IL: University of Chicago Press.

Carrillo, H. G. (2003). Neither *Machos* Nor *Maricones*: Masculinity and Emerging Male Homosexual Identities in Mexico. In M. Gutmann (Ed.), *Changing Men and Masculinities in Latin America* (pp. 351–369). Durham, NC: Duke University Press.

Carrillo, H. G. (2004). Sexual Migration, Cross-Cultural Sexual Encounters, and Sexual Health. *Sexuality Research & Social Policy, 1*(3), 58–70.

Carrillo, H. G. (2007). Imagining Modernity: Sexuality, Policy, and Social Change in Mexico. *Sexuality Research and Social Policy, 5*(3), 74–91.

Carrillo, H. G. (2012). Sexual Culture, Structure, and Change: A Transnational Framework for Studies of Latino Migration and HIV. In K. C. Organista (Ed.), *HIV Prevention with Latinos: Theory, Research, and Practice* (pp. 41–61). Oxford: Oxford University Press.

Carrillo, H., & Fontdevila, J. (2011). Rethinking Sexual Initiation: Pathways to Identity Formation Among Gay and Bisexual Mexican Male Youth. *Archives of Sexual Behavior, 40*(6), 1241–1254.

Casillo, C. (2002). *Outlaw: John Rechy.* New York: Alyson.

Castillo, D. (1995). Interview: John Rechy. *Diacritics, 25*(1), 113–125.

Castillo, A. (2016). *Black dove: Mamá, mi'jo, and Me.* New York: The Feminist Press at CUNY.

Del Castillo, A. R. (Ed.). (2014a). Queer Chicano/Mexicano Bibliography. In A. R. Del Castillo & G. Güido (Eds.), *Queer Aztlán: Chicano Male Recollections of Consciousness and Coming Out* (pp. 337–387). San Diego, CA: Cognella.

Cervantes, V. D. (2014). Still Flaming. In A. R. Del Castillo & G. Güido (Eds.), *Queer Aztlán: Chicano Male Recollections of Consciousness and Coming Out* (pp. 131–142). San Diego, CA: Cognella.

Chaves Pacheco, J. R. (2010). Afeminados, hombrecitos y lagartijos: Narrativa mexicana del siglo XIX. In *México se escribe con J: Una historia de la cultura gay.* México, DF: Planeta.

Chávez-Silverman, S., & Hernández, L. (Eds.). (2000). *Reading and Writing the Ambiente: Queer Sexualities in Latino, Latin American, and Spanish Culture.* Madison, WI: University of Wisconsin Press.

Chavoya, C. O. (2000). Internal Exiles: The Interventionist Public and Performance Art of Asco. In E. Suderburg (Ed.), *Space, Site and Intervention: Situating Installation Art* (pp. 189–208). Minneapolis, MN: University of Minnesota Press.

Colon, E. (2001). An Ethnographic Study of Six Latino Gay and Bisexual Men. *Journal of Gay & Lesbian Social Services, 12*(3-4), 77–92.

Contreras, D. T. (2005). *Unrequited Love and Gay Latino Culture: What Have You Done to My H Heart?* New York: Palgrave Macmillan.

Córdova Plaza, R. (2007). The Realm Outside the Law: Transvestite Sex Work in Xalapa, Veracruz. In H. Baitenmann, V. Chenaut, & A. Varley (Eds.), *Decoding Gender: Law and Practice in Contemporary Mexico* (pp. 124–148). New Brunswick, NJ: Rutgers University Press.

Cortazar, A. (2000). Implicaciones subalternas de un proliferado discurso coloquial en la obra narrativa de Luis Zapata. *Hispanófila, 129*(3), 59–74.

Cortez, J. (Ed.). (1999). *Virgins, Guerrillas, and Locas: Gay Latinos Writing About Love.* Jersey City, NJ: Cleis.

Cruz, J. M., & Peralta, R. L. (2001). Family Violence and Substance Use: The Perceived Effects of Substance Use Within Gay Male Relationships. *Violence & Victims, 16*(2), 161–172.

Cuadros, G. (1994). *City of God.* San Francisco, CA: City Lights.

Cuadros, G. (2014a). Birth. In A. R. Del Castillo & G. Güido (Eds.), *Queer Aztlán: Chicano Male Recollections of Consciousness and Coming Out* (pp. xiii–xv). San Diego, CA: Cognella.

Cuadros, G. (2014b). Coming Out. In A. R. Del Castillo & G. Güido (Eds.), *Queer Aztlán: Chicano Male Recollections of Consciousness and Coming Out* (pp. 59–60). San Diego, CA: Cognella.

Cuadros, G. (2014c). Last Supper. In A. R. Del Castillo & G. Güido (Eds.), *Queer Aztlán: Chicano Male Recollections of Consciousness and Coming Out* (pp. 171–172). San Diego, CA: Cognella.

Cunningham, J. C. (2002). Hey, Mr. Liberace, Will You Vote for Zeta?' Looking for the Joto in Chicano Men's Autobiographical Writing. In *Race-ing Masculinity: Identity in Contemporary U.S. Men's Writing* (pp. 69–94). New York: Routledge.

Cutler, J. A. (2010). Prothesis, Surrogation, and Relation in Arturo Islas's *The Rain God.* In C. Noriega et al. (Eds.), *The Chicano Studies Reader: An Anthology of Aztlán, 1970–2000* (pp. 647–672). Los Angeles, CA: UCLA Chicano Studies Research Center Publications.

Danahay, M. A. (1994). Richard Rodriguez's Poetics of Manhood. In P. Murphy (Ed.), *Fictions of Manhood: Crossing Cultures, Crossing Sexualities* (pp. 290–307). New York: New York University Press.

de Cuéllar, J. T. (2011). *Historia de Chucho el Ninfo.* 1871, 1890. Estudio Preliminar de Belem Clark de Lara. México, DF: UNAM.

Decker, J. L. (1993). Mr. Secrets: Richard Rodriguez Flees the House of Memory. *Transition, 61,* 124–132.

Del Castillo, A. R. (Ed.). (2014b). *Queer in Aztlán: Chicano Male Recollections of Consciousness and Coming Out.* San Diego, CA: Cognella.

Del Castillo, A. R., & Güido, G. (Eds.). (2014). Introduction: Queer Chicano Sexuality, Culture, and Consciousness. In A. R. Del Castillo & G. Güido (Eds.), *Queer Aztlán: Chicano Male Recollections of Consciousness and Coming Out* (pp. xvii–xxxi). San Diego, CA: Cognella.

Días y Morales, M. Coordinadora. (1998). *Juan García Ponce y la generación del medio siglo.* Xalapa, Ver.: Instituto de Investigaciones Lingüístico-Literarias, Universidad Veracruzana.

Díaz Barriga, M. (2001). *Vergüenza* and Changing Chicana and Chicano Narratives. *Men and Masculinities, 3*(3), 278–298.

Domínguez-Ruvalcaba, H. (2009). From Fags to Gays: Political Adaptations and Cultural Translations in the Mexican Gay Liberation Movement. In L. Egan & M. K. Long (Eds.), *Mexico Reading the United States* (pp. 116–134). Nashville, TN: Vanderbilt University Press.

Doring, E. (2014). Growing Up Gay and Latino. In A. R. Del Castillo & G. Güido (Eds.), *Queer Aztlán: Chicano Male Recollections of Consciousness and Coming Out* (pp. 17–23). San Diego, CA: Cognella.

Espinoza-Cuellar, X. C., & Leal-Santillan, E. N. (2014a). To Our Mothers. In A. R. Del Castillo & G. Güido (Eds.), *Queer Aztlán: Chicano Male Recollections of Consciousness and Coming Out* (pp. 61–63). San Diego, CA: Cognella.

Espinoza-Cuellar, X. C., & Leal-Santillan, E. N. (2014b). On Reclaiming Machismo. In A. R. Del Castillo & G. Güido (Eds.), *Queer Aztlán: Chicano Male Recollections of Consciousness and Coming Out* (pp. 271–272). San Diego, CA: Cognella.

Flatley, J. (2008). *Affective Mapping: Melancholia and the Politics of Modernism.* Cambridge, MA: Harvard University Press.

Foster, D. W. (1991). *Gay and Lesbian Themes in Latin American Writing.* Austin, TX: University of Texas Press.

Foster, D. W. (1996). Homoerotic Writing and Chicano Authors. *The Bilingual Review/ La Revista Bilingüe, 21*(1), 42–51.

Foster, D. W. (1997). *Sexual Textualities: Essays on Queer/ing Latin American Writing.* Austin, TX: University of Texas Press.

Foster, D. W. (1999). *Chicano/Latino Homoerotic Identities.* London: Routledge.

Foster, D. W. (2006). *El ambiente nuestro: Chicano/Latino Homoerotic Writing*. Tempe, AZ: Bilingual Press/Editorial Bilingüe.

Garza Carvajal, F. (1997). *Butterflies Will Burn: Prosecuting Sodomites in Early Modern Spain and Mexico*. Austin, TX: University of Texas Press. (2003).

Gaskin, G. H. (2013). *Legendary: Inside the House Ballroom Scene*. Durham, NC: Duke University Press/Center for Documentary Studies.

Gaspar de Alba, A. (Ed.). (2003). *Velvet Barrios: Popular Culture & Chicana/o Sexualities*. New York: Palgrave Macmillan.

Girman, C. (2004). Familiar, Familial Voices: Latino Men Speak Out. *Mucho Macho: Seduction, Desire, and the Homoerotic Lives of Latin Men* (pp. 293–327). Harrington Park.

Gómez-Peña, G. (1994). The Multicultural Paradigm: An Open Letter to the National Arts Community. In D. Taylor & J. Villegas (Eds.), *Negotiating Performance: Gender, Sexuality, and Theatricality in Latina/o America* (pp. 7–29). Durham, NC: Duke University Press.

González, R. (1996). My Literary Fathers. In R. González (Ed.), *Muy Macho: Latino Men Confront Their Manhood* (pp. 165–185). New York: Anchor.

González, R. (2006). *Butterfly Boy: Memories of a Chicano Mariposa*. Madison, WI: University of Wisconsin Press.

González, R. (2013). *Autobiography of My Hungers*. Madison, WI: University of Wisconsin Press.

González, O. O. (2014a). Constructing an Ofrenda of My Memory: A Queer Poz Indio-Xicano Maps His Way Home. In A. R. Del Castillo & G. Güido (Eds.), *Queer Aztlán: Chicano Male Recollections of Consciousness and Coming Out* (pp. 173–227). San Diego, CA: Cognella.

González, O. O. (2014b). Mapping New Directions for a Radical Jotería Agenda. In A. R. Del Castillo & G. Güido (Eds.), *Queer Aztlán: Chicano Male Recollections of Consciousness and Coming Out* (pp. 319–333). San Diego, CA: Cognella.

González de Alba, L. (1981). *El vino de los bravos*. México, DF: Katún.

Guajardo, P. (2002). *Chicano Controversy: Oscar Acosta and Richard Rodriguez*. New York: Peter Lang.

Guido, G. (2012). *Navigating the Abyss: A Queer Chicano Semiotics of Love and Loss*. [Master's thesis, California State University]. Proquest Dissertations and Theses Global.

Guido, G. (2014). My Shadow Beast. In A. R. Del Castillo & G. Güido (Eds.), *Queer Aztlán: Chicano Male Recollections of Consciousness and Coming Out* (pp. 105–122). San Diego, CA: Cognella.

Gutiérrez, R. A. (1993). Community, Patriarchy and Individualism: The Politics of Chicano History and the Dream of Equality. *American Quarterly, 45*(1), 44–72.

Gutmann, M. C. (1996). *The Meanings of Macho: Being a Man in Mexico City.* Berkeley, CA: University of California Press.

Gutmann, M. C. (Ed.). (2003). *Changing Men and Masculinities in Latin America.* Durham, NC: Duke University Press.

Guzmán, M. (2006). *Gay Hegemony/Latino Homosexualities.* New York: Routledge.

Halperin, D. M., & Traub, V. (Eds.). (2009). *Gay Shame.* Chicago, IL: University of Chicago Press.

Hames-García, M., Martínez, J., & E. (Eds). (2011). *Gay Latino Studies: A Critical Reader.* Durham, NC: Duke University Press.

Iglesias Prieto, N. (2011). Coming and Going: Transborder Visual Art in Tijuana. In R. Blanco-Cano & R. E. Urquijo-Ruiz (Eds.), *Global Mexican Cultural Productions* (pp. 175–196). New York: Palgrave Macmillan.

Iglesias Prieto, N. (2014). Transfronteridad y procesos creativos. In J. M. Valenzuela (Ed.), *Transfronteras: Las fronteras del mundo y procesos culturales* (pp. 97–127). Tijuana: El Colegio de la Frontera Norte.

Iglesias Prieto, N. (2017). Transborderisms: Practices That Tear Down Walls. In R. Real (Ed.), *Border Wall as Architecture* (pp. 22–25). Berkeley, CA: University of California Press.

Iglesias Prieto, N. (2018). Creative Potential and Social Change. Independent Spaces of Visual Arts in Tijuana. In M. Peris-Ortiz, M. Cabrera-Flores, & A. S. Santoyo (Eds.), *Cultural and Creative Industries. A Path to Entrepreneurship and Innovation* (pp. 43–62). Berlin: Springer.

Irwin, R. M. (2000a). As Invisible as He Is: The Queer Enigma of Xavier Villaurrutia. In S. Chávez-Silverman & L. Hernández (Eds.), *Reading and Writing the Ambiente: Queer Sexualities in Latino, Latin American, and Spanish Culture* (pp. 114–146). Madison, WI: University of Wisconsin Press.

Irwin, R. M. (2000b). The Famous 41: The Scandalous Birth of Modern Mexican Homosexuality. *GLQ: A Journal of Lesbian and Gay Studies, 6*(3), 353–376.

Irwin, R. M. (2003). *Mexican Masculinities.* Minneapolis, MN: University of Minnesota Press.

Irwin, R. M., McCaughan, E. J., & Nassar, M. R. (Eds.). (2003). *The Famous 41: Sexuality and Social Control in Mexico, 1901.* New York: Palgrave Macmillan.

Islas, A. (1984). *The Rain God: A Desert Tale.* Palo Alto: Alexandrian Press.

Islas, A. (1990). *Migrant Souls: A Novel.* New York: Morrow.

Jaén, D. T. (1987). La Neo-Picaresca en México: Elena Poniatowska y Luis Zapata. *Tinta, 1*(5), 23–29.

Jaén, D. T. (1994). Rechy, John (United States; 1934). In D. W. Foster (Ed.), *Latin American Writers on Gay and Lesbian Themes: A Bio-Critical Sourcebook* (pp. 349–356). Westport, CT: Greenwood.

Jagose, A. (1996). *Queer Theory: An Introduction.* New York: New York University Press.

Jameson, J. (1981). *The Political Unconscious: Narrative as a Socially Symbolic Act.* Ithaca, NY: Cornell University Press.

Keating, A. (Ed.). (2009). *The Gloria Anzaldúa Reader.* Durham, NC: Duke University Press.

Limón, J. E. (1989). Carne, Carnales, and the Carnivalesque: Bakhtinian Batos, Disorder, and Narrative Discourses. *American Ethnologist, 16*(3), 471–486.

Lozano, L. H. y. (2005). *Santo de la pata alzada: Poems from the queer/Xicano/positive pen.* Austin, TX: Evelyn Street Press.

Lozano, L. H. y. (2014a). *Amorcito maricón.* Korima Press.

Lozano, L. H. y. (2014b). Shihuahua, the Place from Which I Write. In A. R. Del Castillo & G. Güido (Eds.), *Queer Aztlán: Chicano Male Recollections of Consciousness and Coming Out* (pp. 7–10). San Diego, CA: Cognella.

Luibhéid, E., & Cantú, L., Jr. (Eds.). (2005). *Queer Migrations: Sexuality, U.S. Citizenship, and Border Crossings.* Minneapolis, MN: University of Minnesota Press.

Macías-González, V. M. (2003). The Largartijo at the High Life: Notes on Masculine Consumption: Race, Nation, and Homosexuality in Porfirian Mexico. In R. M. Irwin, E. J. McCaughan, & M. R. Nassar (Eds.), *The Famous 41: Sexuality and Social Control in Mexico, 1901* (pp. 227–249). New York: Palgrave Macmillan.

Macías-González, V. M. (2012). The Bathhouse and Male Homosexuality in Porfirian Mexico. In V. M. Macías-González & A. Rubenstein (Eds.), *Masculinity and Sexuality in Modern Mexico* (pp. 25–52). Albuquerque, NM: University of New Mexico Press.

Macías-González, V. M., & Rubenstein, A. (Eds.). (2012). *Masculinity and Sexuality in Modern Mexico.* Albuquerque, NM: University of New Mexico Press.

Martinez, M. (2014). Personal Resilience. In A. R. Del Castillo & G. Güido (Eds.), *Queer Aztlán: Chicano Male Recollections of Consciousness and Coming Out* (pp. 143–170). San Diego, CA: Cognella.

Méndez-Negrete, J. (2015). *A Life on Hold: Living with Schizophrenia.* Albuquerque, NM: University of New Mexico.

Miano Borruso, M. compilador. (2002). *Hombre, Mujer y Muxe' en el Istmo de Tehuantepec.* México, DF: Plaza y Valdés.

Miano Borruso, M. compilador. (2003). *Caminos inciertos de las masculinidades.* México, DF: Instituto Nacional de Antropología e Historia, Escuela Nacional de Antropología e Historia.

Mirandé, A. (1998). *Hombres y machos: Masculinity and Latino Culture.* Boulder, CO: Westview Press.

Molloy, S. (1992). Too Wild for Comfort: Desire and Ideology in Fin-de-siècle Spanish America. *Social Text, 31*(32), 187–201.

Molloy, S. (1999). The Politics of Posing: Translating Decadence in Fin-de-siècle Latin America. In L. Constable (Ed.), *Perennial Decay: On the Aesthetics and Politics of Decadence* (pp. 183–197). Philadelphia, PA: University of Pennsylvania Press.

Molloy, S., & McKee Irwin, R. (Eds.). (1998). *Hispanisms and Homosexualities.* Durham, NC: Duke University Press.

Monsiváis, C. (2000). *Salvador Novo: Lo marginal en el centro.* México, DF: Era.

Monsiváis, C. (2003). The 41 and the Gran Redada (A. Walker, Trans.). In R. M. Irwin, E. J. McCaughan, & M. R. Nassar (Eds.), *The Famous 41: Sexuality and Social Control in Mexico, 1901* (pp. 139–168). New York: Palgrave Macmillan.

Monsiváis, C. (2010). *Que se abra esa puerta: Crónicas y ensayos sobre la diversidad sexual.* México, DF: Paidós.

Moraga, C. L. (1997). *Waiting in the Wings: Portrait of a Queer Motherhood.* Ithaca, NY: Firebrand Books.

Moraga, C. (1999). *The Last Generation: Prose and Poetry.* Boston, MA: South End Press.

Moraga, C. L. (2000). *Loving in the war years: Lo que nunca pasó por sus labios.* Boston, MA: South End Press.

Muñoz, J. E. (1999). *Disidentifications: Queers of Color and the Performance of Politics.* Minneapolis, MN: University of Minnesota Press.

Muñoz, J. E. (2006a). Feeling Brown: Ethnicity and Affect in Ricardo Bracho's *The Sweetest Hangover (and Other STDs). Theatre Journal, 52*(1), 67–79.

Muñoz, J. E. (2006b). Feeling Brown, Feeling Down: Latina Affect, the Performativity of Race, and the Depressive Position. *Signs, 31*(3), 675–688.

Muñoz, J. E. (2019). *Cruising Utopia: The Then and There of Queer Futurity.* 10th Anniversary Edition. New York University Press.

Nava, M. (1992). Abuelo: My Grandfather, Raymond Acuña. In J. Preston (Ed.), *A Member of the Family: Gay Men Write About Their Families* (pp. 15–20). New York: Dutton.

Nava, M. (2001). *Rag and Bone.* New York: Putnam.

Nava, M. (2014a). 1966. In A. R. Del Castillo & G. Güido (Eds.), *Queer Aztlán: Chicano Male Recollections of Consciousness and Coming Out* (pp. 123–130). San Diego, CA: Cognella.

Nava, M. (2014b). *The City of Palaces: A Novel.* Madison, WI: University of Wisconsin Press.

Ochoa, J. D. (2012). *Finding familia at UCLA: Joteando in the 1990's—Charting Gay Chicano Political Activism.* [Master's thesis, California State University]. Proquest Dissertations and Theses Global.

Ortiz, R. L. (1993). Sexuality Degree Zero: Pleasure and Power in the Novels of John Rechy, Arturo Islas, and Michael Nava. *Journal of Homosexuality, 26*(2-3), 111–126.

Ortiz, R. L. (1995). John Rechy and the Grammar of Ostentation. In Case, Brett, & Foster (Eds.), *Cruising the Performative: Interventions Into the Representation of Ethnicity, Nationality, and Sexuality* (pp. 59–70). Bloomington, IN: Indiana University Press.

Paredes, A. (1953). Over the Waves Is Out. *New Mexican Review, 23*(2), 177–187.

Paz, O. (1961). *The Labyrinth of Solitude* (L. Kemp, Trans.). Grove.

Perez, H. (2005). You Can Have My Brown Body and Eat It, Too! *Social Text, 23*(3–4 (84–85)), 171–191.

Pérez, D. E. (2006). *Mi familia rara*: Why Paco Isn't Married. *Studies in Latin American Popular Culture, 25*, 141–156.

Pérez, D. E. (2009). *Rethinking Chicana/o and Latina/o Popular Culture.* New York: Palgrave Macmillan.

Pérez, D. E. (2014a). Out in the Field: Mariposas and Chican@ Studies. In A. R. Del Castillo & G. Güido (Eds.), *Queer Aztlán: Chicano Male Recollections of Consciousness and Coming Out* (pp. 277–291). San Diego, CA: Cognella.

Pérez, D. E. (2014b). Toward a Mariposa Consciousness: Reimagining Queer Chicano and Latino Identities. *Aztlan: A Journal of Chicano Studies, 39*(2), 95–127.

Pérez-Torres, R. (1994). The Ambiguous Outlaw: John Rechy and Complicitous Homotextuality. In P. Murphy (Ed.), *Fictions of Masculinity: Crossing Cultures, Crossing Sexualities* (pp. 204–225). New York: New York University Press.

Pesqueria, R. (1999). Daddycakes. In J. Cortez (Ed.), *Virgins, Guerrillas, and Locas: Gay Latinos Writing About Love* (pp. 53–57). Jersey City, NJ: Cleis.

Piccato, P. (2003). Interpretations of Sexuality in Mexico City Prisons: A Critical Version of Roumagnac. In I. McCaughan & R. Nassar (Eds.), *The Famous 41: Sexuality and Social Control in Mexico, 1901* (pp. 251–266). New York: Palgrave Macmillan.

Piccato, P. (2007). 'Such a Strong Need': Sexuality and Violence in Belem Prison. In W. E. French & K. E. Bliss (Eds.), *Gender, Sexuality and Power in Latin America Since Independence* (pp. 87–108). Lanham, MD: Rowman & Littlefield.

Prieur, A. (1998a). Bodily and Symbolic Constructions Among Homosexual Men in Mexico. *Sexualities, 1*(3), 287–298.

Prieur, A. (1998b). *Mema's House, Mexico City: On Transvestites, Queens, and Machos.* Chicago, IL: University of Chicago Press.

Ramírez, R. L. (1999). *What It Means to Be a Man: Reflections on Puerto Rican Masculinity.* New Brunswick, NJ: Rutgers University Press.

Rechy, J. (1963). *City of Night.* New York: Grove.

Rechy, J. (1991). *The Miraculous Day of Amalia Gomez.* Chicago, IL: Arcade.

Rechy, J. (2008). *About My Life and the Kept Woman: A Memoir.* New York: Grove Press.

Reyes, G. A. (2010). *Madre and I: A Memoir of Our Immigrant Lives*. Madison, WI: University of Wisconsin Press.

Rice, D. (2000). Sinners Among Angels, or Family History and the Ethnic Narrator in Arturo Islas's *The Rain God* and *Migrant Souls*. *Lit: Literature Interpretation Theory, 11*(2), 169–197.

Rice-González, C., & Vazquez, C. (2011). *From Macho to Mariposa: New Gay Latino Fiction*. Maple Shade, NJ: Lethe Press/Tincture.

Rodriguez, R. (1982). *Hunger of Memory: The Education of Richard Rodriguez, an Autobiography*. New York: Bantam.

Rodriguez, R. (1992). *Days of Obligation: An Argument with My Mexican Father*. New York: Viking.

Rodriguez, R. A. (1998). Richard Rodriguez Reconsidered: Queering the Sissy (Ethnic) Subject. *Texas Studies in Language and Literature, 40*(4), 396–423.

Rodríguez, R. T. (2002). Serial Kinship: Representing la familia in Early Chicano Publications. *Aztlan: A Journal of Chicano Studies, 27*(1), 123–138.

Rodríguez, R. (2003). A Poverty of Relations: On Not 'Making *Familia* from Scratch,' But Scratching *Familia*. In A. Gaspar de Alba (Ed.), *Velvet Barrios: Popular Culture & Chicana/o Sexualities* (pp. 75–88). New York: Palgrave Macmillan.

Rodriguez, R. (2003). *Brown: The Last Discovery of America*. New York: Penguin Books.

Rodríguez, R. T. (2003). The Verse of the Godfather: Signifying Family and Nationalism in Chicano Rap and Hip-Hop Culture. In A. Gaspar de Alba (Ed.), *Velvet Barrios: Popular Culture & Chicana/o Sexualities* (pp. 107–122). New York: Palgrave Macmillan.

Rodríguez, R. T. (2006). Queering the Homeboy Aesthetic. *Aztlan: A Journal of Chicano Studies, 31*(2), 127–137.

Rodríguez, R. T. (2007). Imagine a Brown Queer: Inscribing Sexuality in Chicano/a Latino/a Literary and Cultural Studies. *American Quarterly, 59*(2), 493–501.

Rodríguez, R. T. (2009). *Next of Kin: The Family in Chicano/a Cultural Politics*. Durham, NC: Duke University Press.

Rodríguez, R. T. (2011). Carnal Knowledge: Chicano Gay Men and the Dialectics of Being. In M. Hames-García & E. J. Martínez (Eds.), *Gay Latino Studies: A Critical Reader* (pp. 113–140). Durham, NC: Duke University Press.

Rodriguez, R. (2014). Chile relleno. In A. R. Del Castillo & G. Güido (Eds.), *Queer Aztlán: Chicano Male Recollections of Consciousness and Coming Out* (pp. 65–69). San Diego, CA: Cognella.

Rodriguez, E. M., & Ouellette, S. C. (1999). Religion and Masculinity in Latino Gay Lives. In P. M. Nardi (Ed.), *Gay Masculinities* (pp. 101–129). Thousand Oaks, CA: Sage Publications.

Román Garcia, L. H. (2014). In Search of My Queer Aztln. In A. R. Del Castillo & G. Güido (Eds.), *Queer Aztlán: Chicano Male Recollections of Consciousness and Coming Out* (pp. 303–318). San Diego, CA: Cognella.

Romo, L. F., Nadeem, E., & Kouyoumdjian, C. (Eds.). (2010). Latina/o Parent-Adolescent Communication About Sexuality: An Interdisciplinary Literature Review. In M. Asencio (Ed.), *Latina/o Sexualities: Probing Powers, Passions, Practices, and Policies* (pp. 62–74). New Brunswick, NJ: Rutgers University Press.

Romo-Carmona, M. (Ed.). (2001). *Conversaciones: Relatos por padres y madres de hijas lesbianas y hijos gay*. Jersey City, NJ: Cleis Press.

Roque Ramirez, H. N. (2001). *Communities of Desire: Queer Latina/Latino History and Memory, San Francisco Bay Area, 1960s–1990s*. Diss. U of California, 2001.

Schuessler, M. K., & Capistrán, M. Coordinadores. (2010). *México se escribe con J: Una historia de la cultura gay*. México, DF: Planeta.

Schulz-Cruz, B. (2008). *Imágenes gay en el cine mexicano. Tres décadas de joterío, 1970–1999*. México, DF: Fontamara.

Serna, E. (1991). *Amores de segunda mano*. Xalapa, Ver.: Universidad Veracruzana.

Serrano, R. M. (2014). Being Frank. In A. R. Del Castillo & G. Güido (Eds.), *Queer Aztlán: Chicano Male Recollections of Consciousness and Coming Out* (pp. 25–33). San Diego, CA: Cognella.

Sifuentes-Jáuregui, B. (2002). *Transvestism, Masculinity, and Latin American Literature: Genders Share Flesh*. New York: Palgrave Macmillan.

Sifuentes-Jáuregui, B. (2015). *The Avowal of Difference*. New York: SUNY Press.

Sigal, P. (2002). Gender, Male Homosexuality, and Power in Colonial Yucatán. *Latin American Perspectives, 29*(2), 24–40.

Sigal, P. (2003). *Infamous Desire: Male Homosexuality in Colonial Latin America*. Chicago, IL: University of Chicago Press.

Sigal, P. (2005). The Cuiloni, the Patlache, and the Abominable Sin: Homosexualities in Early Colonial Nahua Society. *Hispanic American Historical Review, 85*(4), 555–593.

Sigal, P. (2007). Queer Nahuatl: Sahagún's Faggots and Sodomites, Lesbians and Hermaphrodites. *Ethnohistory, 54*(1), 9–34.

Skjerdal, K., Shiraz, I. M., & Benavides-Vaello, S. (1996). A Growing HIV/AIDS Crisis Among Migrant and Seasonal Farmworker Families. In S. I. Mishra, R. F. Conner, & J. R. Magaña (Eds.), *AIDS Crossing Borders: The Spread of HIV Among Migrant Latinos* (pp. 27–48). Boulder: Westview.

Soto, S. K. (2010a). Américo Paredes and the De-Mastery of Desire. In *Reading Chican@ Like a Queer: The De-Mastery of Desire* (pp. 87–120). Austin, TX: University of Texas Press.

Soto, S. K. (2010b). Fixing Up the House of Race with Richard Rodriguez. In *Reading Chican@ Like a Queer: The De-mastery of Desire* (pp. 39–58). Austin, TX: University of Texas Press.

Soto, S. K. (2010c). Making *Familia* from Racialized Sexuality: Cherríe Moraga's Memoirs, Manifestos, and Motherhood. In *Reading Chican@ Like a Queer: The De-mastery of Desire* (pp. 15–37). Austin, TX: University of Texas Press.

Soto, S. K. (2010d). *Reading Chican@ Like a Queer: The De-mastery of Desire.* Austin, TX: University of Texas Press.

Sternad, J. F. (2006). Cyclona and Early Chicano Performance Art: An Interview with Robert Legorreta. *GLQ: A Journal of Lesbian and Gay Studies, 12*(3), 475–490.

Sullivan, E. J. (1988, November). Nahum Zenil's Auto-Iconography ('Mexican-ness' in Mexican painting of the Eighties). *Arts Magazine*, 86–91.

Sullivan, E. J., Arteaga, A., & Pacheco, C. (1996). *Nahum Zenil: Witness to the Self.* San Francisco, CA: Mexican Museum.

Torres, J. (2011). *We the Animals.* New York: Mariner Books.

Torres-Ortiz, V. F. (1997). *Transgresión y ruptura en la narrativa de Luis Zapata.* [Doctoral dissertation, University of New Mexico.] Proquest Dissertations and Theses Global.

Torres-Rosado, S. (1991). Canon and Innovation in *Adonis García:* A Picaresque Novel. *Revista monográfica, 7,* 276–283.

Trexler, R. (1995). *Sex and Conquest: Gendered Violence, Political Order and the European Conquest of the Americas.* Ithaca, NY: Cornell University Press.

Viego, A. (1999). The Place of Gay Male Chicano Literature in Queer Chicana/o Cultural Work. *Discourse: Journal for Theoretical Studies in Media and Culture, 21*(3), 111–131.

Villarreal, J. A. (1959). *Pocho: A Novel.* New York: Doubleday.

Villaurrutia, X. (1966). *Cartas de Villaurrutia a Novo, 1935–1936.* México, DF: Instituto Nacional de Bellas Artes, Departamento de Literatura.

Villaurrutia, X. (1980). *Antología. Selección y prólogo de Octavio Paz.* México, DF: Fondo de Cultura Económica.

Westmoreland, M. (1995). Camp in the Works of Luis Zapata. *Modern Language Studies, 25*(2), 45–59.

Wolford, L. (2000). Introduction to Gómez-Peña. In J. Bonnie (Ed.), *Extreme Exposure* (pp. 276–277). New York: Theatre Communications Group.

Xavier, E. (2008). *Mariposas: A Modern Anthology of Queer Latino Poetry.* Moorpark, CA: Floricanto.

Zapata, L. (1979). *Las aventuras, desventuras y sueños de Adonis García: El vampiro de la colonia Roma.* México, DF: Grijalbo.

Zapata, L. (1981). *Adonis García: A Picaresque Novel.* San Francisco, CA: Gay Sunshine.

Index[1]

[1] Note: Page numbers followed by 'n' refer to notes.

© The Author(s), under exclusive license to Springer Nature
Switzerland AG 2021
A. R. Del Castillo, G. Güido (eds.), *Fathers, Fathering, and
Fatherhood*, Palgrave Studies in Literary Anthropology,
https://doi.org/10.1007/978-3-030-60877-4

Healer(s), 57, 67, 110
Healing, 16, 17, 59, 67, 130,
    147–149, 196
Henry Rios Mystery Series, 238
Heteronormative, 15, 53, 86, 186,
    192, 236, 239
Heteronormativity, 122
HIV epidemic, 188
HIV/AIDS, 9, 119, 128, 182, 183,
    186, 188n7, 192
HIV-negative gay men, 179
HIV-positive gay men, *see under* Poz
    (HIV-positive)
*Hombres y Machos: Masculinity and
    Latino Culture*, 6, 235
Homelessness, 10, 17, 135, 136
Homeless shelters, 136
Homophobia, 12, 15, 44, 83,
    198, 238
Homosexual
    desire, 7
    feelings, 85
    man, 80
Hook-up sites, *see* Tumblr
Hope, 42, 59, 71, 129, 135, 146,
    170, 181, 198, 199, 204n1, 206,
    207, 229, 243, 252
House (a 'family' of people sharing a
    living space involved in the
    Ballroom Scene), 51
Hybrid, 12
Hypermasculinity, 15, 16, 122
Hyperreality, 9
Hypersexuality, 7

I
Identity, *see under* Gay; Mexican;
    Queer; Sexual; Transborder queer
    identity; Transnational identity;
    Two-spirit identity
Illness, *see under* Bipolar disorder;
    Disease; HIV/AIDS; Medicated;

Mental health/illness;
    Psychiatrist(s); Seropositive,
    status, STDs; STIs; Therapy
Immigrant(s), *see under*
    Undocumented immigrant(s)
Immigration, 234, 236
Incest, 186
Incestuous fantasies, 187
Indigeneity, 9, 11
Inequality, 153
Inequity, 153
Infidelity (adultery), 234
Injustice, 9
Intergenerational
    sex, 187
    trauma, 228
Internalized homophobia, 12, 83

J
Jotería studies, 6
Joto
    as faggot, 65, 82, 110
    as gay, 83
    as queer, 43, 44, 83, 86
Juan Crow (anti-Mexican Jim Crow
    laws), 64

K
Kin relations
    as father/son role play, 2
    as fictive kinship (*see under*
        Godfather (*padrino*))
    as fragile, 195

L
Lack of athleticism, 65
Latino(s), 6–8, 11, 13, 16, 117, 120,
    122, 168, 189, 234–241,
    247, 252
Law school, 65

Performance, vii, 5, 10, 16, 42, 52, 112, 119, 122, 169–183
Photograph(s), 80–82, 85, 87
Pocho (Mexican Sp. slang for Mexican American), 222
Poetry, 5, 9, 145
Policing, 15
Political, 64, 70, 84, 92, 245
Poppers (a chemical class of inhaled drugs known as alkyl nitrites), 161, 162, 182
Post-Traumatic Stress Disorder (PTSD), 67
Poverty, 17, 135, 136, 248, 249
Power, 2, 6, 14, 17, 54, 55, 70, 76, 93, 117, 136, 192, 195, 197
Power of Attorney, 117
Poz (HIV-positive), 186n3
  See also Seropositive, status
Prayer(s), 65, 76, 117, 121
Prison camp, 75
Prohibition, 72
Psychiatrist(s), 18, 119, 120, 126–128, 141–145, 152, 153, 170–172, 178, 180, 186, 188n7, 192
Psychological, 8, 144, 198

Q
Quare (an intersectional notion of queer), 51
Queer
  boyhood, 3, 118
  Chicano, Xicano, 1–18
  child, 235
  of color, 16
  consciousness, 11, 14, 18
  identity, 86, 140, 141, 197
  masculinity, 8, 17, 137
  subjectivity, 236, 238
  veterans, 12

Queer sons
  as disidentified with fathers, 241–242
  as similar to fathers, 245

R
Race, 2n3, 15, 92, 163, 188
Racism, 238
Ramírez Berg, Charles, 235, 236
Raza (one's people or ethnic group; race), 261
Reading Chican@ Like a Queer, 51n1
Realness (convincing role playing), 51
Real Women Have Curves, 236
Rechy, John, 8, 237, 242
Recollection, 3, 8, 198
Recovery, 57, 127, 169–183
Rejection, 188
Religion, 69, 118, 196
Resentment, 17, 135, 170, 177, 237
Rethinking Chicana/o and Latina/o Popular Culture, 238
Reyes, Guillermo, 5, 244, 245
Rivera, Tomás, 238
Riverside National Cemetery, 116
Rodriguez, Richard, 6n7, 7, 17

S
Same-sex desire, *see under* Desire; Object of desire
Same-sex relationships, 249
San Judas Tadeo (Saint Jude Thaddeus), 76
San Martín de Porres (Saint Martin of Porres), 76
Santería (pantheistic Afro-Cuban religion)
  Collares (necklaces), 197
  initiation, 196
  Itá (life reading), 196
  priesthood, 196